NASHVILLE'S UNWRITTEN RULES

Inside the Business
of Country Music

Dan Daley

THE OVERLOOK PRESS

WOODSTOCK & NEW YORK

First published in the United States in 1998 by
The Overlook Press, Peter Mayer Publishers, Inc.
Lewis Hollow Road
Woodstock, New York 12498

Library of Congress Cataloging-in-Publications Data

Daley, Dan
Nashville's Unwritten Rules : inside the business of the country
music machine / Dan Daley.
p. cm.
Includes bibliographical references and index.
1. Sound recording industry—Tennessee—Nashville.
2. Country music—History and criticism. I. Title.
ML3790.D28   1997   761.642'09768'55—dc21   96-45691

BOOK DESIGN AND FORMATTING BY BERNARD SCHLEIFER

Manufactured in the United States of America
ISBN 087951-770-0

First Edition
1 3 5 7 9 8 6 4 2

CONTENTS

ACKNOWLEDGMENTS   8

AUTHOR'S NOTE   9

Introduction: Version of the Truth   11

A Little Background Music   21

The Producers, The Princes   40

The Songwriters   134

The Publishers   174

The Musicians   222

Marketing: Radio and Video   272

"Where's the Next Nashville?"   323

SOURCES AND RECOMMENDED READING   344

INDEX   345

To Deborah,
*who saw what was inside
when I couldn't and
believed when I wouldn't*

ACKNOWLEDGMENTS

The author would like to thank the following people for their generous assistance in creating this book:

Robby Clyne, Travis Corder, Peter Cronin, Bobby John Henry and Kari for room at the inn, Michael Hight, Prof. Geoff Hull, Esq., Joli Hummel, Ruth Kennedy, Fred Koller for his library and useful cynicism, Barry McCloud, Susan Nadler, the Nashville Songwriters Association, Susan Niles, Kenny Ozawa, Nick Palladino, Allan Pepper, Ron Pugh and the Country Music Foundation, Denny Purcell, Lisa Roy for her sartorial diversions, Tony Sarno, Howard Sherman, Stanley Snadowsky, Bob Solomon, Joe Talbot for his valuable nit-pickin', Carl Tatz, Jeff and Greta Teague, Bil VornDick, Don Wershba, John and Bobbye Whelan, the Sunset Grill Irregulars.

Special thanks to Missy Baker, Michael Hight, Chris Markferding, Penny Mastrangelo, and Denise Tschida for their editorial assistance.

AUTHOR'S NOTE

The nature of the entertainment business is changeable on a day-to-day basis, and the country music business is no exception. This book is intended as a snapshot of Nashville through the period during which it was researched and written, specifically 1994 through 1996. Many of the people quoted herein will have moved on to other places by the time this book comes out. But the essence of what they say and their place in an ongoing cultural procession remains the same. The quotes attributed herein are from direct interviews by the author, unless indicated otherwise. Every attempt was made to do interviews in person when possible.

INTRODUCTION
Version of the Truth

Myths are useful things, and in country music they are more important than in other genres of American music. Country music deals with everyday life, and it imbues aspects of country life—homesteads, tractors, pets, relationships, guitars—with an emotional, lyrical significance not found in the hormonally driven underpinnings of rock and R&B, or in the more intellectual communications of jazz. These appealing myths of country music provide a homey distraction from the turning wheels of the machine that is the business of country music. Success in Nashville has always been about the twin pursuit of myths and money, and in this book I have attempted to examine the enduring relationship between these two crucial aspects of country music's unwritten rules.

The late Joseph Campbell, the esteemed teacher and philosopher of mythology, wrote, ". . . in a culture that has been homogenous for some time, there are a number of understood, unwritten rules by which people live . . . an ethos, . . . a mode, . . . an understanding that 'we . . . do [things a certain] way.'" Nashville, home of country music, historically, spiritually, and in virtually every other way, has indeed been a homogenous place for much of country music's residence there. And in the business of music in that city over the last fifty years, a way of doing things has emerged and evolved and has, like the myths and legends of country music itself, been passed down from one generation to the next—a way of doing things that remains pleasantly opaque to those who choose to see only the myth and hear only the music.

The business of country music is about the process of reconciling the myth and the money. What I've tried to do with this book is look into the origins and at the present circumstances of the four primary groups of people that make up the country music machine: the record producers, the songwriters, the music publishers, and the musicians. In doing so, the book will look behind the curtain of the myth of country music—not to dispel any of its magic but, rather, to better appreciate it. Those who toil in the engine rooms of country music are legion, and in many respects are the same sorts of cogs, large and small, found in any industry. While each of these groups is found in all other genres of music, in Nashville and in country these players are different: like country music itself in recent years, they combine the clannish characteristics of a small, feudal society with the financial power of a major industry.

When I first began explaining the concept for this book in Nashville, I generally got two responses: "Great idea," and "Make sure you get it right." The consistent thing about these reactions was that they usually came in tandem, and they reflect the sense of independence and apartness that those in the business of country music have historically felt, particularly among the major players—the producers, songwriters, music publishers, and musicians. These four groups of people form a culture unlike any other found in the larger music business, and as such, there are cultural clashes. Nashville's southern location puts it in the region of the United States with the nation's lowest per capita income, yet the Nashville country music industry is a big money churner for the lucky few. As country's success blossomed in the early 1990s, country music and Nashville found themselves bathed in a media spotlight that brought inevitable comparisons with the larger culture to the fore.

I first encountered this palpable sense of underlying anxiety as a trade journalist writing about the recording studios in Nashville. In discussing how Nashville's recording studio business (or at least that substantial part of it not regularly subsidized by a direct connection to a record label and/or producer) related to the larger recording industry, nationally and internationally, I was told often and clearly that many potential clients from elsewhere continue to regard Nashville as a technological backwater. "They're not even sure we wear shoes down here," one studio manager once told me, quite seriously. Hats, yes; shoes, they're not so sure.

On the contrary, Nashville has a higher percentage of state-of-the-art digital audio recording capability than either New York or Los Angeles. There are hundreds of studios in and around the city, and few reside in chicken coops (although more and more of them are in people's homes and garages). Still, the stereotype of the country bumpkin standing shoeless on the side of the Information Highway persists and endures. And it bugs the hell out of everyone involved. The righteous indignation it generates in Nashville is a thin film over a deeply entrenched well of uneasiness about how country music, and by extension, Nashville, is perceived by the rest of the world.

This cultural neurosis has found at least a temporary palliative in the windfall that Nashville received from ballooning country music sales from 1990 through 1995. Aggregate country record sales reached slightly over $2 billion in 1995 (figured at the Recording Industry Association of America's slightly inflated rate of $15.25 per record retail price), half that of rock's $4.1 billion in sales but well above the categories of pop ($1.24 billion), urban/contemporary ($1.39 billion), rap ($825 million), classical ($357 million), and jazz ($369 million). Country's sales gave it 16.7 percent of the prerecorded music market in the United States in 1995, the high watermark for the genre's history. Country concert revenues produced over $126 million in 1995, with the top ten tours, including Reba McEntire, Alan Jackson, George Strait, Brooks & Dunn, Vince Gill, and Tim McGraw, accounting for $108 million of that total. According to Country Music

Foundation statistics, country-formatted radio stations had 77.3 million adult listeners in 1993, 21 million of them converts since 1990. Country radio had reached a zenith of 2,642 stations by 1994, its own high watermark.

Record sales and radio airplay tell only part of the story. Merchandising alone for Garth Brooks was estimated by *Billboard* magazine at $125 million in 1992. Brooks was quiet for most of 1994, but when he released a greatest hits package in December of that year, it sold nearly two million copies in the last two weeks of 1994 and it became the second-best-selling record of the year. Furthermore, Country Music Television (CMT), an all-country music video cable channel, is now a regular feature on U.S. and European cable systems and is also available to 46 million homes in fifty countries. (Gaylord Entertainment—the $690 million country music and media conglomerate that owns CMT, along with The Grand Ole Opry, Opryland, and its adjacent hotel and convention complex—proudly announced in the summer of 1994 that CMT was also available now in Asian markets; no local cable carriers, though, had yet chosen to pick it up.)

Nonetheless, as good as it has been for country music over the last five years, there was still a sense of impermanence about all this in Nashville, one that was detectable even before the sales and radio listenership declines of 1996 became evident. They have been through this before—witnessed previous sales booms, though not as strong as the current one. But this is a condition that has gone on for as long as country music has been an industry. Because, ultimately, it is a product, subject to consumer whim. It is designed to sell and to make its makers money, a basic reality that is rarely said out loud in country, with its emphasis on the myths of country music and the country lifestyle, as opposed to the world of pop and rock music, where dollar signs are acknowledged components of almost everything written about those genres. Money, in the tradition of the old Southern culture that still pervades the New South, is something to be made and spent, but not discussed in polite company. *Nashville's Unwritten Rules* aspires to shed some light on that topic.

With country music's percentage of the music product consumer pie just behind that of mainstream rock through 1995,
there was plenty of money to be made. It was good. Too good,
for some. A "Chicken Little" syndrome began appearing in
1995, as concerns arose about the sustainability of country's
current run, that the tide would recede again, as it had before
in 1955 and 1982. When the tide turned, starting in late 1995,
it was almost a relief. Country showed five straight years of
growth—1990 through 1994—but then, data released by various reporting organizations showed that country record sales
had slipped 11 percent in the first six months of 1996, from the
$2 billion in sales reported in 1995, and that country radio
listenership had declined by 20 percent over the previous three
years. And while the numbers looked healthy for country's live
show market, the larger picture was not; due to more acts touring, the overall industry was down by an average of 12 percent
by mid-1996, according to *Amusement Business* magazine.
(However, Garth Brooks, who accounted for $10 million in
touring revenues in 1994, did not tour in 1995.) Taking a page
from the touring strategies of alternative rock music (e.g.
Lollapalloza), the country music industry tried to combat the
falling profitability of tours by grouping major and new artists
into a single tour. In one instance, Clay Walker, Terry Clark,
James Bonamy, and Emilio were scheduled to tour in 1997 as
a single package, known as the Four-Star Blowout, managed
by subscription-based entertainment system Primestar.

These data were punctuated by the announcement in late
1996 that A&M Records, one of the last of the major labels to
set up shop in Nashville, was folding its operations into
Mercury Records, both of which are owned by Dutch-based
PolyGram Records. On one hand, the closure of A&M Records
was relatively insignificant: the label—started as Polydor
Records in 1994—had only seven artists and only one of
which, Toby Keith, had had any measurable success in terms
of record sales and airplay. The company's two-year existence
had not given it time to develop. On the other hand, A&M's
disappearance underlined many of the anxieties that had
accompanied country music' s meteoric rise over the past five

years. As one of numerous expansion labels such as Decca and Patriot (now also closed), its loss illuminated the inflated rosters of the labels in Nashville, which had mushroomed from six in 1989 to more than thirty by 1996. At the same time as those rosters had grown, the main conduit to bring them to market—country radio—was also experiencing its own decline, and alternative promotional systems were still in their formative stages. And a shortage of executive talent— the prime reason cited publicly by A&M for its closing—contrasted Nashville's proven ability to manage a niche market with its ability to manage a sustained larger industry.

Yet both Nashville and country music have retained their allure for outsiders, particularly those from the entertainment industry. The city's population of just over a half-million is being added to annually, many of whom are refugees from New York and Los Angeles's also-ailing music industries, not to mention riots and earthquakes, most of whom report "quality of life" as their reason for moving to Nashville. (One Nashville radio station cited a probably apocryphal but telling report stating that approximately seven hundred California drivers' licenses a month were being exchanged for Tennessee licenses in 1994; the state had gained 54,000 new residents from out of state that year, 3,000 of whom were from outside the United States according to the U.S. Census Bureau.)

In contrast to the youthful image that propelled country music in the early 1990s, Nashville was also a magnet for aging pop and rock stars; among the new residents were disco diva Donna Summer, Bob Gaudio (the Four Seasons), Michael MacDonald (the Doobie Brothers), Felix Cavaliere (the Rascals), Dino Elefante (Kansas), jazz guitarist Larry Carlton, Al Kooper (Blood, Sweat & Tears, Blues Project), Mark Farner of Grand Funk Railroad fame, Michael Omartian (producer of Christopher Cross and other L.A. pop acts of the 1980s and now producing Christian and country records), and Peter Frampton. Nashville has also become attractive to celebrities from other media, including Tom Cruise and Luke Perry, who have purchased homes in the area in recent years.

Along with quality of life drawing newcomers to Nashville, the draw also seems to be the myth of country music's heritage—which for many satisfies a need to touch, even if figuratively, more traditional values—and the image of what country music has come to represent in 1990s America: a renewed sense of excitement in music; a return to melody; a return to the guitar, the ultimate icon in contemporary western music; and a return to a music that is fundamentally conservative at its core.

But Nashville and country music's futures remain intertwined, giving country much of its strength from something that no other genre does: a highly evolved and sometimes rigid but very stable power structure, which has been in place for over forty years in Nashville's music industry—an industry that has kept the music, and itself, together in a way that no other music format has experienced.

While everyone automatically associates Nashville as the locus of country music, where would you go if you wanted to find the epicenter of R&B music? Memphis, Detroit, Philadelphia, and Muscle Shoals would be fine choices if all you were interested in was the history of the music; R&B moved out of New York years ago in any recognizable form, replaced first by Disco, then Urban/Contemporary, Dance and Hip-Hop. And those last three subgenres have seen a partial migration back to Atlanta, whence R&B came after the 1960s. But while artists such as Bobby Brown, Whitney Houston, and Elton John have taken up residences there, major record labels have little or no significant presence in Atlanta. Those labels, in turn, continue to maintain their headquarters in New York and Los Angeles, but neither has much claim on being the current focal point of anything other than some nonmainstream music bloodlines anymore—such as jazz in New York. And there the strategic planners at major record labels sit, watching the maps, looking for the next Minneapolis/Prince or Seattle/Grunge pairing, and waiting for another cultural shift to manifest the next craze in music in yet another off-road location.

By contrast, Nashville is *the* center of the country music industry and residency there, in some form, is almost always a requirement for those who want to be involved. The few who prosper without a 372 prefix to their zip code, such as Dwight Yoakam in Los Angeles, the Bellamy Brothers in Florida and, before them, Buck Owens and Merle Haggard in Bakersfield, California, are the exceptions to the first of the Unwritten Rules: Thou Shalt Live Here. There are post office box businesses that turn decent profits renting out Music Row addresses for out-of-towners. While it's hip for Hollywood gliteratti to have second homes in Nevada or Montana, their country music counterparts tend to go no farther than Franklin, Hendersonville, or Mount Juliet, all within a half-hour drive of Music Row.

Country music's modern era began in the late 1940s, with the arrival of the legendary Hank Williams, whose innate ability to write simple, piercing songs combined with a voice that stood apart from the radio crooners of the day gave country a new credibility in music, as did the fact that numerous pop artists of the time, including Tony Bennett, Frankie Laine, Teresa Brewer, and Kay Starr, began to cross his songs over onto other charts. His brief appearance on the scene before an untimely and tragic death at age twenty-nine on New Year's Eve in 1952 coincided with the beginning of a new level of autonomy for Nashville record labels, which were owned mainly by such major labels as Columbia Records and RCA Records, based in New York, and Capitol Records, headquartered in Los Angeles (and the first label to open a Nashville division, in 1950). While country was still regarded as a regional music form through the 1970s, many mainstream music artists, from Bill Haley to Foreigner, have temporarily visited to work with the city's studios, engineers, musicians, and producers.

Country is borrowing heavily from pop music today—and vice versa, as the pedal steel guitar on Sheryl Crow's 1994 pop hit "All I Want To Do" indicates—as part of a natural evolution as its makers increasingly come from age groups that have more to do with Lynyrd Skynyrd, Billy Joel, and Megadeth (all of whom did all or part of some of recent recordings in Nashville) than with Hank Snow and Red Foley. But those two artists, and other country music legends of their generation that spanned the '50s, '60s, and '70s, receive a level of respect among the people in Nashville's music industry that a visiting outsider could never achieve—regardless of how many records he or she sold. And while rock artists generally have to wait for postmortem hagiographies or the Rock & Roll Hall of Fame in Cleveland to memorialize them, many of their country counterparts have already been acknowledged and enshrined; the Country Music Hall of Fame has many items from both older and contemporary county artists, and the late Roy Acuff lived rent-free for years in a house on the grounds at Opryland provided by the theme park's owner Gaylord Entertainment.

Fueling the myth is the protectionist policies of the local media, who show respect for country stars in an almost Sicilian manner. Readers of both the fanzines and the local Nashville papers will be kept abreast of Tammy Wynette's illnesses and recoveries and the acrimonious distribution of Conway Twitty's estate, all told in a matter-of-fact sort of way, but it will be tinged with sympathy rather than the lurid over-tones those same stories take on in supermarket tabloids. And while the tabloids have found fertile fields in contemporary country music personalities, even they handle these people with kid gloves most of the time. When the *National Enquirer* launched its *Country Weekly* in early 1994, its executive editor, Roger Capettini, acknowledged to a reporter from the *Nashville Tennessean* that even that veteran of libel litigation was somewhat cowed by country music's closely knit ranks. "If I do something to harm one publicist [in Nashville], it spreads through the town and we're dead," he said. "We're putting millions of dollars into this. We're not gonna screw it up by turning some dirt on one artist."

Roy Acuff enjoyed demigod status throughout his long life before entering the country pantheon of official deity upon his death in 1993. Other veterans of modern country's formative generation, such as Merle Haggard, Waylon Jennings, Marty Robbins, Red Sovine, Willie Nelson, and others, were elevated to the status of near-divinity long before their active careers or lives came to a close, even though they were no longer regulars on music sales charts. This is in sharp contrast with the kind of footnote, filler-item regard most past-their-prime pop and rock acts receive when they fall from sales grace.

The familylike embrace that country music wraps around its members is as much a defensive one as it is borne of Southern manners. The sense that Nashville is held in a lower regard by larger music centers is as truly felt as it is documented in these pages. And those who have worked in Nashville's music business for a long time are vocal both about that perception and their reaction to it.

These pages attempt to relate the stories of some of the people who created the structure that keeps country in Nashville. To say that any organism is the sum of its components is a cliché, and to say that it's the people who make any industry what it is, is trite. But both statements are apt here. The members of country's internal combustion engine—the producers, writers, music publishers, and musicians—are, for the most part, unknown outside of Nashville, and even to some extent within the larger music industry, a fact that reflects the insularity that Nashville, even in its newfound success, both perpetuates and endures. The players are presented chronologically to convey the sense of continuity that is one of the main underpinnings of Nashville. There are omissions because the cast of players is and has been huge. Any apologies due are hereby rendered in advance.

A Little Background Music

MUSIC ROW

I T'S RARE TO FIND a physical location where the leadership and the constituency of music can interface. New York and Los Angeles have the trendy nightclubs, but they are ephemeral, and the hipness quotient required for entrance shuts out many regular fans—and the occasional record company employee without sufficient credentials. Bourbon Street in New Orleans and Beale Street in Memphis offer considerable access to music, but little opportunity to do its business. But in Nashville, there is an intersection where they all come together, even though one group may not always be aware of the other. It's a long dogleg that starts with the several blocks that comprise Music Row—Sixteenth and Seventeenth Avenues South—and adjacent Music Circle, where most of the record labels and a handful of the city's scores of major recording studios are located.

Music Row is high on the tour bus agenda but, aside from more obvious examples of the music business's presence, such as the white curvilinear-fronted edifice that the performing rights organization the American Society of Composers and Publishers (ASCAP) built in 1992, what makes Music Row what it is is opaque to the increasingly upscale tourists that are driven past it in buses every day. According to a Nashville Chamber of Commerce profile in 1994, 73 percent of

Nashville's tourists have had some college, up from 52 percent five years before, and their incomes hovered around $46,000. But despite their good incomes and educations, a tour of The Row is like being driven through the canyons of Wall Street and being told that the financial and economic heartbeat of the world is pumping away behind the brick and granite facades. You come away with a sense of intangibility, of having been told something that can't be empirically proven, even though you want to believe it's true.

The ASCAP building is the joint of the dogleg. Directly across the confluence of Demonbreun and Division streets was, up until recently, Gilley's (it has now been replaced by Gilley's General Store), a 10,000-square-foot, two-story gray faux Victorian building on nearly an acre of increasingly costly Row-area land. Gilley's included a country karaoke gazebo in the parking lot from which country singer wanna-bes would serenade the mixture of old and new Music Row office buildings and wandering tourists from morning till midnight.

To the right of Gilley's General Store is a one-story brick and frame house once owned by Hank Williams, Sr. It was moved there from its original location on Franklin Road where Williams lived for two years after he bought it in 1949, and has been used as a museum, then a nightclub, and now houses a recording studio and publishing company, heralded by a hand-painted sign. To the left begins a long, low-rise block of honky-tonk stores and museum/gift shops that flaunt the mythical names of country music: The Hank Williams Museum; Conway Twitty's Country Store & Record Shop; Loretta Lynn's Western Store; The Randy Travis Gift Shop. It's hard to tell which is the better barometer of fame and immortality—a guitar or stage jacket enshrined in the Country Music Hall of Fame across the street or an ashtray with your name on it. The latter likely generates more income.

Music Row is four streets, Sixteenth and Seventeenth Avenues South—also called Music Square East and West, respectively—bounded at the top and bottom into a rectangle formed by Division Street at one end and Grand Street at the other, divided, as are many Nashville blocks, by an alley that accesses the parking lots behind the buildings. The Row was once a respectable residential address, evident in the lavishness of some of the structures, such as one ornate house on Seventeenth Avenue designed as a scale model of the original Tennessee governor's mansion and that till a few years ago housed Eleven Eleven Recording (named after its address), owned by Waylon Jennings. In spite of the flurry of construction prompted by country music's recent success, much of Music Row is still made up of two-story homes and bungalows. Pending zoning changes, however, could soon make many of the remaining ones available to the expanding commercial zone that the Row has become.

The row became Music Row in the early 1950s, when Owen Bradley, then head of Decca Records's country music division, opened a recording studio in a military surplus Quonset hut on Sixteenth Avenue. Music publishing companies Hill & Range Music and Cedarwood Music were among the early tenants of Music Row, attracted by the then-relatively inexpensive real estate values there as Nashville's encroaching urbanization brought prices down. Prices still fluctuate today, but generally upwardly, with office space going anywhere from $12 to $16 per square foot. And if you can't find the kind of structure you're looking for, you can always build it. MCA Records, Sony Records, and Warner Bros./Nashville have each opened showplaces in recent years that have made their Los Angeles counterparts envious, and record label Capitol Nashville broke ground in late 1996 on a dedicated new home for that company, pulling it out of the somewhat faceless office building on West End Avenue where it had rented space for years. But you can only build if you can find land; the Music Row area had less than 32,000 square feet of late-model office space available as of 1995. Performing rights organization Broadcast Music Inc. (BMI) has torn up its parking lot to put in an office building to accommodate a shift of personnel from New York to Nashville in 1994. Reba McEntire's Starstruck Entertainment, which she owns with husband/manager Narvel Blackstock and which also manages the careers of other such artists as Linda Davis and Mathews, Wright & King, operates a publishing company and several other business ventures including an aircraft charter service, replaced the two-story quad apartment complex on Music Square West that once was home for Kris Kristofferson with a palatial 24,000-square-foot office and recording studio complex.

The Row is changing, as is country music itself. But Music Row also continues to harbor the unique combination of sentiment and commerce that are at country music's foundation. The Country Music Hall of Fame & Museum announced in 1994 that it would move closer to downtown, near the rejuvenated District area and a recently completed metropolitan arena, and just across the Cumberland River from where a new football stadium that will be home to the former Houston Oilers in 1999. The announcement of the Hall of Fame's intent to move tugged the heartstrings of many who saw in the institution—which has been on that site since 1967—a sense of permanence similar to the one country's own history carries with it. But others were equally vociferous about the economic impact of the move. "That business is being disrupted on Music Row is a public policy issue," is the way a local real estate developer and a general partner in Barbara Mandrell Country, a tourist attraction and gift shop across the street, said in an interview.

Even as the Row changes, an element of continuity to country's past remains. Many of the properties along its two main thoroughfares are owned by some of Music Row's founders. The old RCA building at 30 Music Square West, assessed at just over $1.2 million, is owned by Owen Bradley, his brother and session guitarist, Harold, and their wives. They've owned the property since 1963. They also owned what was the only remaining vacant lot on the Row, just across from the CMA headquarters. Chet Atkins owns several properties along the Row, solely or jointly, including one, appropriately enough, at the corner of 18th Avenue South and Chet Atkins Place. Singer Ray Stevens has a string of older residence-type properties along the Row, including five on 17th Avenue South.

Music Row has become the combined Wall Street and Madison Avenue of country, a canyon of granite facades that house the growing legions of workers that are required when a successful business becomes an even more successful industry. While the increasingly corporate countenance of the Row is diminishing its potential for eccentricity, it still has its moments, which have their precedents from earlier generations. A well-remembered event from the mid-1970s is of a would-be recording artist who tried in vain to get an appointment with Chet Atkins at his office on Seventeenth Avenue. In frustration, he ran out in the middle of the street and took all his clothes off, stopping traffic until police arrived to cart him off. He never did get his appointment. In 1996, a similar event happened when an aspiring artist sauntered down Music Row on Valentine's Day wearing nothing but her cowboy boots and cowboy hat. She received a citation for indecent exposure, but like her predecessor, no record deal.

Those who work on Music Row have traditionally been apprentices trained within the industry. It's telling that, while most of Nashville's major label divisions are headed by someone who is—or at least has been—a record producer, none of the New York- or Los Angeles-based main record label offices is so led. Instead, they have long looked to MBA programs for their executive leadership. Nashville has started down that road, as well. Two area universities, Belmont University and Middle Tennessee State University, have well-evolved music business degree programs that can provide in a matter of years some of the basics that used to take decades on the street to acquire, from record engineering to production to publishing and management. Such courses are becoming more common in American collegiate-level schools, with over 200 accredited schools or programs available teaching record production or engineering in the United States. But few of these programs have such an alluring proximity to Nashville. Belmont University, located a few blocks off Music Row, started its music business program in 1972 and now, with 400 students a year enrolled in it, has become the most sought-after curriculum among the school's offerings. The program's alumni include singer Trisha Yearwood and any number of publishing, record company management, promotion, entertainment law, booking agency, and audio engineering people in Nashville.

What the schools can't instill, though, are instincts. Unpaid internships await most of the program's graduates, but to make any money in country music you have to acquire a degree of another sort—one based on what almost always proves to be a lengthy apprenticeship .

A BRIEF HISTORY OF NASHVILLE AND COUNTRY MUSIC

Right from the beginning, Nashville understood the value of tracking trends. Originally named Nashboro by the English/ Scottish settlers who founded it in 1779, it was changed to accommodate a French suffix in 1784 after the United States once again allied itself with France against Britain. The first organized Europeans to reach the area, after French fur traders who set up a trading post near the area's salt spring in 1710, were James Robertson and James Donelson. They situated the city on a bluff overlooking the winding Cumberland River on Christmas Day, 1779. They were followed a year later by the women, children, and baggage trains, much the same way immigrating songwriters and singers do it now.

Like other Anglo settlers who populated the southeast and Appalachian states in the early nineteenth century, Nashville's original settlers brought with them a strain of music traceable to the medieval ballads of Britain. This medieval template aptly describes the structure of the music industry in Nashville—one of dynasties: the Bradleys; the Roses; the Wendells; and numerous other families in which the way Nashville's country music business operates has been handed down from father to son and daughter, and to others not related by blood but by a cultural and economic connection equally sustaining.

Nashville was made the capital of the state in 1843 and throughout the nineteenth century it acquired roots for the future of its music business. Publishers of shaped note music—a rudimentary form of notation in which shapes, rather than the position of notes on a staff, determined pitch and duration—began churning out hymnals for religious groups. But the force that was to make music a perceived cornerstone of Nashville came via another means: technology.

Technology

In the early twentieth century, country music existed in a more primitive form, dubbed "hill-billie music" by the Northern press of the time. The first citation of the term was believed to have been seen in the *New York Journal* on April 23, 1900. The music, based around stringed instruments such as fiddles, banjos, and dulcimers, lived in the hills and hollers of the South, rarely venturing any further.

Much of what did get beyond those mountainous and cultural borders was the result of musical expeditions by Northern musicologists. Ralph Peer, the recording director for the OKeh label, is perhaps the best remembered of these. He spent much of the 1920s and 1930s capturing Southern music on primitive recording equipment, including seminal sessions with the Carter Family and Jimmie Rodgers in August 1927, in Bristol, Tennessee.

Even as early recording machines were transcribing the music that had been hidden in the hills for years and bringing it to a wider audience, another technology was also beginning to make its presence felt. Starting with KDKA in Pittsburgh, Pennsylvania, radio began its days as the premier disseminator of culture in America that lasted until the 1950s. Radio stations owned by their advertisers were common in radio's early days, and the National Life and Accident Insurance Company of Nashville started a station of its own—a 1,000-watt transmitter with the call sign WSM, which doubled as an acronym for the insurance company's corporate motto, "We Shield Millions"—in a studio on Seventh Avenue and Union Street in downtown Nashville in October 1925. The following month, at 8:00 P.M. on November 8, George D. Hay, a former newspaperman for the Memphis *Commercial Appeal* and broadcaster for Chicago-based WGN, introduced an eighty-year-old mountain fiddler named Uncle Jimmy Thompson to an audience of unknown size. Originally entitled the "WSM Barn Dance," it soon became known as the Grand Ole Opry, so dubbed because the program followed a legitimate operatic broadcast. Sponsoring a fifteen-minute segment on the Opry cost an advertiser $100 dollars (it costs over $700 today for the Saturday night show, less for Friday's performance). The artists on the Opry were making five dollars a week and were, for the most part, happy to get it.

The Opry

The Opry struck a nerve, thanks in part to radio's ability to broadcast to the rural parts of America whose musical tastes were not represented in the mass markets of the cities. It quickly became a gravitational core for what was to become country music, preceding the geographical one that Nashville was to become.

The Opry's popularity caused it to move several times in search of larger quarters, from a cramped parlor to two other locations within the National Life Building, and from there through a succession of theaters and even a revival tent in East Nashville. It finally came to its penultimate and best-known rest in 1941 at the Ryman Auditorium, the former Union Gospel Tabernacle on lower Broadway, which sat 3,500 attendees, where it remained until it was moved to the Opryland theme park in 1974.

Even with the Grand Ole Opry, there wasn't enough gravity in Nashville to guarantee the city's destiny as the indisputable home of the country music business. The Opry was but one of several barn dance-type radio shows that sprang up in the 1920s and 1930s, a trend that lasted until they failed to make the transition to television. (*Hee Haw* not withstanding. That program, first broadcast on network television in June of

1969, has been kept alive on The Nashville Network—TNN—in reruns since its last original episode in 1991.) WBAP in Fort Worth broadcast what is generally regarded as the first barn dance in 1923. Sears & Roebuck-owned WLS in Chicago, whose call letters stood for "World's Largest Store" and where the Opry announcer George Hay got his broadcasting start, inaugurated its barn dance program in 1924. Dozens of barn dance-type shows sprang up on radio stations across the country, and were quite popular through the early 1950s.

Throughout the early 1930s country was a ghettoized musical form but one that gained commercial appeal by playing up its hillbilly characteristics. Hay went so far as to apply names to musical entities that did little more than literally wander in from the surrounding hills, and reinforced the stereotypes that continue to plague country music when he encouraged the wearing of denim overalls and other rural accoutrements among Opry performers. Vernon Dalhart, Jimmie Rodgers, the Carter Family, Gid Tanner and The Skillet Lickers and a handful of other country acts dominated what passed for sales charts in those days, when record labels depended largely upon department stores for sales reports, as did *Billboard* when it introduced the first Country chart as "Top Hillbilly Hits" in 1941. In his capacity as Opry manager and chief announcer, Hay's influence shaped the institution and, by association, country music in the pre-Hank Williams era, keeping it closely intertwined with his perception of its rural roots.

The Visual Medium

In 1930, an early brush with another mainstream technology — and country music's first initiation to visual images—was introduced by Gene Autry, a former relief telegrapher with the St. Louis & Frisco Railroad in Oklahoma whose "I Left My Gal In The Mountains" became one of the top recordings of that year. Autry rode a recording career into the movies, starting with a cameo appearance as a singer with Ken Maynard in "In Old Santa Fe" in 1934, and continuing on through a series of singing Hollywood oatburners—and in the process forever, and inaccurately, linked country-and-western music genres. Even though there was no tradition that as yet had established Nashville as the home of anything more than one of several radio barn dances, Autry and other Hollywood cowboys were destined to become regarded as apostates in their time, deacons of country's first schism.

This premodern period of the 1920s and 1930s was critical in country music's development as much for the technology of music as for the music itself. Flat 78 rpm records had replaced the original Edison cylinders; radio had become a national platform for country; cinematic westerns from a rapidly expanding film industry imparted a glamorous Hollywood patina that placed rhinestone jackets and elaborate string ties as a counterweight to the denim overalls that the Opry's George Hay demanded; and the jukebox began to have its first major impact on music, giving nickel-dropping consumers a choice of music. The Opry's success alone, though, still didn't secure for Nashville a lock as the nominal home of the country music business.

THE BUILDERS OF THE MACHINE

One of the evolutionary developments that began to position Nashville as the epicenter of the country music industry was the arrival of a new, more business-minded, artist/performer constituency, who in turn would lay the basis for the first generation of country music executives. Roy Acuff and the Smokey Mountain Boys came to Nashville in 1938 from Knoxville and had won the lead spot on the Opry by the following year. Acuff's recordings of "The Great Speckled Bird" and "Steel Guitar Blues" in 1937 landed him in the top five in country sales for that year. They were recorded on the American Record Corporation label, which was bought by Columbia Records the next year as larger, New York-based record labels began establishing their presences in the South via acquisition of small regional labels. Acuff's "Wabash Cannonball," destined to become a signature song for him, was the number-one record for 1938 in its field.

Contrary to the mentality of many country musicians and Opry performers of the time, Acuff regarded country performing as a business and a full-time career, not as an avocational pastime to fill in the spaces between day jobs. Acuff discovered the economic value of music publishing when he sponsored fifteen minutes of airtime on WSM to sell his songbook. Within the first week he had 10,000 orders at twenty-five cents each and had sold 100,000 copies in the first two months. He remained a fixture with the Opry, its physical and metaphysical figurehead—as both a performer and a businessman—until his death in 1993.

Fred Rose, a composer with equal doses of talent and business acumen, was not the first to realize that country songs had the potential to crossover to more mainstream musical tastes—Hollywood in particular had established that with its singing cowboy films—but Rose was the most efficient and effective at doing something about it; and his was a seminal role in creating a structure that allowed Nashville, not New York, to reap the benefits. Rose, who died in 1954, was a mercurial man, a well-regarded piano player who was with Paul Whiteman's and Fats Waller's orchestras and was a successful pop songwriter from Chicago who took a position as staff pianist at WSM in Nashville in 1942. His vision of music always seemed to include a business marketing component. He wrote under several pen names, including Bart Dawson and Floyd Jenkins, with the idea that country-sounding names would more quickly get songs placed in that genre. He also was able to talk composers Pee Wee King and Redd Stewart into selling them the copyright to "Tennessee Waltz" for $50, a composition that went on to become the state's official song and which has generated millions of dollars in airplay and sales revenues since. A fast chemistry, based as much on business as on artistry, developed between Rose and Acuff. That same year, with $25,000 seed money from Acuff that was returned to him several thousand times over before he died, Rose and Acuff formed Acuff-Rose Publications, a music publishing company that set the tone for publishing and other music ventures in Nashville for years to come.

Acuff-Rose acquired a vast number of copyrights over the years, including those of Hank Williams, Sr. and Ernest Tubb, and it had a substantial hand in developing country artists, becoming the kind of creative publisher that Nashville music publishers have become known for and which was in stark contrast to the "rent collector" mentality that characterized the major music publishers of the day, who preferred to acquire copyrights with proven economic success rather than take chances on the potential of new, unrecorded songs. Most important, though, it kept more of the money in Nashville instead of it simply streaming off to New York. Acuff-Rose was followed in Nashville by music publishers Cedarwood and Tree, which formed a publishing triumvirate that dominated the city's publishing industry until the explosion of new publishing companies in the 1970s.

With an indigenous publishing presence established by Acuff-Rose and a handful of other new publishers, the next element in the creation of a self-sufficient industry was the further development of a locally based record business. Ralph Peer had come to Nashville for Victor Records in 1928 as part of a Southern field-recording tour. Victor had done the first country recordings, with a hillbilly artist named Eck Robertson, in New York in 1922, who had had success with a recording of the song "Sally Goodin'" in 1923. OKeh Records, where Peer began his recording career, recorded Fiddlin' John Carson in Atlanta and Henry Whitter in New York the same year, among many other such rural artists, all three of whom were successful, giving the company a base in the music and encouraging Peer's further field recording travels. Peer, how-ever, believed that his long-term benefits lay in publishing; he worked for Victor without pay on the condition that he be given publishing rights to all the recorded material. These copyrights became the foundation for the Peer-Southern Organization, a music publisher that did well with country music but which ultimately remained corporately aloof from Nashville.

Another field recordist was Art Satherly, a debonair native of England, born in Bristol in 1889, who worked in several capacities in the U.S. entertainment industry during the 1920s and 1930s, eventually becoming a scout for the American Recording Company (ARC). He traveled the South recording country and blues artists on wax disc masters, using hotel room bathrooms and train station waiting rooms as temporary recording studios. In the process, Satherly made some of early country music's seminal recordings, including Gene Autry's "Back In The Saddle Again" and "You Are My Sunshine," Roy Acuff's "Great Speckled Bird," Bill Monroe's "Blue Moon of Kentucky," Patsy Montana's "I Want To Be A Cowboy's Sweetheart," and Bob Wills's "New San Antonio Rose."

The leading record labels at the time, Decca, Columbia, and RCA Victor, all had modern recording facilities in Manhattan (Capitol was based in Los Angeles and had its facilities there); in between their field recording activities and the New York studio facilities were smaller studios in places such as Chicago, Dallas, and Cincinnati, where Hank Williams and other country acts did some of their earliest sessions. Some more sophisticated early recording efforts were made in Nashville at the end of the World War II by RCA Records, which recorded Eddy Arnold in Nashville in 1944, and Decca, which cut tracks with Red Foley and Ernest Tubb there in 1945. In 1947, three WSM engineers—Aaron Shelton, Carl Jenkins, and George Reynolds—established the Castle Studio in the now-demolished Tulane Hotel in downtown Nashville. The Castle marked the beginnings of organized, centrally located recording in Nashville. During the studio's first years in existence, Columbia introduced the 33⅓ rpm LP format (1948) and RCA brought out the 45 rpm single (1949), more durable and less expensive consumer formats that helped create a larger demand for recordings.

By the mid-1960s there were a dozen studios in Nashville, most of them owned by the major recording labels or producers working for them. Today, *Mix* magazine, the leading U.S. professional audio trade journal, lists over 60 significant— i.e., multiple-room facilities with technology investments of $500,000 or more—recording studios in the Nashville area; the Nashville Yellow Pages has over 200 studios, ranging from major facilities to ambitious holes-in-the-wall. The introduction in the late 1980s of powerful, affordable so-called home recording technology easily pushes those numbers to over 500 and are steadily rising.

Transitions of Power

Owen Bradley, staff pianist and bandleader at WSM, moonlighted for Paul Cohen, head of Decca's New York-based Artist & Repertoire (A&R) department, as session leader for Decca recording dates in Nashville, and took over the position of local head of A&R when Cohen left Decca in 1958. The previous year, guitarist Chet Atkins—signed as an artist to RCA in 1947—took over RCA as head of A&R from New York-appointed Steve Sholes after Atkins had apprenticed running sessions at the label's studio on Music Row, which opened in 1955. Decca and RCA were two of the three major record companies still in existence that operated in the United States through the 1940s. By the 1950s, though, the field had widened to include others that would grow into major label status, including Capitol Records (1942 in Los Angeles), MGM Records (a division of the film company in Hollywood, in 1946), and Mercury Records (Chicago, 1947). The period from the end of World War II through the early 1950s also saw the development of dozens of independent record labels representing diverse musical genres based in both the traditional power centers and in other locations. In 1947, R&B label Chess Records incorporated in Chicago, as did Imperial Records in Los Angeles. Atlantic Records and Jubilee Records were both formed in New York in 1948. The contending power centers included Meteor Records (1951) and Sun Records (1953) in Memphis, Duke/Peacock Records in Houston (1949), Trumpet Records in Jackson, Mississippi (1951), and the beginnings of two country music independents, Bullet Records in Nashville (1946) and Dot Records in Gallatin, Tennessee (1950).

The significance of these two seminal transitions of power—Cohen to Bradley at Decca and Sholes to Atkins at RCA—at a time when the overall music industry was growing was monumental in the country music industry's history: they represented the transition to direct management of a Nashville major label division by a locally based executive. Atkins and Bradley shared some common traits: they were musicians, with sensibilities in both country and pop music; they were businessmen aware of the potential of country as a product; and they dealt with music as much as an economic proposition as an art form—as did Acuff and Rose on the publishing side. Furthermore, they understood the need to have a system under which control of the country record-making process was kept in Nashville. The result was the development of a pattern unique to Nashville and country music: the rise of the producer/label division (as opposed to the owner of an independent label) head whose involvement in the music business was much more comprehensive than that of his counterparts in New York or Los Angeles, who by the late 1970s were almost exclusively businessmen. It also contributed significantly to a transition in the role of a music producer from the person who mated song material with artists—the basic definition of the old record industry position of Artist & Repertoire—to someone who, as a musician himself, became considerably more involved in the shaping of the sound and arrangements of recordings. The classic relationships that followed in pop and rock, such as those between

George Martin and the Beatles, and Andrew Loog Oldham and the Rolling Stones owe much to the way in which Bradley and Atkins formulated their artistic positions.

The Nashville archetype of the producer continues to this day—it is not unusual for a single person to be a musician, director of a label's operations, a producer, a publisher, a songwriter whose compositions sometimes appear on the product he produces, and an owner to some extent in a recording facility—to be all these things except the recording artist himself. (While more country recording artists are getting coproduction credits on their recordings, such as Tim McGraw, Alison Krauss, and Patty Loveless, very few country records have ever been produced solely by the recording artist—another way in which country productions differ markedly from pop recordings.) This is a remarkable development and singular in the music industry, paralleled on a wide scale (the phenomenon has been seen in small blues and jazz labels over the years) only recently in Urban music genres.

Country music is a genre that created its own traditions, that stayed firm enough to maintain its own protocols and customs, yet was flexible enough to bend with market realities over the years. The deepening relationship between publishers and producers over the next three-and-a-half decades would form the core of the system that remains central to Nashville's operations today.

This emerging structural core of the modern country industry got its first test in 1957, during a time when country sales and airplay were eroding under the onslaught of rock. It also provided evidence of the organic ability of Nashville's country music industry to respond in a coherent manner to such change with the creation of the Country Music Association (CMA). The Country Music Association was formed in 1958 out of the ashes of the former Country Music Disk Jockey Association (CMDJA).

Radio play for conventional country music was losing ground as stations switched formats toward rock & roll. The burgeoning CMA organized an active offensive against the loss of radio stations, with people such as Bill Hudson, who scanned the radio industry trade publications for stations of any format showing ratings problems and then often personally drove out to explain to the station management why country music would save their ratings. "He would tell them that the country fans were loyal to the artist and thus to the stations that played them and the advertisers that advertised on them," remembers Joe Talbot, a past CMA president. "He'd even tell them which types of advertisers to go after to get the most out of a country audience, such as furniture and auto makers. And it worked."

It did; from 81 stations programming country in 1961, the number rose to over 600 by 1973, and to 1,534 by 1980. Full-time country radio programming counted 2,203 stations as of 1992, after a slight decline in the mid-1980s. The CMA itself was also growing; as of 1995 the organization currently had more than 7,000 members in thirty-one countries, with 700 and other groups affiliated with it. But its crowning achievement was the building of a bridge between the country music industry and its radio network, a relationship that is often strained but one that has helped keep country music an identifiable entity.

In short, never before had a creative music industry organized itself so effectively and so efficiently. In the estimation of CMA director Bill Ivey, the CMA "created an alliance among publishing, radio, and record interests that could affect the financial well-being of the country music industry." The CMA formalized what had been up till then an ad hoc consortium of interests that all shared the common denominator of the financial bottom line of country music as a business.

As I said at the outset, economic success is the final arbiter in country music. If country music began, and continues to describe itself, as music for the common man, then the common man is allowed his financial ambitions and dreams. A good song may be in the ears of the beholder, but the ultimate determination of what's good and what isn't has always been in the song's performance in the marketplace, not on a stage or a recording studio or in a Music Row executive's office.

That conclusion draws contempt from those in its production hierarchy who maintain to a man (and to some extent lately, to a woman) that money is not what country is all about. But the observation requires a slight tilt of perspective to make it fit. It is about money: not money that makes you better than anyone else, but that makes you better than you were, bespeaking a fundamental Christian ethic that doesn't saddle success with any implicit guilt, so long as God and fellow man get their due. More specifically, the nineteenth-century Protestant concept that financial success is a sign of heavenly approval reigns in the country music business. The key to that success, and thus that approval, is hard work. And the structure of the country music business in Nashville conspires to keep it that way: the small circle of record producers works diligently to keep that group compact, while pretenders to those positions work hard to not so much widen it as to acquire a seat when the generational game of musical chairs allows. Despite the enlarged size of label rosters in Nashville, it is still a relatively small coterie of songwriters and producers that continues to dominate the parentheses beneath song titles on charts, while at the same time a wave of new songwriters seeks to enter that realm. In this environment, hard work is not simply its own reward—it is a means to a very specific end. The meek inherit little in Nashville, but true to its Southern social roots they fare better there than the rude and the uninitiated—those who have not learned the Unwritten Rules—who inherit even less. To offer some Grand Unified Theory of Country, Nashville has produced a thousand songwriting, producing, singing observers who collectively and instinctively wrap themselves around a geographic location, three or four chords, and a simple belief in themselves, as individuals and a community, that is unparalleled in any other contemporary form of music.

Nashville and, especially, the four groups who make up its music machine—the producers, the songwriters, the publishers, and the musicians—are what will continue to cause country music to sustain itself. It is a business after all, a money-making machine, and the rules of the country music business that have until now always remained unspoken, will become more evident through the words of the people who follow—and break—these unwritten rules.

The Producers, The Princes

THE RECORD PRODUCER IS a creation of technology and art. The name of the first one is lost to history, but by the 1940s it was a common term in the music industry. And from the beginning, it has been a dual role of managing the creative and practical sides of a recording. The best analogy of the record producer's role is that of a film director's. A producer oversees the entire creative process of a record, including the choice of song material, the choice of recording, mixing and mastering locations, the selection of musicians, and other aspects of the record. In addition, the producer is also generally responsible for supervising and allocating the record's budget. However, the role of the record producer in pop, rock, and other mainstream music genres has undergone considerable change in recent years. In the 1970s and 1980s, the rise of the singer/songwriter artist evolved into that of the artist/producer, with more self-produced records released and more records done as production collaborations between artists and producers.

More recently, the development and proliferation of affordable, powerful digital recording equipment, such as the Alesis ADAT—an eight-track, user-friendly digital recorder—has enabled the current generation of musicians to be vastly more self-contained in terms of creative and production capabilities, allowing them to take their songs and projects to the point of master recordings. Starting in the late 1980s, the thousands of home recording studios that have mushroomed in the wake of this technological development have changed the balance of power in the music industry; would-be recording artists no longer have to go through a long, arduous, and usually futile process of attracting the attention of major record labels, auditioning for them in a club or rehearsal hall, or presenting them with a less-than-master-quality cassette tape, negotiating a development budget for higher-quality demo recordings, and then relying upon the record label to finance, distribute, and promote the master recording.

This revolution in home recording, coupled with the evolution of recording artists into more comprehensive writer/musician/producer entities, has altered the way in which the commercial music industry operates in very fundamental ways. The traditional role of the A&R person of seeking out and evaluating individual artists, sometimes matching artists with producers, has become more like the venture financier who evaluates the commercial viability of producers, record remixers (a more specialized combination of producer and record engineer), and, in the case of Dance and R&B music, club disk jockeys as potential producers for a number of acts that the producer, remixer, or DJ will choose themselves. In other cases, the rapidly increasing number of records—as a result of the ability to write, produce, and record one's own recordings—allow record labels to sign more finished masters, and sometimes groups of masters comprising an entire small record label, which are now run out of homes and small offices, with three or four artists or bands on its roster. This increase in the number of records released every year has turned the music industry into a commodities business model.

At the same time, the number of outlets and applications for music has increased significantly, which also drives the number of recordings and further blurs the role of producers. Alternative music charts, such as college radio and sales charts, club exposure, and ethnic music has segmented the music industry, in the process redefining what a hit is— sales of 100,000 for an initial independent label release are considered highly successful, while the same level of sales would be regarded as a major label failure—and just what mainstream music itself means. Increasingly, the role of major record labels in the United States has focused on marketing and distribution of many more recordings than ever before. Walter Yetnikoff, former chairman of Columbia Records prior to and during the first two years of that company's $2 billion acquisition by Japanese electronics giant Sony Corporation in January 1988, returned to the music industry in 1996 with a new record label that is a model for the next phase of the business. Rather than look for individual artists to sign and then promote, Velvel Records, funded in part by a multimillion-dollar advance from independent record distributor Navarre, takes on the distribution and promotion function for dozens of small independent record labels, providing them with the critical few remaining services that an increasingly cottage-type record industry has yet to figure out a way to do single-handedly.

That, too, has the potential to change massively, however. Alternate forms of music distribution—most notably the Internet—offer significant potential to allow those who now write, produce, and record their own records to market them effectively. Ronnie Montrose, lead singer and guitarist for Montrose, the album-oriented rock band that was a staple of FM radio in the 1970s, released his latest solo record in late 1996—a soundtrack for a CD-ROM video game called Mr. Bones on a label owned by game developer Sega, and recorded at Sega's own studio in Redwood City, California.

In the wake of these changes, the role of the record producer has become a more ambiguous one, and one further outside the internal structure of large record companies. Producers rarely occupy staff positions at major record labels anymore, and there are no longer any producers with significant production credits at the helm of any major U.S.-based record label.

But in Nashville, in country music, things have changed little in terms of the producer's relationship with the record label and the recording artist. The position of the producer is more similar to that of the 1950s than of the 1990s. It is not an unusual occurrence in country music for a single individual to have the authority to sign an artist to a major record label for which that person is an executive of; authorize the budget for and produce that artist's record at a studio at least partially owned by that same individual; and hold, through various means, at least part of the publishing on the songs. That person is the producer, arguably the most powerful individual title in the country music hierarchy.

The role of the country record producer still clings to a tradition that began in the 1940s and which had highly delineated roles for the artist, the songwriter, and the producer, who was often a record label employee working in the A&R department. Many record productions through the 1950s and into the 1970s consistently followed this model. As rock, in particular, became more singer-songwriter-oriented in the 1970s, the artist often transitioned to the role of producer, as well, and successful ones often were able to do so without having to negotiate away percentages of their publishing rights. But rarely do contemporary mainstream music producers find their way back into the formal structure of major record labels anymore.

Major labels—those whose corporate offices are based in New York or Los Angeles—account for nearly half of the 30-odd total labels in Nashville. Of the sixteen major record labels with offices in Nashville, nine or more of them have a major producer within their leadership structure, or have traditionally had one. Included among these are Kyle Lehning (Asylum Records), Tim DuBois (Arista Records, a division of BMG Music Group, which also owns RCA Records), Paul Worley (Sony Records, which includes the Columbia and Epic labels), Scott Hendricks (Capitol/Nashville), Tony Brown (MCA Records), and Jim Ed Norman (Warner Bros. Records). Polydor Records (later A&M Records Nashville), a division of Mercury Records, was run by producer Harold Shedd until 1996. A notable exception is BMG Record Labels Group president Joe Galante, whose New York origins and degree from Fordham University in finance and marketing made him a curiosity when he first arrived in Nashville to work at RCA Records in 1975 through 1989 but he was far less so when he returned again in 1995 to head RCA's Nashville operations, replacing his own handpicked successor, songwriter Thom Schuyler.

There are another dozen or so producers with various affiliations, either with independent record labels, production companies, recording studios, and publishing concerns. For instance, Allen Reynolds produces Garth Brooks and Hal Ketchum and owns recording studio Jacks Tracks; Trisha Yearwood producer Garth Fundis owns Sound Emporium Recording and is the creative director for Almo Sounds Records; Mark Bright, creative director at EMI/Nashville Music Publishing, produces Blackhawk; Don Cook directs Sony/Tree Music, coproduces Brooks & Dunn. Country record producers are integral elements in the formal corporate structure of the Nashville music industry. In fact, the dearth of major label records made by producers not affiliated with any major corporate organization in country music is enough for the *Nashville Business Journal* to note in a front-page profile of independent producer Randy Scruggs, producer of Iris DeMent, the late Keith Whitley, Nitty Gritty Dirt Band, Steve Wariner, and Earl Thomas Conley, among others, in 1994. It can be safely estimated that less than two dozen producers account for close to 90 percent of the major label productions from Nashville, a very different scenario than is found in mainstream pop music.

The collective output of this relative handful of producers is prodigious, thanks to a parallel to the Nashville songwriting community's practice of cowriting songs. Coproduction— sharing record production tasks between one or more producers—allows country music producers to have their names listed as such on as many as fifteen records a year. Some of these coproductions are shared between major producers, such as James Stroud's work with producer Byron Gallimore on Tim McGraw. Another variation are coproductions between a major producer and a recording engineer or session musician, such as Tim DuBois and studio owner/engineer Mike Clute. The level of involvement varies according to the personal and professional style of each producer, some being more hands-on than others.

The tradition of the producer/label chief goes back to the very beginnings of modern country. The two seminal producers in the 1950s, Owen Bradley and Chet Atkins, both ran labels— Decca and RCA, respectively—while producing as many as thirty albums a year. Their output was so large due to the simpler recording processes of the time, before the days of multitrack tape recorders, when entire records were cut in two and three days with no overdubbing. Then, vocals, instrumental solos, and background harmonies were generally done at the same time the basic tracks were cut. If records were still made like that, the productivity of country producers would likely have kept up that pace. Still, with Nashville's average of approximately two to three months to make a record from start to finish, combined with the coproduction approach in which more than one project is underway at a given time, production credits on as many as eight or more records a year is not unusual for the busiest of the top-line Nashville producer. In 1995, for instance, Tony Brown (MCA Records) had credits as producer on eight records; James Stroud did nine; Don Cook produced six and Scott Hendricks produced five. These records were all done while the producers were also running busy major record labels or music publishing companies. Their output contrasts starkly with the often yearlong productions typical in pop and rock music, which allow mainstream music producers to rarely accrue more than one or two album production credits annually.

"Doing What Comes Naturally"

Owen Bradley is sitting with his feet up on a cluttered desk in his studio, a converted barn—known officially and simply enough as Bradley's Barn—in Mount Juliet, a suburb of Nashville surrounded by rolling meadows and woods. Although the barn was partially destroyed by a fire caused by a faulty light fixture in 1980, enough of the original structure remains to get a sense of what sessions were like during that decade when Bradley was using the barn as his main studio in the 1960s, when Loretta Lynn, Brenda Lee, Webb Pierce, Conway Twitty, Bill Anderson, Kitty Wells, and other classic country recording artists made their records with Bradley there.

The recording room is substantial, but space is not at the same premium here as it is in Los Angeles or New York or even on Music Row. The Barn is larger than the Quonset Hut, the third and best-known of Bradley's several studio ventures, which he and his brother Harold (now president of the Nashville local of the American Federation of Musicians) started in 1955 and which, along with the original RCA studio built a block away two years later, served as the anchor for what would become Music Row.

Eighty-one years old in 1996, Bradley, still wearing his trademark nautical cap, led the way briskly through several corridors connecting rooms in the barn, pointing out that the resonant tin roof had to be replaced early on because the rattling noise it generated during thunderstorms forced sessions to halt until the rain abated. While the original recording console is still in place in the control room, his personal office is further cluttered with banks of synthesizers on which Bradley continues to work on new records (he produced k.d. lang's *Shadowland* album there in 1988), simultaneously remastering projects from the 1950s for rerelease.

When he was interviewed by Paul Hemphill for his 1970 book, *The Nashville Sound,* Bradley described his production style as being a referee for "a bunch of musicians getting together and doing what comes naturally." Twenty-four years later, he still uses that description, although, he added, "There's a few less players to keep track of."

Owen Bradley came from within a hundred miles of Nashville, born in Macon County, Tennessee, on October 21, 1915. A crystal radio, a present from his father as he recuperated from an eye injury as a child, opened his mind and ears to the parallel worlds of country and jazz—both regional music forms that were in search of commercial credibility. He was playing piano—obsessed by it, is more like it, he says—by age fifteen, and after quitting school as a teenager to play with a local Cheatham County orchestra, he won a position as an intermission player at WSM in 1935, picking up five dollars per segment. Five years later he graduated to the post of keyboardist and arranger with the eighteen-piece WSM radio orchestra. During the 1940s Bradley led his own orchestras, often playing at the country club functions, at the same time developing a concurrent career doing country music recording sessions; his first was in 1946, a recording of "Blue Mexico Skies" sung by Zeke Clements and done at the WSM radio studios in Nashville. (Radio station auditoriums often doubled as recording studios through the 1950s.)

In 1947, Bradley met Paul Cohen in Nashville. Cohen was then head of A&R for Decca Records and was based out of New York, although Cohen was making frequent trips to Nashville, developing the label's country department, producing acts such as Ernest Tubb and the Anderson Sisters. Decca had been founded in 1934; its roster included Patsy Cline, Kitty Wells, Loretta Lynn, and Conway Twitty. (The label was folded into MCA Records in 1972; in 1994, MCA restarted Decca as an affiliated label to accommodate its then-growing artist roster.) Cohen hired Bradley as pianist and arranger for his county sessions, and when Cohen left to head Coral Records, a Decca subsidiary, in 1958, Bradley was heir apparent to replace him and run Decca's Nashville office. "I was fascinated with Paul's job," Bradley recalled. "He really liked Southern music, which I thought was very unusual for a Jewish boy from Chicago. I had told him that someday when they promoted him I wanted it. So I learned as much as I could about what it was he did."

Bradley emulated Cohen's hands-on style, both managing the label and producing in the studio, which actively encouraged participation by the musicians in arrangements but kept the ultimate decisions, large and small, with the producer. One decision, though, had far-reaching implications: Bradley purposely kept his recording work in Nashville, unlike Cohen who made frequent trips to use studios in Cincinnati and Dallas, both of which were contenders for country music recording capitals in the 1950s. "It was the musicians and the studios that kept me here," he said. "I couldn't get that anywhere else. When you have six or seven guys who know what they're doing, the producer doesn't have to take the load for the whole time." Despite what some of his contemporaries allege was a micromanagement style of producing, Bradley set a tone for those to come after him of relying on a cadre of musicians and engineers to make his records.

In 1958 Bradley took over Cohen's job at Decca, as well as the production of many of the acts he and Cohen had worked on together, including Ernest Tubb, Kitty Wells, and Red Foley. With the musicians as a support team—helping create arrangements and sometimes rewriting songs in the process of playing on them—Bradley refined a production style that emphasized choosing the right songs and getting the best possible vocal performances out of the artists. He drew additional assistance from his own family members on the sessions, including his brother Harold, a guitarist, and his son Jerry, who engineered many of the sessions and went on to become a producer and label executive at RCA Records. The most excitable Bradley ever got was to bound out of the control room and sit at the piano himself to lead a part if he couldn't convey what he wanted through the talk-back microphone from the control room. ("That," said Larry Butler, future producer of Kenny Rogers, head of United Artists Records, and at the time a young piano player who did sessions for Bradley, "was the only time I was nervous on his sessions: having Owen Bradley—the pianist, not the producer—standing over your shoulder.")

Bradley's experience at the helm of a label and as its primary producer exposed him to the relationship between the regional and headquarters offices in the music industry, a relationship that was often a point of contention for Nashville. It reflected the economic and cultural paternalism often shown toward Nashville by New York and Los Angeles label offices, an attitude that viewed Nashville and country music as regional and as a minor revenue generator for labels. It was also a relationship from which Nashville, on occasion, would take pointers from New York and L.A., such as during the era of the "Countrypolitan" sound that blended traditional country instruments and inflections with the smoothness that pop music was demanding, often by exchanging single fiddle parts for orchestral string sections. Related in a published interview,[1] Bradley recalls how he handled a tug-of-war between trying to please New York and widen the appeal— and thus the revenues—of country music, while still letting country artists be themselves:

> "We were always thinking of how to get our records to a broader audience. I used to get a lot of feedback from New York. I sent them [Patsy Cline's] 'I Fall To Pieces.' That record took almost nine months to do its thing, and they said, 'Owen, we could never get that record to play or sell here in New York. Could you make the next one a little more . . .' The didn't say 'pop,' but that's what they meant. And I said, 'Patsy doesn't want to be pop.' They said, '[Country records have] been selling eight thousand to ten thousand records [each]. We could always go back to that.'"

Bradley's response was the lushly orchestrated classic "Crazy," in which he toned down the distinctly country elements like the pedal steel guitar, leaving them present but only subliminally, and letting the shimmering strings dominate the sound. "Probably the finest [record] I've ever been involved with. It's country and a little bit pop, though it's not supposed to be either," he recalled. "[The] steel guitar sounded more like a vibraphone or something." However, Bradley

---

1. *JCM*, December 1994

learned that compromise left him open to reproach from both sides. "Some people really criticized us using the strings with Patsy. You can't please everybody."

A lot of the people who would eventually become the next generation of producers in Nashville, such as Larry Butler and others, were picking up on Owen Bradley's production style, what Bradley defines as a system, such as incorporating a team of players that performed on all his records, instead of using an artist's touring band as had often been done previously. A technical, artistic, and social community was being created and reinforced at each of these sessions—and not just in the studios; Bradley prided himself on having an open door to both publishers and writers, helping establish the song as prime over either the artist or the recording, and in the process making life a bit harder for generations of record label publicists to sell artists to the public. Bradley remembered one example when Loretta Lynn first came to his attention as the singer on a demo of "The Biggest Fool Of All," brought in by songwriters the Gillman Brothers. "They asked me to sign her," said Bradley. "I told them that I thought she was a good singer and maybe sometime later but I want that song *now*." Bradley is also proud of the fact that he never established a personal publishing company during his heyday at Decca. "I had my own private reasons for not wanting one," he said. "And I think I got a lot of real good songs because of it."

But if Bradley ever felt any sense of proportion about the model he was helping create, he didn't let on, and his outlook remained the same as when he went back to making records at the Barn in 1976 after leaving Decca (which by then had become MCA Records). "It was a very day-to-day thing. Hell, you just tried to survive it. Look around at what was out there and meet the competition with something different or something the same. Whatever fits the bill. Whatever you had to do. Whoever you had to sing it. The more hits you had, the more pressure there was. I'll bet there's one thing that hasn't changed: having a big hit was like having to go to the bank with no money in it. You wonder where the hell the next one's coming from."

"We Didn't Know What A Producer Was"

Everybody knows Chet Atkins. At least, they feel they know him, from his classic productions of songs such as Jim Reeves's "He'll Have To Go," Eddie Arnold's "Make The World Go Away," Skeeter Davis's "End Of The World," and Jerry Reed's "When You're Hot, You're Hot," as well as his own substantial output of instrumental recordings spanning five decades, or as he sits picking a guitar in a Cracker Barrel restaurant television commercial, or on stage at Cafe Milano in Nashville, where he began a weekly Monday night engagement in 1996. But as part of Nashville lore, Atkins is best known as one of the two men, along with Owen Bradley, most responsible for creating the pattern that their heirs as producers and label heads have followed to this day.

On a chilly early winter morning, Atkins, a ten-time Grammy Award winner, opens the door to his suite of offices upstairs in a building he owns on Music Row. Past seventy now, he wears his glasses often. But there is much in his presence that still connects this man to publicity photos from the early 1950s that show him holding his Gretsch semihollow-body electric guitar, similar to the ones that he helped design for the company and which were named for him, the Country Gentleman and the Tennessean. The hair is grayer but still has a razor-sharp leading edge across a broad and smooth forehead. His fingers are long and well-articulated. In the photo they caress the strings on the guitar, the thumb wrapped around a rotary pickup selector knob. On this day, they clasp and unclasp as he speaks, slowly and deliberately, tapping the table in the small office kitchen every now and then for polite emphasis.

Atkins was born on June 20, 1924, on a fifty-acre farm near Luttrell, Tennessee, twenty miles from Knoxville. His musical influences from the beginning were varied, from classical (his father was a classical musician, who played violin and piano) to country to blues, and he developed a love for the guitar while still a child, which translated into an adolescence and early adulthood of one-night stands with a diverse array of small combo bands and singers. His early career wasn't promising; he told writer Teddy Bart in his 1970 book *Inside Music City* that he spent much of his time looking for new gigs after getting fired from the old ones, for reasons that ranged from "not being country enough" to "not being commercial enough," "not playing what people want to hear," and other sundry causes. Those criticisms would all be addressed in Atkins's long career as a producer.

Atkins was sensitive to the issue of commericality. When he first came to Nashville in 1946 as a sideman with singer Red Foley, the city didn't yet have a lock on the country music business; significant records were being made in places such as Cincinnati and Dallas. (Hank Williams recorded "Love Sick Blues" in Cincinnati in 1948 and Lefty Frizzell cut "I Love You A Thousand Ways" in a Dallas recording studio as late as 1959.) But Atkins said he felt something about Nashville that would bring him back. "In 1946 there were a lot of places to be, I guess. But the other [radio shows] died out because they tried to please Madison Avenue instead of leaving the music alone like they did on the Grand Ole Opry."

As a young guitarist, Chet Atkins had a recording career of his own as an instrumentalist, and his future hits foreshadowed how much more easily he could balance the demands of country and pop music. He adapted Boots Randolph's "Yakety Sax" into his own version of a Top Five hit called "Yakety Axe" in 1965. A year later he reworked Beatles songs into a guitar instrumental album and recorded and appeared with the Boston Pops Orchestra. Through the 1980s and 1990s, Atkins made a string of collaborative records that alternated between guitar stars of country (Jerry Reed), rock (Mark Knopfler of Dire Straits), and jazz (Les Paul). The musical flexibility that seemed to vex his early employers became one of Atkins's chief assets as both a recording artist and a producer.

Atkins's particular musical vision set him apart enough to be recognized as a talent by Steve Sholes, who was then heading the country music division of RCA Victor Records. Sholes produced early instrumental sides on Atkins, but his real value to Sholes, who often worked in New York City, was Atkins's presence in Nashville, his familiarity with the musicians in Nashville and his ability to communicate with them as one of their own. On a $75-a-week retainer, Atkins would coordinate sessions for Sholes, calling players and booking studios.

Working with Sholes in the studio sparked Atkins's own production ambitions and helped establish what would become Atkins's production style, one that contrasted with Owen Bradley's: relatively hands-off, letting the musicians have a free reign, with his input centered around the song choices, and a pronounced sensitivity to recognizing and fostering talent on every level of the record-making process. "Steve [Sholes] found the songs and signed the artists and matched them together," Atkins recalls. "I learned that from him. He was the first man that ever caused a producer's name to be on an [album jacket]. He wanted to put the engineers on, too, but [the record label] wouldn't let him. They said they didn't have enough room." Sholes also strongly believed that country music's future was destined to be tightly intertwined with that of pop music; he is quoted as saying in 1954 that ten years hence would find ". . . the country and western and pop fields of entertainment so closely allied that it will be impossible to tell the difference without a score card." This was a prophecy that producer and Capitol/Nashville label chief Jimmy Bowen would raise again in the 1980s and one that Atkins himself would come to rue later on when he told a reporter in the early 1970s, 'We're getting the music too pop. I say, let's keep it hillbilly.'"[2]

Atkins got his initial chance to expand his role at RCA when the threat of another national musicians' union strike loomed; an earlier strike had taken place just after World War II and had virtually shut down the pop recording industry. In 1947 he worked for several months with Sholes as a guitarist in the RCA recording studios in New York, which was still the center for most major records, stockpiling future tracks as a hedge against the threatened walkout. Sholes began to let him handle some of the production duties on occasion.

From 1955 to 1957, when Sholes left to become manager of pop singles for RCA, Atkins made a gradual transition to become the Nashville-based head of the division for RCA, taking on an increasing workload of both record productions and label management duties. During that period, RCA became the first label to own a recording studio in the city, a key element in the production infrastructure that was evolving in Nashville. Production was still a function of Artist & Repertoire at the time. A&R was the aspect of the business that discovered and developed artists and matched them to the song material, but it was not a purely creative position— it also had plenty of office paperwork to handle, an issue that still affects the executive structure of Nashville labels. Several major country labels have a tandem top executive arrangement, such as at MCA Records where producer/president Tony Brown's responsibilities are primarily creative and label chairman Bruce Hinton's purview is more financially oriented. (Although Hinton is not a producer, he has a long history of associations with them. He was a partner with Jimmy Bowen in Bowen's private production company, Amos Productions, in Los Angeles in 1967, and later a partner with Warner Records president Jim Ed Norman in the late 1970s. He also started one of the first independent promotion companies in Nashville, which included among its projects the film *Urban Cowboy*.)

"Back in those days, I didn't really know what I was doing," Atkins says. "I was making a lot of hits but I didn't know how. We didn't know what a producer was." Atkins's production style essentially answered his own question, and is regarded by some as the epitome of the "pick the right songs, call the right players, and sit back and shut up" methodology of country music production, and he says little to contradict that view.

But his first foray as full producer, with Don Gibson and the song "Oh Lonesome Me" in 1955, indicates there's more to it than that. Based on a transcript done by the Country Music Foundation of his recollections of the sessions, Atkins was eager to try recording techniques that were then new to Nashville and to country music. Gibson was equally eager; he'd already been signed and dropped once before by RCA, as well as the Columbia and MGM labels. Atkins chose "Oh Lonesome Me" and "I Can't Stop Loving You" and, despite the urgings of Gibson's publisher Wesley Rose to "keep it country," used the more aggressive playing of Troy Hatcher, the Knoxville drummer who played on Gibson's original demos of the songs, and had recording engineer Jeff Miller place a microphone directly in the bass drum, a trick learned during the New York sessions, rather than rely on a microphone placed elsewhere in the room to pick it up. These and a few other recording and playing techniques imparted a distinctly different sound to the records; the backing tracks were more distinct and the low end had more punch, perfect for bass-heavy jukebox speakers. Recording technique was being combined with song and musician choices to lay the foundations for the Nashville Sound.

The unwritten rule that says not to play on sessions you produce can be traced back, in part, to Atkins, who concedes, "I had better success when I didn't [play on records I produced]." There were some special cases, he said, but for the most part, "I found . . . that if I was [out] in the studio all the time I'd miss something and be unhappy with the session when I got through. Once in a while I'd play on a tune but most of the time I stayed in the control room and listened."

When Atkins began making records for RCA as a producer, his salary started at $7,500 per year, and he was making full LP recordings on budgets that topped out at around $3,000. "When I started out making a lot of hits, I got them to raise [my salary] to thirty thousand. I just held out. I knew [RCA] would, because they didn't have anybody else," he recalls. Commenting on the increased pressure on producers today to churn out hits, he didn't seem to feel the same urgency to get that next hit that Bradley said he constantly experienced. He recalled Nashville as a halcyon place where the few producers could coast a bit in between hits. "If you didn't have a hit for a while there wasn't all that much pressure . . . The company was making a hell of a lot on the hits we did have because they weren't paying much royalties. That's a big difference between now and then."

Atkins's heyday as a producer came during the time when albums were made in the course of a day or two, and when both artists and producers were given a longer term with the label in which to prove themselves. And due to the lower budgets expended on records then, it took less time for a label to recoup its investment and begin making a profit from a record and an artist. Atkins remembers with affection the fact that Steve Sholes stuck with him for the three years between when he started making records as a recording artist in 1947 and his first significant chart successes in 1950. "It doesn't happen that way anymore," he says, tapping the table for emphasis. "You get one or two shots and that's it."

Making records with multitrack recording, in which various aspects of a final recording, such as vocals and instrumental overdubs are recorded separately, consumes far more time and its advent in the 1960s made record-making lose some of its luster for Atkins. "The records have become much slicker and technically better, and the songs are more cleverly written than they were back then," he says. "But I think what's missing is the heart, the excitement that you got having musicians all play together, the cohesiveness . . . of a live band all in the same room. You don't get that when you record in layers." And the old days of Nashville still hold fonder memories for him than the present when it comes to songs. "Those were true hits in those days," he stated. "Today, [records] are hyped to number one. Now record companies, they move something up to number one. It's all hype."

As a label executive, though—he was promoted to vice president of RCA's country division in 1968, the same year Sholes died of a heart attack—Atkins undoubtedly experienced much of what he laments on the business side of the music. During his term as head of the label's Nashville operations, Atkins signed and guided the careers of far more artists than he produced, including Connie Smith, Bobby Bare, Charley Pride, and Waylon Jennings (although he produced some sides with many of them, including Elvis Presley). But it was, Atkins notes, "a very different kind of business then; the money changed the level of pressure."

So did technology. Multitracking reduced the individual output of producers by demanding more of a producer's time for each project. That, combined with an increasing administrative workload at RCA, caused Atkins to gradually pull back from production and eventually leave his position at RCA by 1980, handing the reins over to Owen Bradley's son, Jerry. "There was a conflict within me," he recalls. "I finally got sick and stressed. It was too much work. I remember I went to work one day and about the middle of the morning I looked down and my shoes didn't match. And I said, 'I believe you've been on the job too long.'"

Atkins, who says he no longer reads the music industry trade papers anymore and describes himself as "out of it" in terms of staying abreast of current industry business developments, remains as shy and introspective as his contemporaries described him in the 1950s. He has returned to the public eye more in recent years; in addition to his weekly gig at Cafe Milano, a new weeklong music festival was scheduled to start in Nashville in June 1997, called Chet Atkins's Musician Days. Yet one wonders how his personality and talent would have weathered the pace and expansiveness of Nashville in the 1990s. He and Owen Bradley are far from museum pieces, but they are talismans of another era of the country music business. A time when it was a little slower, a little surer, a little safer. His status as chairman emeritus of the industry in Nashville is secure. But what it took to get there is reflected in a recollection by singer Marty Stuart: "Chet told me one time, 'Work your ass off, but never be number one in this town because they'll be through with you.'"[3]

Atkins mused on his hands, guitarist's hands, wondering aloud what was in them and how they connected him, spiri-

---

3. CMA *Close Up*, May 1994

tually and physically, to all that happened throughout his career, regarding them as though, for a moment, they were no longer connected to him. He looked out the window of the kitchen onto a changing Music Row, saying, "It's a very different business now in some ways. It's become a visual business. We used to have hits with people and the public never knew what they looked like. They just liked the songs. They bought the songs. But now they put [out] some guy or girl that they think's handsome or good-looking . . . and [they] all sound alike." He paused and with a half smile added, "But they look great."

Bradley and Atkins set the tone for years to come, creating what was to be called the Nashville Sound, a combination of recording techniques and esthetic sensibilities that, despite the advent of multitrack recording and a host of other technological innovations such as digital CDs, hasn't changed much in the intervening years. Their approaches creatively, artistically, and technically to record-making and to their positions as label heads would influence future generations of producers. The combination of label head and producer would coalesce under such people as Jimmy Bowen, Tony Brown, and James Stroud. But Bradley and Atkins established a mold that has endured.

"That's Just The Way Things Were Done . . ."

Jerry Kennedy has the patrician's visage often seen among successful members of Nashville's second wave of producers as they approach late middle age—trim and youthful looking, Cadillac comfortable in a roomy but simple office off Music Row where he runs a production company that still works with the Statler Brothers, with whom he has done records since 1970, and packages rereleases for direct marketing of older artists such as pianist Floyd Cramer. While Kennedy's production credits are substantial, including Roger Miller hits "King Of The Road" and "Dang Me," Roy Drusky, Dave

Dudley, Jerry Lee Lewis, Tom T. Hall, Johnny Rodriguez, and early Reba McEntire records, his career represents a more stable time in Nashville and in America in general, when people stayed with record labels like they used to stay with jobs at IBM or AT&T—virtually for life. Kennedy headed Mercury Records for two decades, from 1962 to 1983. The start of his long tenure at Mercury Records began in the early 1960s when Shelby Singleton, then a promotion man for Mercury (and who would go on to run the label till 1966, then become an independent label owner—Plantation Records—and producer, most notably of Jeannie C. Riley's "Harper Valley P.T.A."), brought him up from Louisiana as an assistant. Other assistants in the office included future country stars Ray Stevens and Jerry Reed.

The rise of the Countrypolitan sound as country made more crossings into pop radio, the influence of country on pop records, such as the Beatles's recording of Buck Owens' "Act Naturally," and the continued popularity of Rockabilly and other variations on country music in Europe and the United States had notched up the rate of production in Nashville. More producers were needed for more records. Kennedy originally looked at the position as a way to fill in his income gaps as he established himself as a session guitarist in Nashville, reflecting the fact that the term "producer" had not yet acquired the esteemed connotations that it would take on some years later. But the label position grew larger as Singleton's career shuttled him increasingly between Nashville and New York as vice president of A&R for Mercury before taking him to his own production company in 1967. In one of the earliest acquisition moves upon an American entertainment company by a foreign one, Netherlands-based Philips bought Mercury in 1961 and by the following year had expanded the company to a trio of labels: Mercury, Smash, and Philips. "We had three labels and all these guys were crying for product," Kennedy recalls. "Back then A&R meant producing, so all three us—me and Jerry and Ray—were assistants *and* producers, and we were all playing on each other's records."

Kennedy's first session as a producer came in 1962, within months of his arrival. Singleton's flight from New York's Idlewild Airport was snowed in. He called Kennedy and informed him he was now not only the guitar player on the next day's Teresa Brewer session but the producer, as well. "I had only worked the other side of the glass up to this point," he says, referring to the thick vitrine that separates the control room from the studio. "And all of a sudden I found myself over here. But the thing was that I was used to working with all these [musicians]. Had I been thrown like that into a session in L.A. or somewhere and I didn't know them personally, it could have really been a traumatic thing."

Kennedy's experience illustrates the simplified nature of production at the time, and how it was based on Bradley's and Atkins's patterns, as well as the much lower pressure of the Nashville music environment. "All I was essentially doing was, it was up to me to say, 'Yes, this is a take,' or, 'Let's do one more.' The whole [musician] team was like a production unit. As a producer, you found the songs and you go with a sort of picture in your mind of what it was supposed to sound like, and [the musicians] filled in the colors. If it wasn't heading in the direction that you pictured, you got up and said something. I kind of got the bug on producing and the next week Shelby gave me a Rex Allen session. The song was 'Don't Go Near The Indians' [which went to Top Ten on country charts and Top 20 on the *Billboard* Pop Chart]. And I said to myself, there's nothing to this. This is easy."

There were no conflicts of interest to speak of, Kennedy claims, directly linking the methods of Atkins and Bradley to the dual roles of label head and producer. "If you think about it, it was that way all over town, from Chet and Owen to Ken Nelson [head of Capitol Records's Nashville division starting in 1952]. That was the way it was done. All the decisions were folded into one person, and back then budgets were low, so that may have been part of it."

Mercury had its own publishing companies at the time, but in a relatively rare instance, Kennedy's contract with the label contained a conflict-of-interest clause prohibiting him from having his own publishing concern. It didn't seem to bother him either way: "I saw eyebrows going up in town over Billy Sherrill [composer and producer of Tammy Wynette, Barbara Mandrell, Charlie Rich, and George Jones] writing a lot of what he recorded . . . writers and publishers griping and complaining. But everything he was doing was going number one; he wasn't loading up albums or a guy's repertoire with dog songs. If it works, I don't think a label's gonna step in and say, 'Hey.' I always thought that was the only rule: find the best song and marry it with the right act."

At this point, Kennedy paused and reflected, then adds an observation on the current climate in which the producer's gut feeling about which songs would be hits is undermined by a marketing-driven, committee-like approach to choosing songs. "I'm not sure it's treated that way now. There's a joke going around town now: a songwriter goes up to a producer and says, 'Hey, I dropped a song off over here last week. Did you like it?' And the producer says, 'I don't know; I'm the only one that's heard it so far.'"

With a corporate environment comes the need for consensus. And corporate machinations have affected Mercury as they have the other labels in town. Jimmy Bowen revived the dormant Liberty label in February 1992, to provide what was Capitol/Nashville with a clearer identity, and MCA in 1993 announced the return of the Decca label to accommodate bulging rosters. In early 1994, Mercury, owned by PolyGram, announced they would spin off a new label, Polydor, which takes its name from another dormant rubric in the Philips inventory (Philips owns PolyGram Records).

By 1996, each of those moves came home like a roosting chicken as the business began to contract. Liberty returned to the name Capitol after Bowen left. Polydor's fate was more complex—in 1995 it changed its name to A&M Nashville, a division of the Los Angeles-based pop label, also owned by PolyGram. Though Harold Shedd, a producer (Billy Ray Cyrus, among others) who served as vice president of Mercury then president of first Polydor then A&M Nashville, remained on through the changes, A&M Nashville reported to A&M's

New York office. In November 1996, Shedd left and A&M closed its doors, an event for many in Nashville which heralded more viscerally the onset of a period of contraction in country music than the relatively abstract midyear reports of country sales being down over 10 percent. All artists on the former Polydor/A&M Nashville were then optioned back to Mercury Records, PolyGram's sole remaining Nashville division. However, only one—Toby Keith—was picked up.

Decca's own future as a label seemed uncertain at the end of 1996, as was the case with several of the independent labels that opened in Nashville in the mid-1990s, such as Magnatone Records, which was part-owned by Richard Speer of Speer Communications (son of the founder of the Home Shopping Network and owner of a Nashville-based music channel start-up in 1995, MOR Music, which spun Magnatone off in 1996). But the revival of the vintage label names reflected both the need for an expanded machine in Nashville and a yearning to maintain its links to the old days, times which were rapidly receding from memory as the country music industry underwent striking changes. In one stroke Bowen further insulated Nashville from corporate offices in Los Angeles and New York and, by removing the word "Nashville" from the label, eliminated the historic sense of geography that remains part of country music, bringing country perceptually closer to pop music. The name Decca conjures up the golden days of that very isolation, which is contrasted with the appointment by MCA Nashville chief Tony Brown of Shelia Shipley Biddy, who began as a receptionist at Monument Records in 1976, as the first female executive to become the general manager of a Nashville label. Polydor recalls the heyday of R&B and soul; it was the home in the 1960s and 1970s of James Brown, Alicia Bridges, and the Atlanta Rhythm Section, and the label's debut occurred coincidentally with the release of *Country, Rhythm & Blues*, in 1994, a tribute record that paired country and R&B singers in duets and expresses a link between the two genres. All of this was a further example of the image consciousness of a Nashville that sometimes seems to root around in its past like an adolescent in an old toy box, looking at the past with a combination of guilty nostalgia and an adult's eye for the now-valuable Mickey Mantle rookie card buried near the bottom.

Jerry Kennedy remembers an incident in which the late songwriter/singer Roger Miller was about to leave RCA Records. Miller stopped by Kennedy's office and inquired as to whether Kennedy would be interested in signing him. In contrast with the complexity that accompanies deals between labels and artists today, the quaintness of such a meeting, without lawyers or managers, is emphasized by the fact that Kennedy called Chet Atkins at RCA as soon as Miller left and asked not whether Miller's imminent departure was accurate or about the circumstances surrounding it, but simply if it was all right with Atkins if he talked to Miller about it. "That's just the way things were done; we all touched base on things like that back then. I'm not sure it would be the case today. Back then, there was a sense, a feeling, that I don't feel anymore. Maybe because it's so big . . ."

"It Was Like Going To School . . ."

Larry Butler is the only Nashville-based producer to win a Grammy in the Producer of the Year category, in 1979. (Tony Brown was nominated in 1994.) Besides several awards, however, Butler occupies a place at the confluence of country, pop, and that comprehensive swatch of television—the Movie Of The Week. "The Gambler," Kenny Rogers's 1978 hit song, was immortalized in this manner and has since spawned four sequels, several of which featured contemporary country artists, such as Reba McEntire, in acting roles. It's the enduring vestige of the *Urban Cowboy* era of country, which saw country music sales rocket to nearly 15 percent of total record sales—nearly as high as 1993's 17 percent market share—temporarily supplanting pop and foreshadowing the current country boom.

Butler produced the record "The Gambler," written by Nashville songwriter Don Schlitz, and a wall of his Music Row office is nearly covered with a Recording Industry Association of America plaque in which RIAA-certified platinum records are displayed: the frame is close to bursting, barely holding seventeen silver discs. Its presentation was slightly premature; the record went on to sell over twenty million units.

Butler's office is on Eighteenth Avenue South, a block off Music Row and around the corner from the United Artists Tower, where Butler headed that now-defunct label for a decade starting in 1973. The Pensacola, Florida, native came to Nashville as the piano player in a Florida band, Jerry Woodward and the Esquires, on a road trip in the early 1960s. Producer/publisher Buddy Killen, then at Tree Publishing, heard him play at the Black Poodle Club in Printer's Alley and told him if he ever considered moving to Nashville permanently, there would be work for him. Butler made that move in 1963 and began climbing steadily through the Nashville session ranks, except for a brief hiatus in Memphis, where he and Memphis-based producer Chips Moman formed The Gentrys, a studio-based band that charted with pop hits "Keep On Dancin'" and "Every Day I Have To Cry Some."

Butler combined the country approach he learned from doing sessions for Bradley and Atkins with pop elements picked up working with Moman in Memphis. "I brought in some different influences to production," he said, leaning back in a chair in his office, which is wallpapered with many of the other sixty-five gold and platinum awards he's received over the years as a producer and songwriter. "But trust me, it was like going to school. I learned and did what has always made this town what it is today as far as production. And that was that there are certain rules you have to follow: keep it simple, walk in with a great song and a great singer."

In 1969 he returned to Nashville from Memphis and walked into his first label position, staff producer at Capitol Records. "I was sitting at Tree one day and [songwriter] Curley Putman says to me, 'Ken Nelson [head of Capitol's country division] is looking for a producer.' I literally jumped up out of my chair and went running down there and by the time I got to the top of the stairs I was completely out of breath. The receptionist tells me that [Nelson] is in a meeting and I told her I'd wait. Finally Nelson comes out of the meeting and I tell him I'm here about the producer's job. Ken tells me it's already been filled. So I said, 'Well, okay, I'll tell you this: I don't know who you hired and I don't want to know. They could never do the job for you that I could do.' Then I got up and left. The next morning Nelson called me and told me I had the job." Within a few months, Butler had his first hit as a producer, "Seven Lonely Days" for Jean Shepard.

Subsequently, after a short stint as a staff producer at Columbia Records under Billy Sherrill, where Butler produced Johnny Cash, Butler was offered the chief executive slot at United Artists Records. It was in that position that he met Kenny Rogers, whose career as the front man for The First Edition—notable for the pop hits "Just Dropped In (To See What Condition My Condition Was In)" (1968) and "Something's Burning" (1970)—was waning. The two met in 1978 at a Houston restaurant, which led to discussions about taking Rogers's career country. "He maybe didn't want to go as country as I ultimately took him, but that's where he wanted to go," said Butler of the meeting.

Rogers certainly had a grounding in country, with cuts such as "Reuben James" and "Ruby Don't Take Your Love To Town," both hits in 1969. But the lure of mainstream music sales and airplay for country artists was already making any number of Nashville producers and artists starry-eyed and making country radio nervous. Butler wanted some confirmation of his intuitive hope that Rogers could be both viable on the larger pop market but could also be palatable to country radio. He called a number of managers and program directors at country stations in Southern states and got what he felt was a mandate to take Rogers full-bore country. "Lucille" was the first single, and it hit number one in 1977. Other major hits from their collaboration included "Love Or Something Like It," "She Believes In Me," and "Coward Of The County."

"The Gambler" was the biggest of them all and it worked on both country and pop charts, and for Rogers at least, it continues to roll on with its own momentum in made-for-television movies.

Butler's own forward motion continued, as well. He left United Artists Records in 1983 to form his own production company, producing records for Charlie Rich, Mac Davis, Don McLean, John Denver, Debbie Boone and other acts, a move that would be matched by other producer/label heads in the future, like Jimmy Bowen, to gain greater freedom of action at a time when labels still took their cues from headquarters offices. Meanwhile, he parlayed his song sense (he was also a successful composer, having cowritten with Chips Moman B.J. Thomas's career-maker "Another Somebody Done Somebody Wrong Song") into a publishing venture, administered by CBS Songs, signing writers Mickey Newbury and Dean Dillon. That company rang up eight Top-Ten charting records over the next two years. The only dark cloud was a large one, however; in 1986 the IRS disallowed a substantial investment deduction from the early 1980s. Butler had to sell interests in several recording studios, including Eleven Eleven Sound and Sound Emporium (which was bought first by Roy Clark and subsequently by current owner, producer Garth Fundis), as well as other real estate investments.

Larry Butler pushed the edges of the envelope of country music by venturing as deeply into pop production techniques as much as he did. But while he learned his craft during a conventional Nashville apprenticeship, a predilection toward mainstream music seemed inherent in him. "The Gambler" and subsequent Rogers records he did reflect that, as do his early compositions, such as the Poppies' 1966 pop hit "Lullabyes Of Love," and his crossover productions with artists such as Mac Davis, Debby Boone, Don McLean, and John Denver. In the course of developing a sense of where the lines between pop and country crossed, he obviously had the opportunity to observe both genres from various perspectives. So Butler's current pursuit, Nashville Music Consultants, a business formed in 1993 that provides song and artist evaluation for a one-time fee, seems both opportunistic and appropriate to the present times in Nashville. "There's a need for something like this these days," he said, but not necessarily because the bloated rosters of Nashville were becoming more than the labels could handle. They were, as evidenced by the roster reductions that started in 1996 and which were expected to continue for months to come, but also because the rules that had served country music so well for so long—the emphasis on the song, the apprenticeship learning system, the pulling of producers from the ranks of musicians—was showing strain as the number of artists and record releases increased. And who better than a producer, someone who learned through the ranks, who understood the complex nuances that make up the relationship between a song and singer and understood as well that that relationship was a parable for life itself, to help Nashville sort itself out? In 1996, Butler formed one of the many new independent record labels that Nashville has seen start up in the mid-1990s. And its initial signings reflect Butler's preferences for music he's familiar with: B.J. Thomas and Highway 101.

The circumstances may have changed, but the rules haven't, Butler says reflectively; the emphasis on the song remains. But, he learned as a producer that leaning country over into pop alternately seduces and victimizes. "Back when I did 'The Gambler,' country albums were selling two hundred to three hundred thousand units, and that was good sales. But pop albums were selling one and two million units. Wouldn't you want to sell two million albums? But I tell you, I fell victim to that, too. We started getting away from the very thing that we knew how to do best—country records. All of a sudden, mine and other country records started sounding overproduced, overdone, too many strings. It was easy to fall into it."

At the same time, Butler is all for experimentation in country production, and his equivocation underscores the bottom line rule in country that, if it sells, it's good. "It's almost like a disco thing at this point, that you've got to have so many beats-per-minute [an electronic measure of tempo used often in Dance and Urban music]. But the people obviously enjoy dancing to it. Only a fool would ignore that because it's the hottest thing in country. Radio—only a fool would ignore that barometer. But that doesn't mean the song isn't still the main thing. You can have both. It's okay to go out on a limb once in a while, as long as you come back. The rules haven't changed."

Larry Butler is quintessential Nashville, of the glory era just before this one, when country music rode the 1970s into the plush pit of *Urban Cowboy* and the reassembly of the pieces in the 1980s. After working at three labels and running one of them, staying a record 624 weeks—12 years—consecutively on *Billboard* charts as a producer or writer, owning several studios, and running a successful publishing company, Nashville Music Consultants is perhaps a way of holding pieces together at a different moment in time, a way of staying active in a game that few players ever really get out of, at least voluntarily. "It's up to each individual to go to school every day [here], to fine-tune with the times," he observes. "Otherwise, your phone won't ring quite so much, and when it does it'll be praise for what you did yesterday, but it won't have anything to do with what's going on tomorrow. It's understood that you've got to keep your membership up in the club, so to speak."

"This Isn't Kroger's; This Is The Record Business"

"Jimmy Bowen is the only carpetbagger to ever come here and flip the bird at everyone and everything and still be that successful." So said Joe Talbot in the pithiest of the many comments about the one who is regarded by many as the most pivotal and controversial of modern Nashville country producers. Jimmy Bowen has been involved in three labels in Nashville—MCA (twice), Electra/Asylum/Warner's (Electra/Asylum merged its operations in 1983 with Warner's and in the process Bowen became nominal head of Warner Bros. Nashville; Asylum later became a separate Nashville label), and Capitol/Nashville. He is credited with turning MCA from a financial basket case to the city's leading label by 1985. He also founded the independent Universal Records in 1989 that was merged the following year into Capitol/Nashville, which he renamed Liberty Records in January 1992, part of a marketing strategy to position the label for a broader diversity of acts and to reinforce the Nashville division's identity. His Nashville production roster included Mel Tillis and Red Steagall in the late 1970s and extended to include records by Suzy Bogguss, George Strait, Reba McEntire, Eddie Rabbitt, the Oak Ridge Boys, Crystal Gayle, the Bellamy Brothers, John Anderson, John Berry, and Eddie Raven by the 1990s. Bowen is also credited with turning many of Nashville's music industry business and recording practices around, from establishing a separate business affairs department at Liberty to introducing digital recording and pop music-level budgets to Nashville.

While his is a success story, Bowen's experience with Nashville also reveals a man who used Nashville's quirks to his own benefit as much as he purported to change them. He readily acknowledges that he started his own rumor about jumping ship from MCA to RCA in the late 1980s in a bid to enhance his contract renegotiations with MCA, and then complained about the quality of the rumor mill in Nashville when his own rumor didn't get around accurately enough. He is also regarded as having fired more label staffers than anyone else in the history of the town's music industry; and he also paid lip service to the most powerful organization in country music after the Grand Ole Opry—the Country Music Association—at the same time that he set up his own organization, the Nashville Entertainment Association (formerly the Nashville Music Association). Whatever Bowen has been, he's been successful, and he contributed substantially to changing Nashville's music industry.

Bowen used the fraternal network that the two previous generations of producer/label heads had developed to his advantage. On the subject of rumors, he said straightforwardly, "It's getting more difficult. When I first came here you could start a rumor on Monday and by Thursday or Friday it would still be relatively intact. I had it out that I was going to RCA and by the second day the Row had it that I was going to Columbia." As for the ethics of using rumors as a negotiation ploy, he said flatly, "This isn't Kroger's; this is

the record business. I didn't invent how to negotiate."
(Bowen's penchant for encouraging rumors also shadowed
the announcement of his retirement, due to health reasons,
from the chairmanship and CEO position of Liberty Records
in March 1995. Several sources reported rumors that Bowen
was planning to start up another label of his own, and
Charles Koppelman, then chairman and CEO of EMI
Records Group North America, parent company of Capitol
Records, was soon reported fending off such rumors.) On the
matter of the lack of job security at his labels, Bowen says,
only half joking, "The way I stay sane is to expect [perfection]
out of everybody except me." But the man who has been
married five times leavened the statement with the recording
studio metaphor, "Sometimes it takes a while to get a good
take."

Prior to his establishment of the NEA, the CMA, as the
official organization of country music, was Nashville's ambas-
sador to the larger music industry. The establishment of the
NEA was viewed as a challenge aimed at the historical structure of the country music industry in Nashville—the "good ol'
boy" culture that Bowen proved on many occasions to be more
than willing to utilize but still a challenge that Bowen reveled
in. "The CMA was a tightly run and controlled trade organization, probably one of the best ever," he said. "Financially
well-off and well-run but under the control of a small group of
people. But a lot of people in country music were using
Nashville as the excuse for why their stuff didn't get a wider
audience. They weren't fixing their real problems, which was
their music or their songs or their productions. So [I gave
them] another organization, somewhere to go, something to
bounce things off of. And it worked wonderfully." The NEA
runs, among other events, the Nashville Extravaganza, an
annual display of local noncountry music acts that has been
more ambitious that successful, since a major noncountry
artist has yet to emerge from Nashville.

Bowen was also not afraid to take on even larger organizations. In 1985 when the Tennessee state government
proposed a tax of between 5.5 and 7.5 percent on the music

industry to raise revenues, Bowen organized a movement that would have relocated the industry to Kentucky. The tax idea died in committee.

Bowen's production background began with Norman Petty, who produced Bowen's first attempts as a recording artist in 1957 and garnered him a one-time hit, "Party Doll," on Roulette Records. Bowen's first Nashville performance came that year when he was invited to play the Grand Ole Opry. The man who would start the trend of increasing the presence of drums on country records was not allowed to use his own drummer at that show unless he stayed behind the curtain and played with brushes instead of sticks.

Without a follow-up hit to "Party Girl," Bowen moved to Los Angeles in 1961, after a stint as a disk jockey in Boulder, Colorado. Signed as a songwriter to American Music Publishing, he and another young songwriter, Glen Campbell, began using a local studio for song demos and Bowen began getting his first hands-on recording experience. "We had to turn in five demos a week to get our seventy-five-dollar pay-checks," he recalls. "So we recorded tracks on Fridays, wrote the lyrics over the weekend, and recorded Glen's vocals on Mondays." The experience resulted in laying the foundation of a Bowen's production style, with an emphasis on letting the project determine how long a record would take and on a minimum of producer input between the artist and the vocal performance—things, says Bowen, that Petty taught him. But his obsession with controlling every other aspect of the session came from elsewhere. "I used to go out and hang out at Gold Star Recording [Studios, in Los Angeles] and watch Phil Spector produce," Bowen remembers of his experience with Spector, whose thickly arranged "Wall Of Sound" production techniques created hits—and sometimes entire acts—for the Ronettes, Darlene Love, the Righteous Brothers, Cher, Dion, and George Harrison. "He was a whole 'nother kind of producer. It was absolutely his music, his record, he was in total control. He didn't even have artists; what he had were great singers and he decided what names they'd have as artists later. If you have an artist worth a damn, then you help them with the music, not do it for them." Jimmy Bowen's production style came from a synthesis of Petty and Spector's production approaches, one in which Bowen would strive to control virtually every aspect of the production (including running the label, if he could), while building a safe cocoon for a singer to become intimate with the song.

Bowen's big production break came in late 1963 when, after two years of working in A&R at Chancellor Records in Los Angeles, he was offered an A&R/staff producer position at Frank Sinatra's new label, Reprise Records. The connection had been made through a mutual friend, Murray Wolf. "I got a call one night from Palm Springs and Murray said, 'You got the job. Hang on. Frank wants to talk to you.' I'm sitting there, twenty-six years old, and Frank Sinatra came on the line. He said, 'James, glad to have you aboard.' Click. And I thought, well, I can work for a guy like that."

Bowen's intuitive understanding of the economics of the music business became visible early in his stint at Reprise. Mo Ostin, then head of A&R at Reprise and the future head of Warner Bros. Records, offered him a $150-a-week salary as a staff producer. Bowen countered with an offer of $100 a week and a 1 percent royalty on anything he produced. Participation in sales royalties for producers was uncommon during an era when most producers were still salaried staff A&R men. Ostin looked at it as a savings of $50 and accepted Bowen's bid. One of the first artists Bowen produced at Reprise was Dean Martin, with a song called "Everybody Loves Somebody Sometime." The record was hugely successful, and Bowen had a piece of it worth far more than $50 a week. Bowen and Martin went on to record twenty-six hit singles, and fifteen gold and five platinum albums. During this time, Bowen also worked directly with Sinatra, producing his later period signature hits "My Way" and "Strangers In The Night."

Bowen's studio and executive persona were evolving quickly, and the Los Angeles entertainment business environment was embraced by the Texan in Bowen. Ray Kelley, a veteran Los Angeles session player who played in the string sections on many of Bowen's Los Angeles sessions, recalled, "He had a pretty imposing personality. He wasn't a tyrant, but he was very directed, very driven. He was also pretty flamboyant, and he knew how to have a good time. There was one session where we all showed up at nine A.M. and he was sleeping one off in the backseat of a stretch Mercedes limo in front of the studio." Another engineer he worked with in Los Angeles at the time recalls coming into the studio and finding Bowen wrapped in a sleeping bag. With the covers still over his head, he would call out directions during the session.

The distinctions between record label executive management and producers had become clearer and more established in pop music by then, with production duties shifting to independent producers and away from A&R staffs, which were becoming more concerned with marketing their artists as their numbers proliferated as rock music grew from a niche into an industry. Bowen, however, hewed to an older model, wanting to be a producer first—he maintained his own independent production company, Amos Productions—but also wanting to retain the clout that accompanied an executive position. He moved up the corporate ladder in Los Angeles, eventually heading MGM Records by 1974. But as an executive, Bowen found himself with less and less time for the studio. As a producer, he began working with more contemporary pop acts, including Kim Carnes and future Eagles members Don Henley and Glenn Frey. But the business and lifestyle changes in the L.A. music industry that accompanied that growth were taking a toll: records were costing more—upward of a quarter-million dollars—and taking ever longer to make. "I didn't have the patience to sit around [in the studio] with four or five people on different drugs taking days trying to figure out an eight-bar intro," he says of the time. Nashville, with its highly structured recording methods and seasoned musician base that made records quickly, continued its embrace of the producer/executive paradigm, and its songwriting community to which Bowen had often looked for songs for Sinatra, Martin, and Campbell, seemed the best place to redirect his vision of a production career.

He arrived in Nashville in October 1977, and quickly became at home with the antiestablishment types that congregated at the Glaser Brothers studio on the Row—owned by recording artists Tompall and Jim Glaser and one of the homes of country's Outlaw movement in the late 1970s—getting what he calls "a three-year crash course in country." He was also evaluating Nashville business practices. "When I came here, producers were getting a hundred and fifty to two hundred and fifty dollars per side [the legal industry term for one recorded song on an album or a single] and a point-and-a-half to two points per record," he recalls, referring to the percentage points of a recording's sales price that are part of a producers' compensation. "But it really didn't matter because they weren't selling records, so it was all just an exercise in paperwork. The sound of the records was way behind, too, ten years behind pop." Bowen compared that to the $1,500 to $2,000 per side that producers had been getting in Los Angeles for major rock records and set his fee at $500 per side for his country productions. "I heard about how the heads of CBS and RCA were at a party one night. One of them said, 'Are you going to use that damn Bowen?' and the other one said, 'Shit, no, he's too expensive.' They're always real nice to you when you come in just to do some business. But when you move here they get real uptight. Like any other small Southern town. That's what the music community here is like. A small Southern town."

The first major country Nashville recording he did was with Mel Tillis, and the economics of that record illustrate the difference between Bowen's previous experience and what he found upon his arrival. When the album *Love's Troubled Waters*, was done in 1977, Bowen laid out the recording and production bills on Tillis's desk in his office. "He was so upset, he couldn't talk," remembers Bowen, a reference to Tillis's trademark stuttering. "He said, 'Th-th-th-th-thirty-eight thousand damn dollars,' Bowen!' Now, his last album had cost fifteen thousand and sold forty thousand copies. I said why don't you give this one a chance and see how it does. Fortunately for me, it did about a hundred and fifty thousand units. It was a turning point in Nashville economics, but no one knew it at the time. Waylon [Jennings] had left RCA for the Glaser Brother studio so he could cut the way he wanted; Willie [Nelson] had to leave here and go to Texas just to be Willie Nelson; Dolly had to leave here and go to California to be Dolly Parton. The factory, do-it-this-way-or-else mentality was strangling these people to death creatively."

When in 1978 MCA Records offered him the position of vice president and general manager, Bowen seized his opportunity to again combine an executive position and production. He stayed at MCA only briefly before moving to Elektra/Asylum. He promised that company $30 million in revenues in a year; he delivered $29 million, signing Crystal Gayle, Conway Twitty, Hank Williams, Jr., and the Bellamy Brothers. "They said when I came in here that I taught Nashville how to make a forty-thousand-dollar record for a hundred and forty-thousand dollars," Bowen observes. "They were right. And sales show it."

Nashville always equated sales with success, but required a certain protocol of the members of its fraternity; fortunately for him—and undeniably for Nashville—Bowen's abrasiveness was counterbalanced by results. Frictions on the local level were offset by his relationships with MCA's Los Angeles-based record label headquarters, where he had some leverage through personal relationships. At the same time, those ties also brought him more autonomy, and allowed him access to increased corporate funding, which he used to increase recording and marketing budgets and produced increased profits that he reinvested in his Nashville label divisions.

Jimmy Bowen doesn't seem to feel the need to be liked, but he demanded respect. He has a remarkable memory for anything he perceives as a slight, and that has resulted in strained relationships with any number of people in Nashville, including two producers whose careers he nurtured, James Stroud and Tony Brown. While both generously acknowledge Bowen's influence and mentoring, they reflect the difficulty in dealing with him personally. Brown, who inherited Bowen production clients Reba McEntire and

George Strait at MCA and ultimately Bowen's executive position there, flatly refused to work with Bowen when MCA considered bringing him back a third time. Stroud's observation was pithy and pointed: "I loved him like a brother but sometimes I just wanted to bop him."

Bowen's introduction of more complex, more expensive digital recording technology and higher budgets paved the way for the glossier sounds that characterize country music now. (Several recording studios in Nashville assert to having the first digital multitrack decks, but most acknowledge wanting to please Bowen as a client as the impetus for making that investment.) Bowen recalled in a self-penned interview[4] that, "When I first came to Nashville . . . my first thought was that somebody must have had a big sale on shag carpeting. [Carpeting was often used to deaden the sound of studios and, by extension, the records that came out of them.] It was all over the place, on the floors, on the walls. The sound would just shoot into that shag and never come out again. There wasn't a sound loud enough to last more than half a second in any one of those rooms." This was at a time when rock and pop records were heavily using the ambient sounds of large, live spaces for recordings. "Of course, [country records] didn't really have drums then, or at least none you could hear. They used brushes most of the time, but I knew that a generation grows up with certain sounds and the last couple [of generations] had grown up with a strong beat. They'd never start taking country seriously until it gave them that sound, and until it caught up with L.A. and New York music production. The whole town was about ten years behind the times [in terms of production]. . . . The music publishers had become the producers, and usually if a [country music] publisher can hear the lyrics, he's satisfied with the production."

With an almost missionary zeal to raise the threshold of the sound of country records, the effect of Jimmy Bowen's productions opened the door to a much more comprehensive merging of rock and country productions, an effect that

---

4. *EQ* Magazine, April 1992

remains audible today—loud snare drums, rocklike guitars, a glossy production sheen that was radio-friendly to a wider range of formats. Without abandoning the song as the core of the production philosophy, Bowen stretched the rules in Nashville sonically, artistically, and business-wise. And it shows in those who succeeded him.

"You Either Make Dust Or You Eat Dust."

James Stroud is a large man, intimidating in stature whether sitting around his recording studio on Music Row, or at a negotiating table. He is the contemporary quintessence of a third-generation Nashville power broker/producer: aside from his credits as a country producer, most notably Clint Black, Clay Walker, Tim McGraw, the Charlie Daniels Band, the Bellamy Brothers, Lee Greenwood, Tracy Lawrence, and several noncountry productions including the Neville Brothers and Melissa Ethridge, he also was, until early 1997, head of Giant Records's Nashville office; he is co-owner, along with former BNA Records chief and one-time Lorrie Morgan producer Richard Landis, of Loud Recording studios; and he is a publisher with hits such as "Third Rock From The Sun" and "She Can't Say I Didn't Cry" from writers signed to his Stroudavarious and Stroudacaster music publishing companies. His productions between 1993 and 1994 sold a cumulative total of nine million units, three million of which were for *Common Thread: The Songs Of The Eagles*, which also garnered him a CMA award for 1994 Album of the Year. In one week of 1994 he was listed as producer or coproducer on four of the top 20 *Billboard* singles. He was named Producer of the Year by the Academy of Country Music (ACM) in 1989 and earned *Billboard*'s Top Country Producer nod in 1990, 1994, and 1995.

Born in 1949 in Shreveport, Louisiana, Stroud came to Nashville in 1981 as a session drummer after stints throughout the South, first in Jackson, Mississippi, and then in Muscle Shoals, Alabama, where he was house drummer for blues label Malaco and drummer on records by King Floyd, the Pointer Sisters, Gladys Knight & The Pips, Dionne Warwick, and on Paul Simon's *There Goes Rhymin' Simon*. He's the drummer on Bob Seger's "Old Time Rock & Roll." Engineer/producer Ed Seay (producer for Martina McBride and Pam Tillis) remembers Stroud as a brash young man who strolled into a Paul Davis session Seay was engineering in Atlanta in the early 1970s and blew everyone away with his playing. In search of bigger records to play on and higher session fees than were found in the South at the time, Stroud moved to Los Angeles in 1977 before returning to the South and Nashville in 1981.

Producer David Malloy brought Stroud to Nashville that year to play on Eddie Rabbitt's debut record, which spawned "Driving My Life Away" and "I Love A Rainy Night." "I knew David and [producer] Steve Buckingham, both from L.A., and that was it," Stroud recalls. "I had seven hundred bucks in my pocket and no regular [session] accounts. I took every session I could, including demos." Within a few months, he and the late Larry Londin were the two main session drummer calls in Nashville, and Stroud was playing as half of a battery with another Los Angeles migrant musician, bassist David Hungate, a former member of the pop band Toto. The Los Angeles connection was beginning to create a clique of its own in Nashville—as a drummer Stroud picked up producer Jimmy Bowen, then at MCA Records, as well as Jim Ed Norman, a producer (Anne Murray, Hank Williams, Jr., Crystal Gayle, Johnny Lee, Janie Fricke, Charlie Rich), both of whom had come from Los Angeles a few years earlier.

It was during this period that Stroud, who still regarded himself as an R&B drummer, began to learn the rules of the session world in Nashville. "To work in this town you had to understand the structure," he says. "Especially back then. Some key people did most of the work here, and you had to get in with those guys or you just didn't work. Producers, label heads, publishers, certain session players. I remember getting in with Reggie [Young, a guitarist]; he helped me a lot. [Keyboard player] David Briggs was one of my big brothers and he helped me get a lot of [sessions]. But what you did, though, was you had to fend for yourself. If someone called you for a session, you had to take that date or that client or that account away from somebody else. The competition was pretty intense between me and Larry and a few other players." He pauses. "You either make dust or you eat dust."

Stroud wanted to produce, the natural channel for that intensity of ambition in Nashville. His initial attempts at it were tentative and restricted to a secondary tier, with stabs at developing new artists. That changed when he shifted his focus toward publishing in a move that was patterned on similar, earlier transitions by people such as Tom Collins (see the Publishers section). Jimmy Bowen also had his own publishing company, Great Cumberland Music Group, and producers Bob Montgomery, Steve Buckingham, Billy Sherrill, and Norro Wilson were also successful publishers. In 1984, Stroud started The Writers Group out of a small house on Music Row, initially signing Fred Knobloch, Tom Schuyler, and Paul Overstreet, the same trio that started the writers-in-the-round at the noted songwriters' showcase club, the Blue Bird Cafe. "What had been happening was, I was playing for [producers] Tom Collins, Billy Sherrill, and Larry Butler along with Jim Ed and Bowen. I was learning from them an older, more traditional Nashville approach [to production]. I was learning from them as a player what to do as a producer, but I couldn't figure out how to get the dadgum song. I looked at Collins, who had success as a producer through his publishing company. And Collins and Sherrill would always say to me, 'it's the writers, it's the publishers. Go to those people.' I started my own publishing company to learn that side so I could be a better producer. I picked Fred and Tom and Paul because they had been friends of mine and because I thought they were the best writers for the kind of productions I wanted to do."

He also picked them based on their potential as recording artists; not something new to Nashville's publisher/producers such as Collins and before him Fred Rose, but in doing so Stroud was laying the groundwork to that approach—Nashville publishers today routinely consider the songwriters' recording artist potential with the reasoning that cuts are much easier to get if the writer is also an artist recording his or her own songs.

Stroud financed The Writers Group with capital raised privately, and sold the company profitably in 1987. Along the way, he used his session work as a song-pitching conduit, slipping tapes to producers' assistants before sessions started. "If I was playing for Jimmy Bowen, I knew what the next four or five projects were he had coming up, so I'd pitch for them." That was a procedure that required a lot of finesse as country producers are constantly deluged with song tapes and not all took kindly to having tapes passed to them by musicians they were paying double-scale at sessions. But Stroud learned the protocol and chose his moments.

Stroud had another unconventional angle for pitching that got songs listened to. The building that housed The Writers Group had a perfect view through a bedroom window into the house next door. "Every afternoon at three-thirty the couple who lived there would come home and raise the shades and make love. We found out about it by accident at first, then we got the whole staff up there, watching. So I called a couple of producer friends of mine and said you've got to come over and see this. It got all over town and we wound up with a regular group of producers who couldn't wait to come over and listen to our songs at three-thirty every day."

Stroud garnered the ultimate Nashville credential as a result of The Writers Group: a number-one song. "Baby's Got a New Baby" achieved that status in 1984 for SKO, the group formed by Schuyler, Knobloch, and Overstreet and produced by Stroud for the short-lived MTM label, owned by actress Mary Tyler Moore and then-husband Grant Tinker and part of their Los Angeles-based entertainment production company. The tracks for the record were originally recorded as a publishing demo and leased by Stroud to the label. The sale of The Writers Group, which had accumulated a number of successful copyrights such as "On The Other Hand," "Diggin' Up Bones," "Forever And Ever, Amen," and "I Fell In Love," was precipitated by an offer from Bowen for Stroud to join

MCA Records as a producer and member of the A&R staff; company policy prohibited an employee having a publishing company as a conflict of interest.

Stroud followed Bowen to Capitol Records in 1986 as vice president of A&R. During that time Stroud met Clint Black through a mutual friend, Bill Ham, Black's manager and the man to become the capital force behind Stroud's next publishing venture, Stroudavarious Music and Stroudacaster Music. Meeting in a Houston club, Stroud heard Black play live and decided to record Black with musicians from his own band. This was then and still now a rarity in country record productions and one of the major differences between country and rock artists. "I had a theory that if I could find an artist with a good live band and good songs, I'd like to go in and cut an album in country music the way we used to do it in pop music. I listened to Clint and loved him and the band and the songs. So we went to the club and during the day we'd work on the songs and at night we'd play the arrangements for the crowd. If you listen to that first Clint Black record, it's very loose, very live sounding, very spontaneous, because it wasn't just a session players' record. It was a band record. After that, Charlie Daniels called me and we did *Simple Man* the same way and it went gold."

Stroud came to Nashville knowing what it took to play on a hit song but not what it took to pick one. By playing on them in the closely knit Nashville environment, with its heavy overlap of job descriptions, he says he came to understand what constituted a hit. Even when that wisdom was absorbed, it was still a matter of developing instincts. But it wasn't enough if the song was still king in Nashville anymore, as Bowen and Jim Ed Norman were proving; the sound of the record was becoming increasingly important. Pop and rock musicians traditionally had more input into the record-making process in Los Angeles, if only because they were often integral to the writing and arranging of records as members of the bands or extended entourages of artists; in Nashville, that function had become relegated more and more to the B team—the demo players—upon whose work the arrangements were often based. "I learned that a good producer would take the demo and tear it apart and make it a little bit better or a little bit fresher," Stroud explains. "Billy Sherrill could take a demo apart in five minutes and explain it and you knew what he wanted. You let the professional side of the musician take over and you didn't have to play it more than a couple of times and it stayed sounding fresh. The bad producers didn't know what they wanted and they'd try this and they'd try that and wear the artist out singing, trying to figure out what was wrong."

Stroud's—and country's—secret weapon was its small but extremely deep pool of talented studio musicians in Nashville, known unofficially as the A Team. Relying on them, however, was and still is a double-edged sword; the very efficiency with which they work has also contributed to a widely held criticism that many of the records that come out of Nashville sound alike. Stroud's use of Clint Black's band members on Black's records was a hedge against that.

Stroud came to head Giant Records in 1991, after it was formed the year before by Irving Azoff in a custom label deal distributed and funded by Warner Brothers Records. Azoff, one-time manager of the Eagles, had known Stroud from his days as an L.A. session player. His first choice had been Tony Brown, who had worked at MCA when Stroud was there under Bowen and who now heads the Nashville office of that label. Brown chose to stay and Stroud became Giant's first Nashville office head. In that position, he produced the label's first gold-selling artist in 1993, Clay Walker, and weathered a small but turbulent controversy surrounding the release of *Common Thread: The Songs Of The Eagles*. The record, as much a strategic marketing effort to capitalize on country's then-emerging Yuppie audience as it was a musical tribute to the band, had a number of country recording artists—Vince Gill, Diamond Rio, Suzy Bogguss, and Stroud's own artist Clint Black—doing versions of Eagles songs, and 8 percent of the record's total of 20 percent royalties were to be donated to former Eagle Don Henley's Walden Woods restoration project. The record attained gold status within ten days of its late

1993 release, but not before the Tennessee state Charitable Solicitations Division had launched a probe into the distribution of its nonprofit revenues. The situation led to public and industry criticism. Stroud and Giant asserted—successfully, as far as the state was concerned—that the problem was attributable to a mistake in the wording of the original letter of intent. *Common Thread* hit double platinum in early 1994. Stroud likes the concept of various artist-recordings; in 1996 he coproduced for Giant Records the all-star charity single "Hope," a benefit for the music industry-favored T.J. Martell Foundation and which featured John Berry, Vince Gill, Little Texas, Tim McGraw, Marty Stuart, and Travis Tritt, among others.

Stroud's experience with the Eagle's tribute record underscored his own assertive nature, but it also reflected his long-standing personal theme of pushing country music's and the Nashville industry's structural limits. The Eagles record and others that followed by Stroud and other producers show how the realms of production and marketing could be pushed closer together. Yet, his moves have to be construed as variations on a theme—assertive, yes, but well within the structure that Nashville had historically provided. Stroud's numerous hats—label head, studio owner, publisher, producer—are worn in a balancing act that was common in Nashville. In keeping with his approach of looking for and signing writers that have potential as recording artists, he coproduced a record released in 1994 for Robert Ellis Orrall and Curtis Wright. Wright was signed to one of Stroud's publishing companies at the time, and Stroud had once signed him to a deal at Capitol Records. It's these interrelationships that cause some publishers to roll their eyes at the mention of Stroud's name as they watch the share of the chart available to publishers not directly connected to record companies and producers diminish. Stroud counters by referring to the inherent checks and balances in the Nashville system in which a producer's viability is determined by how many of the songs he picks become hits. "If the song is right, I do it," he says vehemently. "Curtis doesn't get special treatment, nor do any other writers. A hit song is a hit song and I'm in competition with [producer and Arista Records president] Tim DuBois and Jimmy Bowen and everyone else and if that's what it takes to win, that's what I'm going to do. I don't play games about it, and that's where my temper comes in, because if I'm accused of it, it bothers me.

"There's more of a pop mentality in country now, and producers are looking for artists who can write their own songs. I produce so many records [that] I don't have time to look for all the songs for all the artists. The artists are more complete now. Look at Vince Gill; he writes them and performs them and plays on them."

The balancing act is limiting the number of productions Stroud can do, as it does other label heads/producers in Nashville. They've developed a methodology similar to the one that's evolved for songwriters. Coproductions are rampant in Nashville these days, a way to maximize participation in an album and do a lot of them. Stroud coproduced Clint Black's first record with Mark Wright (who was named head of A&R for the Decca label in 1994). "I schedule them so that I can finish one record and then start right in on another," he says. "I schedule the ones like Clint Black first because he writes his stuff and I don't have to look for as many songs. John Anderson writes some of his own stuff. For Tracy Lawrence we do song hunts." Stroud does his administrative work in the morning, then works in the studio from the afternoon through the evening. The fact that Clint Black is an RCA Records artist would seem to compound conflicts further, but not in Stroud's eyes. "I told Irving [Azoff] that if I was going to run this label, I had to keep my artists. He said that was fine with him."

Getting as many productions as possible could be wise, considering that Stroud, like many others of his stature, is well aware of the cyclical nature of country music's success over the years. "We'll run our course and someone will take my place," he said. "People will get tired of it like they do of other types of music. It's a cycle. It'll go away at some point."

"Radio's Never Going To Play This"

Josh Leo looks more than a bit like Dustin Hoffman, circa *Midnight Cowboy*, with a trimmed beard that girds his oval, early-forty-ish face. Just as Hoffman's Ratso Rizzo character made a personal crusade of fighting a society that refused to give him his due, Leo's observations on Nashville's music industry sound like those of the habitual outsider. Leo seems to revel in maintaining that stance, but if he's progressed further into the production structure than an outsider might usually have, it's not by virtue of either his ability or willingness to play its politics. He is an L.A. rock guitarist who is unabashed about his passion for what Los Angeles pop artists such as the Eagles and Linda Ronstadt did with and to country music. Leo's résumé includes production credits on records for K.T. Oslin, Restless Heart, the Nitty Gritty Dirt Band, Paul Brandt, Kathy Mattea, Lari White, Ray Vega, and Alabama. But other credits—Robert Ellis Orrall, Foster & Lloyd, Andy Childs, Juice Newton—reveal a distinct pop side—both his and country's. Also unique among non-Southern-born producers, Leo has held an executive position at a major country label: he was head of A&R at RCA Records for a fractious two years, from 1990 to 1992.

Brought to Los Angeles by an MCA Records contract as a member of a young rock band from Kansas City that self-destructed within months of signing its deal, Leo quickly landed in the upper-tier club and session circuit in Los Angeles, becoming an insider with that lofty crew in large part due to what he called "one good night on stage at the Roxy" in Los Angeles, playing behind J.D. Souther. Some of the people at that show—Jackson Browne, Bonnie Raitt, engineer/producer Val Garay—began calling Leo for session work, and he became adept at the triple-guitar harmonic clichés that characterized the SoCal sound of Souther, Ronstadt, the Eagles, Warren Zevon, and Andrew Gold in the 1970s.

Leo fell in with the writers of the SoCal Zeitgeist, as well, penning a song that found its way onto a session for Trisha

Johns that was being produced by Dixie Gamble. Interestingly, Johns was the ex-wife of Jim Ed Norman and Gamble was the former spouse of Jimmy Bowen. That established a connection for Leo with the Los Angeles-Nashville axis that was forming in the 1970s. Shortly thereafter, Bowen cut a song Leo had cowritten with pop songwriter Wendy Waldman in Los Angeles for Crystal Gayle, "Baby What About You," which went to number one on the country charts. "That's when I started thinking, I'm in the wrong town," said Leo.

If Nashville was to become the right town, it wasn't immediately apparent to Leo. He tried to establish himself within the musicians' community, where he played what he called "washed-out Eagles three-part-harmony guitar parts" on sessions for his country *arriviste* benefactors Bowen and Norman, who were now producing in Nashville and whose West Coast pop sensibilities were creating a demand for the kinds of sounds Leo specialized in on country records. "If it wasn't for them I would never have made it as a musician [in Nashville]," he said. "The Nashville session guys felt threatened about all the people moving here from Los Angeles at the time. They thought we were going to come in, take all the money, rape the women, and leave. If you wore a black leather jacket to a session they made fun of you. I walked into a control room in a studio once early on in Nashville wearing one and one of the musicians said, 'Let me guess, you just got in from L.A.,' and the whole control room started laughing."

Leo says he alternately tried to assimilate and maintain his West Coast attitude, which was not an easy balancing act in the days before there were places such as the Sunset Grill to hang out in Nashville, and a time when Los Angeles, like New York, still had deeply held negative connotations for Nashville veterans. On the one hand, he acknowledged a story in which, when asked to play a solo on a country session by Jim Ed Norman, he played it standing on a chair, much to the amazement of the traditionally sedate and usually seated Nashville A Team musicians. On the other hand, he concedes, "I also came to realize that what they lacked in energy, they made up for in chops. When I would go back to Los Angeles and do sessions there, I found myself realizing, Jeez, there's some good players here but no discipline. I mean, I remembered being on sessions in L.A. that went for hours and you were starving and it wasn't cool to ask for a food break. Here, you get a break every three hours. I began to realize that the rules in Nashville had some reasoning behind them."

Leo ultimately wanted to produce. He had one production credit under his belt from Los Angeles: ex-Poco bassist Timothy B. Schmidt's 1982 solo record. Jim Ed Norman had explained the rules to him in 1982 when Leo first began doing sessions in Nashville: move here and get in line. Norman eventually gave him a shot on a few Pam Tillis singles early in her career, none of which charted but gave him a basic production portfolio, a necessary calling card for a producer.

Leo waited it out, doing sessions, until 1987, when producer Paul Worley demurred on doing another Nitty Gritty Dirt Band record. Leo did half the tracks on that record, *Live Two Five.* which produced two number-one singles, "Fishing In The Dark" and "Baby's Got A Hold On Me." It gave him the hit-record legitimacy he needed to open other Nashville doors. A relationship with Joe Galante, another former outsider who was heading up RCA Records in Nashville in the 1980s, brought him the act Alabama, who, under coproduction with Leo and Larry Lee, turned out three platinum and two gold albums, spawning a dozen number-one singles.

But his success with country acts remained tinged with a defiant West Coast sonic component. With the three-part guitar harmonies came the louder snare drums and more complex processing on sounds that were standard techniques of Los Angeles and New York rock records but still alien to much of country music, elements that Bowen and Norman were also experimenting with in conjunction with their country record productions. Those production techniques helped precipitate what Leo jokingly called "Snare Wars," a period during the late 1980s in which the relative volume and sound of the drum on records took on a significance among producers and engineers that rivaled the rest of the instruments in the production and, to a degree, the song itself. This

was the ultimate irony in Nashville, where the song was sup-
posedly supreme and where the Grand Ole Opry wouldn't
even allow drums onstage thirty years earlier. "We used backwards echo [flipping the tape over and recording reverb in
reverse] on the first Dirt Band record I did, and that was all
people could talk about," he recalled. A review of Kathy
Mattea's 1994 release *Walking Away A Winner* compelled a
startled reviewer[5] to comment, "Producer Josh Leo has
stacked so many guitars on some tracks that at times it's
almost dizzying . . . Now and then they even play backwards."

Success with Alabama, a very legitimate country act,
allowed Leo more latitude for the application of contemporary
pop recording techniques, which reached a logical conclusion
with the release of 1992's *Big Iron Horses*, by Restless Heart,
which spawned the number-one Adult/Contemporary (A/C)
radio format *pop* single, "When She Cries."

When juxtaposed against the fact that the single reached
only number eight on the country charts, "When She Cries"
became a point of either meditative contemplation or outright
annoyance and alarm within the Nashville music industry,
particularly among the country radio community. It almost
single-handedly precipitated a simmering debate within the
radio and records community, with radio watching the
normally staid pattern of one country-formatted station per
market explode into highly competitive multiple-station
markets, and the records community watching country music
sales rapidly expand and chafing at country radio's penchant
for conservative programming but with nowhere else to go for
the exposure needed for sales. Moon Mullins, a country music
radio consultant, summarized country radio's concerns,
focusing on that particular song: "Take a stance against the
rock- or A/C-oriented 'country' tunes—we don't need 'em. Let the
competition play them. . . . Country labels, heed this warning.
Attempting to make crossover music . . . eventually produces the
same old formulaic, noncountry pop Pablum of the past."[6]

5. *Country Music* Magazine, July 1994
6. *Radio & Records*, May 7, 1993

Big Iron Horses was Restless Heart's first album after the departure of lead singer Larry Stewart for his solo career. That they wanted a pop direction was evident from their inquiries to pop producer Don Was, a Los Angeles-based producer who has produced records for major artists in pop and country, including Bonnie Raitt and the Rolling Stones, and country acts Willie Nelson, Travis Tritt, and The Highwaymen. Leo was still in his A&R position at RCA, and found that Was had several projects ahead of him before he could even consider Restless Heart. Leo, who had earlier produced two cuts for the band's greatest hits record, was the band's second choice. "They thought it was over for them without Larry," he said. "Me and the band sat in a room at RCA and they said, in effect, we know this is our last record, so please let us do what we've always wanted to do. It was like this was their last dying request."

In many ways, Restless Heart and Leo were perfect for each other: both wanted to make pop records in a country milieu and both had been stymied before in that effort, although each was able to put enough of a pop sense into their previous records to make it quite clear that they were not strictly country artists. Restless Heart had five records prior to *Big Iron Horses*, culminating in *Fast Movin' Train*, which scored them a distinctly pop-sounding country hit with the title track in 1992.

Marc Beeson's "When She Cries" was "definitely a country song when its demo came across my desk," Leo remembers. "But it had some of the pop elements we were looking for, and I picked up the guitar and started playing eighth notes to the beat. Lyrically, we thought, 'The girls are gonna love this . . .' By the time we had recorded it, it was the one song that at the end of every session we'd say, 'Let's hear that one again.' But at the same time, we said, 'radio's never going to play this.'"

Not country radio, anyway, as it turned out. "When She Cries" was released to country radio first, which made sense, considering Restless Heart's country track record. But RCA's pop division, based in New York, decided to release it to pop stations, as well. Leo said that impatience on RCA's part to widen its audience cut the song off too soon for country stations as pop radio quickly accepted it. "[RCA's] country division told them to wait, that releasing it to pop stations would piss off country stations if they start hearing it on competing stations in the same markets, and that's just what happened. It stalled out at number eight on the country charts but went to number one on pop."

Once "When She Cries" had established its ascent on the pop charts, RCA Records's New York office essentially took over the marketing of the album. Within a few weeks *Big Iron Horses* had sold about 150,000 copies, at which point "Tell Me What You Dream" was quickly added to the next edition of the album. Not part of the original recording sessions, the song, written by Leo, Nashville writer/musician Vince Melamed, and Poco bassist Timothy B. Schmidt, was picked by RCA's New York office as the second single off *Big Iron Horses*. In what is an historical nightmare scenario from the point of view of Nashville's Old Guard, a country division's headquarters office was again encroaching on Nashville's purview as a crossover hit record materialized. Underscoring the fact was that "Tell Me What You Dream" was originally scheduled to appear on saxophonist Warren Hill's record on the label— with Restless Heart as guest vocalists; instead, the song was cut by Restless Heart with Hill as guest instrumentalist. "Tell Me What You Dream" was never released to country radio and hit number one for three weeks on *Billboard*'s pop chart.

"That caused us even more problems with country radio and really fired up the debate over whether we had turned our backs on country," recalls Greg Jennings, the band's guitarist, who a year and a half after the two singles climbed the pop charts found himself part of a disintegrating band that had lost both its record deal—RCA dropped the band in mid-1994—and two of its founding members, Stewart and keyboard player Dave Innis.

The story of "When She Cries" is a kind of morality play that outlined how close country music had now come to mainstream pop music, yet how isolated and vulnerable to the dominion of its label headquarters Nashville remained, as well as how isolated and narrowly defined its primary exposure medium—country radio—was. Leo contends that the way that "When She Cries" or any other record that he's produced sounds is simply the result of his own influences and preferences, with a grounding in country only to the degree that the artists bring with them. "What I'm saying is, this is my idea of country. You've got twenty-year-old kids with record deals saying they grew up listening to George Jones. No—they grew up listening to James Taylor and the Eagles. People are finally coming out of the closet and copping to the fact that they listened to the Eagles, which is not something they used to readily admit here. People don't play George Jones and Merle Haggard records anymore, so how can twenty-year-old country artists be influenced by them?"

Leo's own position at RCA was relatively short-lived. Conflicts with Jack Weston, then RCA's vice president and general manager and Leo's counterpart and equal on the business side of operations, were increasing. The matter came to a head when RCA Records's president Joe Galante, former head of A&R in Nashville and then running all the label's national and divisional operations from New York, installed songwriter Thom Schuyler as head of the Nashville office. "We butted heads on musical terms," Leo recalled of the few months he and Schuyler worked together. Referring to his release from RCA, Leo said, "I felt like a horse with a broken leg and [Galante] did me a favor by shooting me." (Galante himself put it more prosaically by commenting, "There are people who are meant to be executives and people who are meant to be production people; Josh was meant to be a production person. It was wrong for him to be in that position. I put him there because I liked what he was doing . . . Unfortunately, by doing that, I was hurting him.")

With more Los Angeles musicians than ever on Nashville's A Team, Leo seems a bit more comfortable with the music that country makes today. His leather jacket rests easier on his shoulders now—when he chooses to wear it. And he wears his tenure as an executive at a Nashville record label like a campaign ribbon. "Now my selling point to the labels' A&R people is, 'Hey, I had your job and I know the pressures," he says, still with a tinge of the L.A. *arriviste* in his words. "I can deliver a commercial record on time and on budget. And I don't want your job. I did it and I didn't enjoy it. I'll do what you want me to do [with a record] if you just let me go as far as the line allows at the moment."

"They Drove Big, Flashy Cars. *They* Were Flashy"

On the night of February 24, 1994, MCA Records unveiled its new Nashville headquarters building. The motif was anything but pure country: a loud stew of rock, dance, and uptempo country music—MCA artists, of course—pounded through the cavernous garage on the street level of the new building, ricocheting off the corrugated sheet metal dividers placed around the space on which the label's publicity department had spray-painted such graffiti phrases as REBA RULES. Outside, the car valets hired for the occasion were working for five dollars an hour, jockeying Mercedes 500s and Lexus sedans to a parking lot a quarter-mile away, running back and politely snatching tips along the way.

Inside, scooting between trays of puff pastries and smoked salmon, MCA Records President Tony Brown moved quickly and lingered only momentarily at each of the dozens of small groups that formed on the floor, listening more than talking. His office on the third floor of the new building is tasteful but sparse with his desk at one end of the room of plush chairs and gray carpeting that's obsessively orderly.

MCA/Nashville is the apotheosis of country music's business success. The country division's domestic sales in 1992 were over $120 million, representing over a third of MCA Records's total annual sales of $344 million—which accounted for 11.6 percent of the U.S. domestic music business that year. Well over half of the label's roster had attained gold sales status. As both the president of MCA/Nashville and current producer for established, radio-friendly MCA acts such as Reba McEntire, George Strait, Wynonna Judd, and Vince Gill, and occasionally straying further afield with the lyrically Dylanesque alternative singer Todd Snider and the often-uncategorizable Lyle Lovett, Brown is arguably the most versatile—some say most powerful—single entity in Nashville. But while many laud the relative eclecticism of his production range, it is overwhelmingly his mainstream country productions that have garnered him sixty-two number-one singles and over fifty million units thus far in his career.

Brown's observation, "Personally, I prefer things the way they are," is polite and amorphous, like many of his initial comments as he warms to an interview. He is animated to talk about how Nashville's producer/star system that has more in common with the Hollywood of the 1930s than anything in contemporary music, and yet has signed and produced some of the edgiest country acts, from the skid-row country of Steve Earle to the eclectic oddness of Lyle Lovett to the pop-diva-in-cowboy-boots style of Wynonna Judd. He repeatedly defers questions whether he has ambitions in production that exceed country's realm with a Cheshire cat smile. "I'm already making pop records here in Nashville; they just happen to be country records," he says.

Born in 1946 in Greensboro, North Carolina, where his father was an evangelistic preacher, he came to Nashville in 1966 to start his professional playing career as the piano player for the Oak Ridge Boys. He spent much of his early years working on gospel records and trying to get on the A Team of session players, interspersed with road gigs, including a stint with the Sweet Inspirations, Elvis Presley's touring band, from 1975 until Presley's death in 1977. (He still wears a green malachite ring that Presley gave him.) He subsequently played with Emmylou Harris and Rodney Crowell/Rosanne Cash, keeping his hands on the keyboard even as his careers at the recording console and conference table were beginning to take shape.

Initially, his gospel and pop influences predominated, but it was his time playing with Emmylou Harris, whose tra- ditionally rooted country sensibilities and relationships with early country-rockers such as Gram Parsons helped bridge the generation gap in country in the 1970s and 1980s, who Brown credited as opening his eyes to what country music was, and could, become. "She is a major inspiration for what is happening today," he told an interviewer for *Mix* magazine in 1993. Talking about the roots of the synthesis of rock & roll, pop, and tradition that comprise the state of country music at the moment, Brown observed in the same interview, "The glamour of what a Kenny Rogers was doing at his biggest fascinated me as much as the redneck aspect of Alabama selling five million albums, because they tapped into that Southern rock & roll thing that was missing [from country]. I started analyzing everything about country music and loving the idea of trying to figure out why this act would happen and why that act wouldn't. Sometimes I like diving into areas where I think it's a little dangerous."

Brown's diverse background in gospel, country, and rock led to his first A&R position in 1978 at Free Flight Records, an ill-fated pop custom label venture sponsored by RCA Records that was based partially in Nashville but which ultimately answered to RCA Nashville division head Jerry Bradley, who balked at some of the pop-level budgets for Free Flight artists. More often than not, Bradley's decision that a country record should cost $30,000 won out over Free Flight's putative mandate to develop competitive pop artists and records. As the Free Flight experiment wound down, Brown spent two years in Los Angeles before returning to Nashville and RCA in 1980, where he signed Alabama and several other acts to the label before going on the road full time with Rosanne Cash and Rodney Crowell. He went to work in the A&R department at MCA Records, brought there by Jimmy Bowen in 1984, the year in between his early Grammy Award years in the Soul/Gospel categories for "I'm So Glad To Be Standing Here Today" by Bobby Jones & New Life with Barbara Mandrell and Shirley Caesar's "Martin." Brown won Grammy Awards again in 1991 and 1992 for work with Vince Gill and Lyle Lovett; he was nominated numerous times for Grammys, including as Best Producer in 1994, a prize that had only once before been won by a country producer (Larry Butler in 1979). He would come to head the A&R department, running the label in concert with MCA/Nashville's then-president Bruce Hinton. In 1993, in a negotiation shadowed by the courting of Brown by several other labels including Sony, MCA Music Entertainment chairman and vice president of MCA, Inc. Al Teller offered him the presidency of MCA/Nashville at a reported salary of $1 million with a bonus of twice that amount. (Hinton was elevated to chairman of MCA/Nashville.)

His time in Los Angeles provided Brown with both a reaffirmation of where he ought to have been—Nashville—and with a perspective that few who have spent all their time in that city have. The first was underscored by a sense of insecurity he perceived about himself while there. "I went to every party I could go to in Beverly Hills because, being young white trash from North Carolina, I figured I better do this while I had the chance," he says with a laugh. Brown's references to his own humble and Southern origins often sound self-deprecatory but are natural and earnest. "Then I realized my Camaro just didn't hold up out there . . . I came back with a whole new respect for Nashville. . . ."

In moving into the executive suite, he went from cruising Camaros to considering the impact of a daily nonstop flight between Nashville and London when American Airlines introduced that short-lived venture in 1994. He made the transition between the two sound easy. "You think that's not important until you get higher up in the executive position in the music business," he says. "You start realizing that's the . . . thing that can make Nashville grow. Not just hit songs being cut here but actually attracting more creative people, more of the business. And the only way you can attract more of the business is to be convenient."

That thinking is broad, and it underscores Brown's statement in an interview with BMI's house publication in the fall of 1993 when he said, ". . . I think country music as a genre is not ever going to be totally accepted . . . because it's really a more narrow art form, such as jazz and real R&B . . . diluted versions of [those forms] end up being crossover . . . most of the [genres] that are really true [to their origins] don't sell very much. . . . Country music as we know it has limitations."

Tony Brown's response that he is already producing pop records is playfully evasive, but echoes the sentiments of his predecessor and one-time mentor Jimmy Bowen about the position of country music in relation to pop. Yet he is more than passingly familiar with the names and accomplishments of his cohorts on the other side of the musical fence, more so than other producers of his term and stature in Nashville. He, more than any other contemporary country producer, has been nominated by his peers on larger platforms than country music's, including Producer of the Year by the National Association of Recording Arts & Sciences's Grammy Awards and the more technically oriented *Mix* magazine TEC Awards. While his success and his workload indicate that music comes first for Brown, at the same time he seems to enjoy a level of celebrity that extends beyond Nashville.

When Brown first got to Nashville he found a place in which "celebrity executives" such as Billy Sherrill and Jerry Bradley controlled the town's music business. "Guys like [Elvis Presley producer] Felton Jarvis," he said. "They drove big, flashy cars. *They* were flashy. It was show business." He said he missed that aspect of it during the early 1980s. The flash was being replaced by a more controlled corporate charisma. Within a few years, people such as Arista's Tim DuBois, a songwriter but one with a degree in accounting, marketing maven Joe Galante at RCA, and attorney Ken Levitan (Rising Tide Records) were running labels in Nashville.

Brown's ascension to the leadership of MCA Records in the wake of Jimmy Bowen, though, underscored the role of personality that still plays a significant part of country music's upper echelons. The internecine celebrity of the Nashville music industry was alive and well. Bowen, ever the self-acknowledged doyen of that milieu, maintained that the tension that accompanied Brown to MCA's leadership was engineered by him intentionally to goad Brown into making a career move. "[Brown] was always a little timid," Bowen said in an interview that appeared in the May 1993, issue of *GQ*.

In attempting to get Brown to assert himself, "sometimes you almost have to make somebody hate you to get them to come through . . ." Bowen had left in 1989, but when MCA considered bringing him back, the backbone Bowen contended he was trying to elicit from Brown was considerably evident, as Brown reportedly told Teller he would not work with Bowen. Teller dropped his pursuit of Bowen, and Brown had the mandate he was looking for.

(At the annual Country Radio Seminar in March of 1994, Brown participated on one of the panels, whose members were introduced with brief, comedic videos in which they starred. Participating enthusiastically in a parody of his own status, Brown's video opened with him being measured for a custom suit in his office. When his assistant, Renee White, enters that office to tell him that he has phone calls on hold from several Nashville power brokers as well as "the writer from *GQ*," Brown tells her to put the writer through, he'll get back to everyone else. At the conclusionof the tape, Brown is shown signing his autograph onto an eight-by-twelve glossy of himself. He leaned into the camera and said, "Should I sign this, 'To Jimmy?'" Cocking an eyebrow, he paused and added, "Or *Mister* Bowen?'")

Brown has picked his way carefully but forcefully through the thickets of Nashville music business politics, looking for a kind of star quality in artists and songwriters that didn't fit the traditional mold. While working at MCA in 1985, he took a ride to Gulf Shores, Alabama, at the urging of Noel Fox, a publisher who told him he ought to listen to Steve Earle, then signed to CBS Records, where his brand of harsh lyricism and edgy guitar country-rock was not being understood.

"Steve was trying to get off CBS. They didn't like any of his new songs. He started playing me the stuff he was writing, like 'The Fearless Heart.' While he was down there . . . he was on the phone arguing with his girlfriend in Texas and he wrote 'Guitar Town' about that. He wrote 'Hillbilly Highway' down there and he wrote 'Good Ol' Boy' and I was around him watching all this go down. I thought, 'This guy is killing me.' I started getting chill bumps. Steve

Earle . . . didn't look that different from Hank Jr. and Waylon and those guys. He's just a good ol' boy kind of guy. I thought I'd found the next Waylon. And everybody started tapping him as the next Springsteen or Cougar and that's really what confused the issue.

"So I played this stuff for Jimmy Bowen. So, of course, Bowen's first reaction was, 'The guy can't sing. If you can make me like his voice one iota, you can sign him.' So I went out to a studio and we cut 'Good Ol' Boy' and we really worked hard to get Steve to get his vocal just right. We . . . just cut the hell out of the demo and played it for everybody. How can you deny that song? It's not about singing. Bob Dylan's not about singing. Tom Petty's not about singing. So we cut that and Bowen let us cut a record and we cut *Guitar Town* [and] not for one second did I think we were pushing the envelope. I just thought it was good stuff."

Tony Brown had heard what everyone else was hearing, but he was hearing it, listening to it, in a different way, with ears that had not simply come from Los Angeles but rather that had been there and back. If Steve Earle would not prove to be the future of country music, he did point the way it could go—a more sophisticated lyricism in which a much wider range of topics and emotions were on the table, and with a harder, rock-and-blues edge musically. In the case of Lyle Lovett, whom Brown also signed to MCA and produced after seeing him paired with Nanci Griffith doing an *Austin City Limits* broadcast, the distinction between what country wanted and what country could be for him became clearer.

"I knew when we mixed Lyle's first album—which were his demos—that . . . Lyle's subject matter . . . was a little more out there than Steve, and Steve was basically dealing with issues that country music knows about. Lyle was dealing with issues that I knew were beyond the realm of what most country people want to talk about. Plus Lyle looked back then the way he looks now. I was taken with Lyle the first time I saw him on stage."

Brown is very concerned with business; many regard him as doing the Nashville balancing act of label head and producer better than anyone before him. At the same time, they also acknowledge that he spends more time in the studio than others in his position, and his percentage of coproductions is lower than most other label head/producers. (And unlike other contemporaries and predecessors, Brown has never owned a recording studio; his personal publishing venture is limited—a copublishing deal with MCA Music begun in January 1993, with a single writer and which grew only slightly to a stable of four composers, very small by Nashville publishing standards.) Under Brown and Hinton, MCA/ Nashville reduced its inherited roster—well before the economically enforced rounds of roster cuts that started in late 1996—and concentrated on a core of existing artists, such as Vince Gill and Reba McEntire, while focusing a limited number of new signings that they would intensively develop. Artists that often could test the flexibility of country esthetically and commercially, such as the Mavericks and Trisha Yearwood.

Yet Tony Brown's personal intensity about music—country and otherwise—is still paralleled by his fascination with the personalities of those who make that music. For him, one does not come without the other. It's a slight but pivotal departure from the Nashville tradition that puts the song above all else. His early memories of Nashville's most colorful leaders have been seasoned by time spent in the global capital of entertainment celebrity, Los Angeles. And the continuing influx into Nashville's music business of people from there dovetails nicely with Brown's personal experience. Of anyone in Nashville, Tony Brown would have understood both Lyle Lovett's music and his haircut. The migration from Los Angeles and New York to Nashville hasn't and won't change Nashville, in Brown's view. "We'll change them," he'll say. Because ultimately the insularity that many in Nashville had complained of for years has now become as much of a barrier for keeping traditions in as keeping larger influences out. "We sort of enjoy being isolated, even though we whine about it all the time," he said. "But if we became totally like L.A. and pop music, I think the thought of that scares everybody to death.

I don't really care what's going to happen ten years from now. All I really care about is what's happening right now. It's changed from when I got here, but as you've noticed, it hasn't changed all that much."

"People Where We Come From Like To *Dance*."

The traditional role of the Nashville producer—the marriage of songs to artists—is becoming more complex as dance mixes become more common in country. Brooks & Dunn's "Boot Scootin' Boogie" propelled the duo's first album, *Brand New Man*, to triple platinum in 1992. The song, the flip side of "Neon Moon," the album's third number-one single, was a dance remix that sold 400,000 cassette singles alone that year, stayed at number one on the country charts for four weeks, and entered the Top-50 of *Billboard*'s pop chart. More significantly, "Boot Scootin' Boogie" was the first major country record to use remixing techniques reserved for Urban/Contemporary dance records. A conventional record mix involves taking the separate elements of the recording process—basic tracks, instrumental solos, vocals combined on anywhere from twenty-four to forty-eight individual tracks on tape per multitrack machine—and blending them together, along with electronic processing such as reverb and delays. Dance remixes, on the other hand, allow the remixer almost as much freedom as the original record producer (although often little of the credit); the remixer generally keeps only the original vocals and replaces instruments, percussion, and effects, usually with purely electronic instruments.

On "Boot Scootin' Boogie," virtually all but the vocals on the original tracks had been stripped away and a combination of electronic and acoustic instruments replaced them, with an emphasis on the bass and the snare drum—the bottom and the beat: the basic elements of any dance remix. The success of the record has helped move along a country dance business that came into being in the late 1980s. Country promotion

departments and independent promotion companies now ser-
vice hundreds of country dance clubs nationally with records
and remixes in much the same way their U/C counterparts do.
Country dance remixes, such as Confederate Railroad's
"Queen Of Memphis" and "Trashy Women," and Alan
Jackson's "Chattahoochee," have become a routine part of
record promotion. TNN airs three dance-oriented programs:
"Club Dance," "Dance Line," and Dancin' At The Hot Spots."
Most importantly, though, country dance remixes offer record
companies and artists another way around the bottleneck of
country radio, since the remixes go directly to clubs. The
result makes for an interesting contrast in music; according to
Wynn Jackson, president of Country Club Enterprizes, Inc.,
an independent dance club record promotion company that
services over 400 such clubs in the United States and Canada
and which produces the Country Dance Music Awards,
"Somewhere late in the night, the D.J. will throw in something like 'Back In Black' by AC/DC or an extended urban
record. If they know what they're doing, they can segue [into
a country record] and no one leaves the floor because the
grooves work well together."[7] (In a sort of more sedate and
primitive prefiguration of the country dance remix and rap's
turntable scratching, 1950s country disk jockey Joe Allison
recalled that he would take 78 rpm records on his radio show
and randomly skip across their grooves. "I'd say, 'Boy, that
was a great chorus by Chet Atkins. Let's listen to that again."
'And I'd pick up the needle and set it down just about where
his chorus was. If you were pretty good, you could do it.")[8]

The idea for the "Boot Scootin' Boogie" remix came from
someone for whom the seeds of a future production career
were planted while he was driving a tractor on a farm in
Oklahoma. Scott Hendricks would listen to a combination of
stone country and the Eagles while working as a teenager on
farms in the 1960s, blasting tapes in the cockpit of an
International Harvester combine in the fields surrounding

7. *Music Row*, August 23, 1993
8. *Radio & Records*, October 7, 1994

Clinton and Sentinel, Oklahoma, near where he was born in 1956.

Hendricks went to college at Oklahoma State and formed a band there with two people who would become key later in his career: Tim DuBois, who taught accounting at the college while he worked on his songwriting and who would go on to become head of Arista Records in Nashville; and Greg Jennings, who became the guitarist for the band Restless Heart. Jenning's guitar virtuosity led Hendricks, a guitarist himself, to reassess his own talents and turn to studio engineering as his route into the music business. Having learned recording in a rudimentary two-track studio on the college's campus, Hendricks moved to Nashville in 1978, taking his degree in architectural acoustics first to a studio design company, then to the Glaser Brothers' recording studio on Music Row, where he worked as an assistant and often hung around all night watching Jimmy Bowen work until the management finally hired him as a staff engineer. He eventually became a freelance engineer in Nashville, working with other producers, learning the formulaic, fast-paced Nashville production approach from them.

DuBois, looking for an outlet for his songwriting, approached Hendricks in 1984 about doing a record with the nascent band Restless Heart. After a few false starts looking for some free time in studios, the two wound up in Sound Stage Studios where they cut seven songs in one day for what would become the first Restless Heart record. It gave Hendricks a production credit as well as an engineering one. Having his name follow the phrase "Produced by . . ." on a record in Nashville conferred a new level of possibilities for him. Simply engineering records would no longer be enough.

Scott Hendricks obtained that credit during a time when Nashville was undergoing a major change in how country records sounded and were made. Producers Bowen, Jim Ed Norman, and others who came to Nashville from the Los Angeles rock music milieu had brought new sensibilities and the need for higher record budgets to country. And the previous generation of country record producers, which were drawn mainly from a pool of musicians such as Bradley, Atkins, Butler, and Stroud, were now being infused by engineers such as Kyle Lehning, who produced Randy Travis's seminal New Traditionalist record *Storms Of Life*. As country records became more complex during the recording process, recording engineers began to take on a new level of importance, just as they had in pop and rock music. Their mastery of an increasingly sophisticated (and to many producers in Nashville, increasingly mysterious) recording environment gave them a unique perspective and an advantage in transitioning toward production. Specialization in certain areas of the recording process became more common in Nashville; several engineers became quite successful doing "pitch-fixing"—using algorithm-based digital audio workstations to correct pitch flaws in artists' vocals. While engineer/producers such as Jim Malloy (who produced Dolly Parton's sister, Stella) had used their combination of creative and technical talents successfully in the past, the growing number of people who could engineer and produce would bring Nashville's recording structure to a point where the sound of the record was virtually tantamount to the song.

It was during this time that Hendricks began specializing in mixing records, performing that task for producer Jerry Crutchfield's work with Tanya Tucker and Lee Greenwood. "It gave me a different perspective as to what I thought should go on a record in the first place," he said. "I grew up listening mostly to singles on the radio driving that combine. I'd only hear the top songs mostly. I knew what a good [single] was supposed to be and what it was supposed to sound like."

Brooks & Dunn came together in what could be described as a marketing accident, with the sort of synchronicity that has brought Nashville to where it is today. In 1989, Ronnie Dunn had won the Marlboro National Talent Roundup, a country music battle of the bands, and part of his prize was forty hours in a studio with a Nashville producer. Barry Beckett did the production with Hendricks engineering. One of the songs on the session was "Boot Scootin' Boogie." In the course of the production, Hendricks became enamored of

Dunn's voice and songwriting and asked him to send him more songs after the session was over, which he then took to his friend Tim DuBois, who had since become president of Arista Records. DuBois didn't share Hendricks's enthusiasm at first. But a few months later, Hendricks and DuBois were attending a University of Tennessee football game and DuBois mentioned to Hendricks that he was looking for a duo act for Arista. He had a tape of two singers he thought would work well together. One was Kix Brooks. "Coincidentally, I had one of Ronnie Dunn's tapes in my pocket," Hendricks recalled of the afternoon. "I told Tim that I thought this was who should be the other half of the duo act." DuBois, now listening in a different context, quickly agreed.

Just before the release of *Brand New Man*—which Hendricks coproduced with Don Cook, the original producer DuBois had in mind for Kix Brooks—Hendricks was on the road watching another of his productions, Alan Jackson, working in a Texas nightclub. There it occurred to Hendricks that people dancing to country were responding to some records and not to others—records that had bottom ends like rock records. It got them up on the dance floor faster. He came back to DuBois and suggested a remix of "Boot Scootin' Boogie" along the lines of a dance club mix. DuBois questioned whether the song had single potential at all, much less as a dance remix, an idea that neither Brooks nor Dunn were comfortable with at first. Hendricks pursued the idea, first with Keith Thomas, the producer of Vanessa Williams and other pop/R&B and Contemporary Christian music acts, who has a studio in nearby Franklin, Tennessee. Thomas liked the idea but told Hendricks that he was too busy with other productions to get involved at that point. He did, however, suggest another engineer, Brian Tankersley, a Los Angeles producer and remixer who had done remixes for the *Dirty Dancing* soundtrack and Smokey Robinson, and who had recently moved to Nashville. Hendricks gave Tankersley the tapes of the song, which Tankersley took to his home studio and from which created a one-minute rough sketch of what a remix would sound like. Hendricks took this back to DuBois, who then gave Hendricks a $10,000 budget and said try it.

The creation of the dance mix was a curious mixture of country and Urban studio approaches, tinged with trepidation about how country audiences would react to the venture. This was illustrated by the first meeting between Ronnie Dunn and Tankersley, who jokingly introduced himself to Dunn by saying, "Hi, I'm the guy who's going to ruin your career." Harmonica player Terry MacMillan was called in and he played various parts to the tracks that were then reassembled using a sampler, a digital recording device that allows engineers and producers to digitally capture and then manipulate the speed and pitch of recordings and place them anywhere in the song.

After the parts were cut, Hendricks played the traditional role of Nashville producer, sitting back and letting the musicians work, but this time the musician was a dance remixer. "It went pretty quickly once we got started," Tankersley recalled. "The half-time breakdown part in the middle of the song, I thought that up in the car on the way to the studio and we had it down in ten minutes."

The politics of production were apparent in Hendricks's next move, which was to play the song for selected groups of Arista staffers before playing it for DuBois, building up enthusiasm for the remix, then playing it for the label head with some of those staffers present. DuBois was suitably impressed, as were the radio and country audiences that they all were apprehensive about: "Boot Scootin' Boogie" received the 1992 Single of the Year award from the Academy of Country Music and undoubtedly helped land Brooks & Dunn the ACM's top vocal duo honors. The record helped drive the proliferation of country-themed dance clubs which, according to *Billboard*[9] now number approximately a thousand, and of which between 600 and 800 hundred use live D.J.s. In the wake of "Boot Scootin' Boogie"'s success, Sony/Epic Nashville compiled and released the first major-label country remix album, *Steppin' Country*, in 1993, with two accompanying videos.

---

9. July 17, 1993

After a decade as an engineer to Nashville producers, Hendricks had learned what the rules were, and how they were changing. As an engineer-turned-producer, he went to another, more specialized, engineer and in doing so contributed to changing the way country records were made. The art of using recording technology had attained the same level as the playing of a musical instrument. But the possibilities were considerably broader, and new technology allowed producers and engineers to manipulate the very DNA of a recording and the song itself.

At the same time, Hendricks's realization of the need to build consensus in the increasingly corporate atmosphere in Nashville's music industry reflects the changing nature of the country music business, one that combines the historical conservatism of country music with the innately cautious restraint of a large company in a highly competitive and increasingly crowded market. He was keenly aware that he would need broad support at the middle level of the label's management in order to gain the absolute backing needed at the upper executive levels to get the record out and properly promoted. A combination of those talents, honed over the years, brought Hendricks to the presidency of Capitol Records in May 1995, succeeding Jimmy Bowen. For years, country had been pulling much of its creative and lyrical influences from rock. As more and more people with mainstream musical backgrounds came to influence country, it affected the budgets of those records. "Boot Scootin' Boogie" marks where country began to change the way the records were made.

But what's *not* different about "Boot Scootin' Boogie" is as remarkable as what is: In applying Tankersly's remix techniques to the song, Hendricks was simply drawing on a talent, no differently from any other producer in the past had chose a certain musician for a certain instrument. And despite the emphasis on the sound, a deep and personal belief in the song was still as much the key for Hendricks, as it was for Chet Atkins and Owen Bradley before him.

The other producer on Brooks & Dunn records also had extensive studio experience, although not as an engineer. Don Cook came to Nashville in 1972 from Cariso Springs, Texas, where he started writing songs at the age of fourteen and began making demos out of them almost as soon. A self-professed "folkie" at heart who combined that influence with the Rolling Stones, the Beatles, and Atlantic Records's R&B singles, Cook chose Nashville out of a combination of its reputation as a music center and his desire to stay in the South.

He got his first publishing deal with Acuff-Rose, signed there by Don Gant, who he followed four years and a few successful cover songs later to Tree Music. Cook now sits behind a desk there, as Tree's senior vice president. From 1976, when he had his first real hit with Bobby Wright's recording of "Lovin' Someone On My Mind," until 1990, Cook's career track in the Nashville music industry was purely as a writer. He came of age with the first cowriting generation of Nashville composers, and had cuts in collaborations with writers such as Rafe Van Hoy, Bobby Braddock, and Curley Putman, starting out with a $100-per-song contract with Tree. "I turned in an amazing number of songs when my rent was due," Cook laughs as he recalled those days.

His writing relationship with Kix Brooks, who in 1989 was trying to build a career as a solo artist on Capitol Records, would become pivotal to his entry into the producers' club of Nashville. When he and Brooks wrote the song "Lost And Found" that year, Cook began producing the demos of that and the collaborations that followed (some written with Ronnie Dunn after they were teamed into an act by Arista Records). Many of those demos found their way onto the Brooks & Dunn debut record the next year, including "Brand New Man," "I'm No Good," "Cool Drink Of Water," and "My Next Broken Heart." Other songs were cut by other artists, such as "Who's Lonely Now," a number-one hit for Highway 101 in 1989.

Cook maintains that he and Brooks had no strategy planned for writing for a specific artist's project for Brooks; just that they seemed to click well as cowriters. But when Arista Nashville President Tim DuBois heard the song demos, he took a substantial chance on pairing Cook, who had no production credits to his name, with Scott Hendricks, based on Cook's demo productions. Producer Paul Worley, who headed Tree prior to Cook's ascendancy there, encouraged Cook to try his hand at production. "I was sort of reluctantly being pushed into [production]," Cook says. "I was very happy being a writer. Until this opportunity came along, I didn't want to compromise my quote—integrity—unquote—as a songwriter by being a producer and having people accuse me of making records just to record my own songs."

That sensitivity that Cook felt at the time is one that runs long and deep in Nashville, harking back to the 1960s when Billy Sherrill removed that taboo with a string of very successful self-penned hits for Tammy Wynette, George Jones, and others. But the relatively high level of production volume that country music has, compared to pop and rock, brings an internal checks and balances system into play that keeps longevity as a producer dependent upon producing hit records regardless of who wrote them. Producers have been known to put their own songs, or those of writers whose publishing they own, onto their records. The practice may annoy publishers and songwriters by cutting off one more record slot to them, but as long as those songs turn out to be hits, it no longer raises eyebrows as high as it used to in Nashville.

Cook's first meeting with Hendricks took place in Tim DuBois's office at Arista on Music Circle South in 1990. Cook recalls it as "uncomfortable" at first, a feeling that quickly passed. Perhaps understandably; both pairings—Brooks & Dunn as artists and Cook with Hendricks as producers— were being made as much as a business imperative as an artistic one.

Cook approached the production of *Brand New Man* the same way he had the original demos. He used the same assortment of musicians that had played on the demos, including Brent Mason on guitar and Lonnie Wilson on drums. And he wanted to use the same cultural references as the demos: "[To] make a record that the people where we come from will enjoy. Ronnie's from Oklahoma, Kix is from Louisiana, and I'm from Texas. And the people where we come from like to dance. They like to *dance*. That's just what they do . . . We made a record for the people in those three states, probably. We're very fortunate that a lot of other people liked it, too."

Very fortunate, for all concerned. Cook's career as a producer took off after the success of *Brand New Man*. Within three years he had done records with Mark Collie, Michael Martin Murphey, Conway Twitty, Marty Stuart, Larry Boone, James House, and Shenandoah. Perhaps the one production client that has brought him almost as much attention as Brooks & Dunn is The Mavericks, whose retro-sounding platinum-selling *What A Crying Shame* in 1994 cast country's net well beyond the bounds of traditional country radio. His rapid rise as a producer underlines the quickened pace of Nashville in the 1990s at a time when songs compete with sonics on records. Cook still writes and considers himself first and foremost a songwriter, although he complains that he has little time for it now between productions and his position at Tree. As for his induction into the elite producers' fraternity, Cook is equanimous. "The funny thing is, I didn't try to join," he observes. "I was pushed into the club. And I like it, but I'd be very comfortable leaving the club, too. I just like being part of the process."

But within Cook's own assessment of his initiation lies the fact that as country music grows, the fraternity itself will need to grow. The comfortable interrelationships between the few who do most of the country records Nashville puts out will feel the effects of growth, as well. Even with rosters pared down from the 200-plus artists at country's peak in 1995, the golden baker's dozen of producers will not be able to keep up a level of productivity to match the output of all of Nashville's labels. But the vicissitudes that bind them will remain the same as they have been for some time. They'll have to maintain a successful production record over the course of many records, meaning that the songs can come from wherever, as long as they become hits. The recording methods and the thinking that goes into them will likely change significantly. But as Cook puts it, "If you take a one-hundred-thousand-dollar budget and make ten million [dollars] with it, everybody in town won't care what you do. They don't care if you stick a bone in your nose and dance around the console. If you can [make a successful record], they'll want you to do that for them. It's a real superstitious, quirky process that gets people to this point. I try not to analyze it very much, because it never has done me any good to analyze it."

"I Have Not Been Back To L.A. Since"

Like a number of other successful engineers and producers, John Guess appears in endorsement advertisements in professional audio trade magazines. In a 1994 ad, Guess holds his hands in front of him in a Tai Chi stance as a German-made microphone floats between his outstretched hands. You're not quite sure whether he'll catch it or not. A telling image for someone who was then on the cusp of becoming a Nashville producer.

John Guess is sitting in Masterfonics, a Nashville recording studio where he engineered many sessions before founding his own studio nearby on Music Row in 1995. He is wondering aloud when his production of Michelle Wright will ever be finalized. "They cut like twenty-two sides on her with various producers and I got four sides and then they asked me for three more," he says. "So hopefully I'll have maybe six cuts on the album whenever it comes out."

A common phenomenon in pop and rock, the concept of multiple producers for individual tracks (versus the idea of a complete coproduction between two producers) on a country record is relatively new. But John Guess came of age as a producer in Nashville at a time when things like that were changing.

As of early 1995, the only complete country production on which Guess had the sole producer credit was Linda Davis's debut record (he would go on, in 1996, to produce an album for Reba McEntire, for whom he engineered several previous recordings); he had coproduction credits with Tony Brown on

Kelly Willis, Chet Atkins, and Suzy Bogguss on their 1994 collaboration, and Deanna Carter with Jimmy Bowen. After ten years of engineering in Nashville, Guess learned that the transition to producer remains a lengthy one.

Guess's beard and his six-foot-plus frame make it easy to imagine him as one of the lumberjacks that worked the hills of northern California, where he was born in 1942. And he might have been one, had he not found music at an early age with the release from the network of small towns and winding roads of that region. In 1953, he was nine years old and singing in local dance halls like the Moonlight Gardens in Chico, opening for traveling country acts such as Lefty Frizzell and Ray Price when they passed through. Bob Wills was ready to take him along when he was twelve and Guess was ready to go till his parents intervened.

It was after he got out of the army and settled in Los Angeles a decade later that he would deal with music so directly again. A deal with Kapp Records and later with Capitol Records produced three records and little else, but introduced Guess to the technical side of the business. In the mid-1960s, following the classic apprenticeship path of the recording studio business, he took a job cleaning the studio at Hollywood Sound Recorders in Los Angeles studio and moved up through the ranks until he became an engineer there. In 1969, Jimmy Bowen, then at MGM Records, sent over a Sammy Davis, Jr. tape for mixing and Bowen and Guess met. Bowen liked the mixes enough to hire Guess for several more sessions, and later as an A&R assistant at MGM Records. Guess got more grounding on the business side of music when he became head of A&R at the recently merged Polydor/MGM label in the early 1970s.

Guess and Bowen stayed in touch over the years after Bowen had moved to Nashville, with Bowen attempting to lure Guess with promises of coproductions and complaints about how Bowen's own musical visions were being less than well-served by the engineers in Nashville. Intending to move into a producer's role in Los Angeles, Guess held Bowen off for several years while he remained in Los Angeles and engineered rock and pop sessions for Rod Stewart, Donna Summer, Jermaine Jackson, and Christopher Cross.

"He would call me every now and then and try to get me to move down here and I'd just tell him, no, I'm happy in Los Angeles," Guess recalls. "He finally talked me into coming out [to Nashville] to have me mix George Strait's *If You Ain't Lovin' It, You Ain't Livin'* album for him." The 1987 trip had an effect on him—at the same time that Nashville was becoming a haven for many in the Los Angeles music business, L.A. itself was becoming less and less a place Guess wanted to live. And the New Traditionalist movement of the mid-1980s reawakened Guess's own roots in traditional country music. The combination was overwhelming. After a few trips back and forth and some effort convincing his native-Californian wife, he and his family moved to Nashville for good in August 1988. "And I have not been back to L.A. since," he adds.

His initial engineering work was for Bowen, and when those projects would dry up Bowen's imprimatur was enough to get him around the studios working for other producers. Surprisingly enough, considering it was Bowen who had brought him to Nashville, it was Tony Brown who gave Guess his first coproduction credit—Kelly Willis's *Well Traveled Love* album in 1990—after Guess had done engineering projects for Brown, notably Patty Loveless, George Strait, Reba McEntire, and Vince Gill.

There were two things Guess noticed as an engineer in Nashville that differed from his experiences in Los Angeles with pop: the records were recorded and finished much faster in Nashville; and secondly, engineers were being relied upon more and more by country producers to supervise ever-larger portions of projects, which in turn freed the producers up to juggle more projects simultaneously and to pay more attention to the increasingly complex business side of their then-expanding label rosters. After spending the better part of a year engineering a single pop production, Guess was initially astounded at how quickly country productions moved. He estimates that Jimmy Bowen was perhaps the king of this: "He would have engineers doing various things on a project—one recording the basic tracks, another doing overdubs, another mixing it. How Jimmy works is, he would sometimes make the artist the coproducer . . . which allowed him more time to do more projects."

When Tony Brown brought Guess on board the Kelly Willis project, Guess was nominally the coproducer but his role in the most traditionally critical aspect of country record production—song choices—was nonexistent. "Tony made it very clear he was going to be the decision maker," Guess says. "I could give some input, but I had no say in the selection of material." But Guess had more latitude in terms of creative control over things such as instrumental overdubs.

The experience whetted Guess's appetite for more productions, but it would be three years before another opportunity came about. He calls the period "a long, dry spell" in which he continued gaining considerable success as an engineer but in the process fearing he was further pigeonholing himself into that niche to the possible exclusion of production. "Bowen said to me, 'Well, find an act,' but when you're engineering in the studio every day it's impossible to do."

Then Guess heard a song demo sung by Linda Davis. "I'd never seen her. I didn't know anything about her," he remembers. "I just heard that voice and said, 'Yes.'" Davis had just switched management from Strait's long-time manager Erv Woolsey to Starstruck Entertainment, a company owned by Reba McEntire and her husband, Narvel Blackstock. Guess called Bowen for help in tracking her down only to find out that Bowen planned to produce her himself. "Timing is everything," Guess laughs in retrospect. But it was clear that Guess felt disappointed that, having finally found an act he believed would establish him as a country producer, it had already been snapped up by one of Nashville's chosen few.

Bowen did two records with Davis on Capitol/Liberty, neither of which resulted in any significant sales. So, after what he regarded as a decent interval, Guess approached Blackstock directly about producing Davis. In the wake of the lackluster performance of Davis's first two efforts, Blackstock preferred to wait longer, hoping to reposition

Davis at another label. In the meantime, Guess was engineering for Tony Brown on McEntire's *Greatest Hits Volume II*, which would contain a new single, the duet "Does He Love You." Several artists, including Trisha Yearwood, were considered as the vocal partner for McEntire. As the recording progressed, Davis was called on to provide a "scratch track" vocal—a guide performance—for the unfilled second vocal track. That day, at Emerald Recording on Music Row, Davis was vocally spectacular. When the session was done, McEntire listened to the playback and said to Tony Brown, in Guess's recollection of the moment, "Now if whoever you get to sing that part doesn't beat Linda's performance, which one of you is gonna tell that to whoever we were gonna get to sing it?"

"Does He Love You" was a bona-fide hit, reaching number one on the country chart in 1993 and helping to propel McEntire's *Greatest Hits Volume II* record to sales of nearly four million units. (The song was never released in a commercially available single version for public sale; only to radio.) Guess felt his belief in Davis's talent verified, and must have suspected he and Davis were fated to work together. After another round of near misses, they finally did. Tim DuBois, president of Arista Records, and Blackstock agreed to let Guess produce Davis's next solo outing, her first on Arista, based on some demos Guess had done with Davis. *Shoot For The Moon* was released in February 1994, and was the first real Guess production, one on which he had control over both the song choices and the production. Unfortunately, the record's performance was sluggish, staying on the *Billboard* country album chart for just one week in May 1994, and peaking on *Billboard*'s Top-200 Albums chart at the number 124 position.

Guess attributed some of the responsibility to a shakeup in Arista's promotional staff at the same time as the release, which blunted some of the emotional disappointment for him on his first solo production outing. But he was also personally humbled by the experience; it was a quiet but significant epiphany that studio engineers who become producers all undergo and that signaled the transition from one level of existence in the music business to the next, but was also a transition of responsibility and an emotional rite of passage. "I realized that [as an engineer] I used to be able to go home after the session was done and not worry about it anymore," he reflects. "Now I worry more because my name's on the record as producer, whether it's a success or not." As for being a member of the producers' fraternity, Guess seems to feel that simply having produced is not sufficient; full membership requires hits: "So far as feeling like I'm one of them, I don't feel that yet. Until I have that major success as a producer, then maybe I'll have that feeling."

"That feeling" was felt by the end of 1996, when McEntire's *What If It's You*, which Guess coproduced with the artist, went to number one in the first two weeks of its release on *Billboard*'s Country Albums chart in November of that year.

"They May Not Have Played Us, But They'll Remember Us"

The inclusion of more engineers in the ranks of country music producers will have an inevitable effect on how country music sounds. The basic golden rule of production—pick the right song—seems secure enough for now, but engineers—and by extension, the hundreds of musicians and songwriters who now have affordable and powerful recording equipment in their homes—will push the envelope of how country defines itself even further. As daring as it seemed at the time, "Boot Scootin' Boogie" pales by comparison to "Dance," a track from the 1993 Twister Alley debut record on Mercury Records. It was produced by Mike Lawler, at the time an A&R staffer at Mercury Records as well as a session keyboardist and one of this new generation of producer/engineers empowered by "project studio" technology. "Dance" makes heavy and intensive use of drum machines and electronic gating techniques—an effect that creates dynamic contrasts in volume and processing effects on certain key tracks of a recording—that have been in use on dance and U/C records for a decade. The song got some play on CMT but country radio barely touched it. If "Boot Scootin' Boogie" blazed a new trail in country record production, it also drew a line in the sand regarding how far it could be taken. If "Achy Breaky Heart" drew barbs for its content—or lack thereof—even that criticism remained focused primarily on the song; in the case of "Dance," the song was subsumed by the track and its production, which was all about sound and attitude.

Mike Lawler speaks with an almost syrupy Southern accent, but a conversation with him is an experience in coherence for other reasons. His voice is tinged with a barroom-bred asperity and his sentences skip around like a needle on a scratched record, veering onto tangents with frightening speed before returning to the point. He will often apologize for sounding "scattered" while in the same breath telling a listener he is not crazy. The Cooter, Missouri, native started his professional career as a musician playing keyboards for James Brown's revue; his second professional gig was playing synthesizer keyboards with Porter Wagoner in the early 1970s and in doing so, becoming the first synthesizer player on the stage of the Grand Ole Opry. He has also played with the Allman Brothers and Steve Winwood (for several years a Nashville resident) on tour and on Winwood's 1988 *Roll With It* album, and has been a session player on numerous country records. Most recently, he succeeded with "Lonely Too Long," which Lawler cowrote and which Patty Loveless had a country hit with in 1996.

Lawler claims he discovered Twister Alley in 1989, and says he waited until their then-lead singer, Shellee Morris, came of legal age before signing them to Mercury—she turned eighteen in December 1991. In making the record, much of which was done at his home studio, Lawler raised some eyebrows by loading the record with songs he'd written; of ten songs on the recording, Lawler had cowritten seven. He raised them further by making the record by primarily using electronic sequencers and drum machines, rounding out the production with members of the band and an occasional part from a local session musician. Working in his home studio, he also recorded the songs in sections—working on a verse here from one song and chorus there from another, regardless of their sequence—rather than using one of the regular Nashville studios with musicians all there tracking ensemble. Records are made like this—nonlinearly, with parts shuttled from sequencers to tape recorders and back again—all the time. But not country records.

Some other producers in town had miffed reactions to Lawler's approach; one replied to the question with a terse, "No comment." Lawler himself could care less. Little of the protocol that exists between generations in Nashville was evident in his words. "The same people play on all the records here—there's two drummers, two bass players, four guitarists, two fiddle players, and two piano players, and they play on all the records," he says. "And it sounds like it. Don't get me wrong, they're all great players. But we're in a format of cloning hits, and it sounds like it. And the bosses own the studios and sign the budgets and they make sure every bit of the hundred and twenty thousand dollars [is spent] and that makes the mortgage on their two-million-dollar studios. And they don't want to hear about people like me doing it in their basements. I don't worry about how much I can make off the budget. Hell, if I'm producing one of my own songs, I don't even charge for it. I'm just tired of all this mediocrity. I love this job and that I can do it here. Every three months I call up Owen Bradley and I say 'thank you.'"

As Lawler describes it, Twister Alley begins to sound less like a country record and more like what country could become, a template for the *auteur* of country music's future. Writer/producers such as Billy Sherrill and publisher/producers such as Tom Collins might have been more self-contained than many producers in country, but they still needed the common ground of the studio and its live musicians. The studio and live musicians constitute much of what separates country music from other genres.

Lawler is sincere in his praise of the Nashville musicians

and studio engineers who follow the rules of production in Nashville, while at the same time he often does not use them on his productions. In response to why he would pull so heavily from dance production techniques to make a country record, he pointed out that country is borrowing heavily from rock for its sounds, a point well taken, and which adds a certain sibilance to the "no comment" reaction that Lawler's name elicits from some Nashville producers.

Accessibility to affordable, sophisticated recording equipment, the sort that previously required lots of capital, something that young producers rarely have enough of, has dramatically changed pop, rock, and Urban music. Thousands of independent records are now released each year, some on microscopic labels with only one artist—the one who made the record—and when taken as a group they had become the second largest single force in record sales by 1996, after Time/Warner. The force of this technology-driven change is about to descend on country music. And homemade records will take the production process further away from the controls of Music Row, allowing more influences to propagate within country.

The concepts for the songs on the Twister Alley debut record—if not the songs themselves—existed in Lawler's mind before the record was made, even before he met the band. The concept for the record itself was brewing in his brain before there even was a Twister Alley. It was an idea that was waiting around for some kind of structure on which Lawler could drape his vision. That assessment is confirmed by Paul Lucks, former general manager for Mercury in Nashville and later Twister Alley's manager. "Mike Lawler had a concept looking for a band," says Lucks, who was leaving Mercury in 1993 after seventeen years around the time that the band's record was close to completion. He remembered that the feeling at Mercury about the act was generally good, and that Lawler's radical production approach wasn't viewed with any major concern. "Mercury had been going out on a limb all along," he said. "Billy Ray Cyrus and the Kentucky Headhunters weren't exactly safe signings in the beginning."

Upon its release, country radio ignored "Dance" except for a few scattered stations that were going with a so-called Young Country format. "Dance" was added to about sixty stations, but SoundScan was showing the equivalent of 1,500 unit sales per week during the latter part of 1993. "That was very good, relative to airplay," Lucks says. The single charted at the lower end of the *Billboard* Country chart, and the CD made it only to the "Heat Seekers" chart, a starting point on the climb to sales and airplay charts. Its total sales as of March 1994, were around 85,000 units. The record's performance didn't dampen the band's evaluation of its own chances. At a country radio convention in 1994, before the record had run its course, Amy Hitt, the other female vocalist in Twister Alley at the time, looked over her shoulder as she stood at the Mercury Records booth and said of radio, "They may not have played us, but they'll remember us."

Lucks observed that Twister Alley is both an anomaly and a portent of things to come for country music. "There's lessons for everyone in it," he says. "The music industry is bigger than Nashville; the boundaries that seem limitless in other parts of the music business are narrower in Nashville. Lyle Lovett had to leave the format and the structure to break in it, and so did k.d. Lang," an observation that recalls Jimmy Bowen's own comments on how Dolly Parton and Willie Nelson had to pry themselves out of the comfortable country music way of doing things to realize their personal musical visions. Lucks then added, "The thought processes in this community sometimes baffle me." Either way, at the time at least, Lucks was willing to bet Twister Alley's sophomore record on Lawler, as well.

Lawler points to synthesizer work he's done on country records, such as George Jones's 1993 *High Tech Redneck*, as examples of how Nashville embraces the technology and the techniques of contemporary music production but how the rules will only let those influences go so far. Noting how many master sessions start out by listening to the publishing demo of the song and pulling the master recording's arrangement from that, he asserted that what he was doing was using technology to bypass the traditional structure of how country records are made, using digital technology to eliminate the line between what is a demo and what is a record. When a studio full of musicians listens to a song demo before the master session starts, they interpret what another musician has done with a part of the song—the drum groove, a guitar lick, a bass pattern. What they play may incorporate all, some, or none of what was played on the song demo.

In the home studio environment, sequencing replaces the interaction of live musicians. A sequencer is essentially a digital road map of a song on to which any number of instruments, sounds, and rhythms can be attached and replaced or added to at any point. Run as computer software, sequencers can reduce each quarter note of a musical measure to as many as 256 individual points, allowing for a tremendous amount of expression where notes and rhythms are placed. Drum machines and synthesizers can be reprogrammed (or their sounds changed even as the parts they play remain), guitar licks and vocals can be sampled digitally and then inserted precisely over and over again.

"'On Lonely Too Long' I had done all the parts in my basement studio for the demo and when it came time for Patty to do the song, they just asked me to bring the stuff over to the studio," says Lawler. "If it wasn't for the fact that her vocal was a fifth up [in key] from the demo, I would have just done a data dump from my computers to theirs. Studio musicians used to brag about being able to cop the demo; hell, the demo was the record in this case. That's what I had been doing with Twister Alley—making the record in my basement and making a master from the start instead of a demo that a bunch of musicians would then copy. And what people were giving me hell for in 1993, now everyone in Nashville does it that way. They give the keyboard player a tape and say go home and make us come up with parts and then bring it back and we'll synchronize what you played at home with what everyone else played in their homes and put it all together in the studio. That's the way records are done now. I just think a lot of people were kind of pissed off that they hadn't thought of it before I did."

The same digital technology and techniques that Lawler is so assertive about are used consistently throughout country recordings today—sampling, digital editing, and fixing of vocal accuracy, and other tricks of technology. But for the most part they are used as ancillary parts of the process of making country records. The basic premise of the country recording session, though, remains as it has for the last fifty years: a group of musicians playing together behind a singer while a producer sits on the other side of the glass in the studio's control room and guides the session.

What Mike Lawler represents is the ability to do all this alone. If the producer in country music is singular in his ability to run record labels, sign and produce artists and write songs, the producer still has a high degree of interaction with others who affect the outcome of the process and the producer's creative interpretation of a song, from the song-writer's own vision of the song to that of the label's marketing manager. Removing the historical constraints of that interaction from producers has provided them with formidable creative freedom. But freedom is always a mixed blessing, and what personal recording technology can do for country's esthetic limitations has to be also considered in the context of how it will change what country music is: from the sum of many creative parts to the vision of one person.

Mike Lawler says he is grateful to Nashville, for a certain tolerance if not outright acceptance, and despite his unorthodoxy, he is grateful in a very basically and fundamentally Nashville sort of way. "I'm especially thankful to our forefathers, like Owen Bradley, who also has his own studio," he says. "For giving us this town to ride this gravy train through."

"I Looked At Nashville As A Business . . ."

Not every country record producer has played by its production rules over the years. Fred Foster abided by the rule that states that "Thou Shalt Live In Nashville," but when Foster started his Monument Records label in 1958, it would give country music an alternative development site for artists who otherwise might not have had a chance before he arrived.

Foster got into the music business almost as a joke, teaming with singer Billy Strickland and writing songs on the spot for nightclub customers. But Foster's epiphany occurred when he was working at a local record store in Washington, D.C., on the same day that Hank Williams, Sr. died—New Year's Day, 1953. "I called up the local MGM Records distributor and asked him how many pieces of Hank Williams product he had on hand," Foster remembers. "He said he wasn't sure, but I told him to send every piece he had to me at the record store on Irving. Every bit of display material, everything to do with Hank Williams. He asked me if George Friedman, the owner of the store, knew I was doing this, on New Year's Day, no less. I lied to him, 'Yeah, oh, sure he does.' Turns out he had twenty thousand pieces of Hank Williams product."

Two days later a truck pulled up, and within hours the small store on Irving Street was stacked floor to ceiling with Hank Williams records. George Friedman was not amused when he walked in that morning and saw them. "He was freaking out, running around and screaming at me, 'What have you done?' I told him I was going to make him a lot of money. All he had to do was run one ad on the local country radio station that said he had the entire Hank Williams catalog at his store. He calmed down and we ran the spot. The next morning when I came to open the store there was a line outside five blocks long. That's when I learned the power of merchandising. I called the MGM distributor back and ordered another fifty thousand pieces."

Monument Records—named for the Washington Monument in a moment of inspiration as Foster saw the obelisk from an airplane window—and its publishing arm, Combine Music, were started five years later, capitalized with less than $1,000 of Foster's savings and a lot of good luck in the form of free advice and services from a number of Nashville establishment people, including Chet Atkins, who spotted the young Foster on his first recording session and helped assemble its musicians, and songwriter Boudleaux Bryant.

Monument's first release, produced by Foster, was Billy Grammer's record of Foster's adaptation of an old traditional British folk song, "Got To Travel On" in mid-1958. Monument chugged along but truly took off with the signing of Roy Orbison. It was publisher/producer Wesley Rose, owner of Acuff-Rose Music, who brought the Texas singer to Foster in late 1959, mainly, Foster said, because he knew he had something in Orbison but wasn't sure where he fit into country music. Orbison had been produced by Chet Atkins on RCA, but with little success. "Wesley said I could have Roy for Monument on the condition that I make him sound the way Chet did on RCA because Wesley liked that sound, even if it didn't sell records."

Sales of the first four Roy Orbison records on Monument were unspectacular; Foster only met Orbison on his first session in the studio in Nashville and Foster was still chafing at Rose's dictum about how the records should sound. Foster kept looking for songs he thought could be a hit, visiting publishers but coming up empty. Orbison had played "Only The Lonely" for him earlier, but Foster said its structure was too awkward, with the chorus initially consisting of only that line coupled with a thirty-two-bar verse, which was two to four times the conventional length for either a country or a pop song at the time. He had also played "Come Back To Me, My Love" for Foster. "Trouble was, it was a teenage death song, too much like 'Teen Angel,'" he recalls. "And you can only have one teenage death song every twenty years. But there was this vocal figure on it, and one morning at breakfast it came to me that if we put that into "Only The Lonely" we'd have a hit. So I walked over to Roy's room at the Anchor Motel downtown and knocked on his door and told him. He wasn't sure it would work but we wound up cutting it a day or two later over at the RCA studio." It became one of 1960's top records worldwide.

Foster continued to produce Orbison through his landmark "Pretty Woman" cut in 1964. It was as good for Foster as it was for Orbison, giving Foster credibility with Nashville even as he pursued pop chart success. He used

Nashville's studios, its publishers and songwriters, and its musicians; but he used them differently, spending an entire day on one or two songs and planning the sessions carefully in advance, rather than just relying on choosing a good song and counting on the musicians to come up with a fast arrangement. "The studio was costing me money, so I always knew what I wanted when I walked in," he says. "But we still took as long as I thought we needed to and I listened to any suggestions the musicians had. I do remember, though, that for 'Pretty Woman' we even went into the studio knowing the guitar lick ahead of time."

Orbison's pop hits were lucrative for Monument, which Foster was building into an oasis of pop music in Nashville, and for Wesley Rose, who typified the country establishment of the time (he both published and managed Orbison). But despite their joint success, Foster was doing things differently from how they were done in Nashville, and there was constant conflict between the two, professionally and personally. "Wesley told me I was ruining Nashville," says Foster. "And he wasn't the only person who ever said that to me there."

For one thing, Foster was increasingly using musicians from both Muscle Shoals and Memphis; these R&B-style players were more receptive to his way of making records, and he eventually convinced some of those musicians to come to Nashville permanently. "The old guard down here was trying to do four songs in three-hour sessions," he says. "I looked at Motown, where they had a house band which went into the studio and stayed there all day until they came up with something everyone was happy with. I wondered how the hell we were supposed to compete with Motown [Records]. I started out doing two songs a sessions and got down to doing one per session pretty quickly. I couldn't get a regular band in Nashville until the Memphis guys got here, so I just went in and kept doing takes until I thought it was right. Not everyone connected with those sessions liked that."

Foster's Combine Music was different, too, signing edgier songwriters than the establishment was used to, including

Tony Joe White, Billy Joe Shaver, and Dolly Parton, all of whom had their first releases on Monument.

Kris Kristofferson was a former Rhodes scholar and army veteran who came to town in 1965 to be a songwriter but didn't look like either. Recalls Foster of their meeting, "I had an understanding with Bob Beckham, who I'd hired to run Combine, that any advances to writers over a hundred dollars a week we had to discuss. He called me one day and said there's this guy he'd found who was making seventy-five dollars a week at another publisher and we had better sign him now and he needed to approve a hundred and twenty-five dollars a week. I said bring him on out.

"So Beckham walks into the office with Kris and he's got on this old brown leather suit, which was in pretty bad shape, and the sole of his right boot would flop out every time he took a step. He didn't look too successful, you understand. I learned early on never to ask a songwriter to sing only one song 'cause he'll sing you his best song and you'll never know how deep his well is. So I said you need to sing me four songs. He was definitely nervous. By the time he had finished his second song I was thinking, 'Man, something's wrong here. No way can these songs be as great as I think they are. He sang 'De Valia's Dream,' 'Jody And The Kid,' 'To Beat The Devil,' and 'The Best Of All Possible Worlds.' I said I'd sign him on one condition; if he also signed to Monument as a recording artist. He said you've got to be kidding, but if you're crazy enough to ask me, I'm crazy enough to say yes. And so he signed." Kristofferson, as a writer, immediately began having hits for artists like Ray Price, Roger Miller, and Johnny Cash; he had a number-one hit as an artist on Monument Records with "Why Me," in 1973.

Kristofferson's sales success as a recording artist eventually led Monument to a distribution deal with Columbia Records, in which Columbia would distribute and market Monument product. When Columbia president Clive Davis was ousted in 1973 (he went on to form Arista Records), however, the deal soured, as did a subsequent distribution arrangement with PolyGram. By 1982 the label's output, so dependent upon Foster as its main producer, was slowing down. Then came a series of financial blows in the form of a Knoxville bank failure, that sent Monument into bankruptcy despite the label's success. A group of former Monument artists, led by Dolly Parton, attempted a financial rescue of Foster and the label in 1984, but to no avail. Combine Music's deep pool of songs became one of the first of Nashville's main music publishing companies to go into the corporate meat grinder of catalog acquisitions that began around that time, when they were purchased by U.K.-based Thorn-EMI.

Foster and Nashville did not always see eye to eye, but by bringing and developing pop artists in Nashville he helped broaden the city's music industry. "I was always considered an outsider in Nashville, and I always considered myself to be that, too" he says. "I looked at Nashville as a business, from a business point of view for things like location, as a good place to raise a family, and to have fun in the studio and make records. It was always cliquish and resistant to change. And ultimately with what's going on now it may wind up like New York or L.A. I hope not, though, 'cause it's a real friendly place."

"There's a machine . . . in Nashville"

When Dwight Yoakam climbed the stage at the 1994 Grammy Awards in Los Angeles to take his prize for Best Country Vocal Performance, Male, for "Ain't That Lonely Yet," his acceptance speech was short, almost curt. Had the Grammy Awards been held in Nashville (they were once, in 1973), Yoakam might not have been there to pick up the award at all. The Pikeville, Kentucky, native has always been more at ease in Los Angeles than in Nashville. His records are made at Capitol Records's recording studios on North Vine Street in Hollywood, in the same studio room that Buck Owens and Merle Haggard made many of their non-Nashville country records in the 1960s.

Yoakam's records, which painstakingly re-create the fast-tremelo-and-cheap-reverb ambiance of those earlier recordings, are produced by a white blues guitarist from Detroit named Pete Anderson—a man who has his own issues with Nashville. Anderson passed through Nashville on his way to Los Angeles in 1972, at nineteen, stopping only long enough to drop off a tape. He didn't return until Yoakam's first major label record, *Guitars, Cadillacs, Etc. Etc.* was released in 1986. Today, as one publisher commented with a laugh, "He won't even come here to pick up checks."

"Country music wasn't a geographic thing for me; it was a cultural and economic thing," says Anderson, sitting behind the console at Encore Recording in Los Angeles on a break from a mixing session. "What I really wanted as a white kid playing the blues was black audiences to like me doing it. Being white and playing blues puts you on the bottom rung. And I guess that's when I started realizing that country was closer to my life."

Anderson played country in the honky-tonk bars of the west end of the San Fernando Valley in the 1970s, occasionally getting gigs at the Palomino (the spiritual heir to L.A.'s earlier country mecca, the Riverside Rancho nightclub), but more often than not at places such as Hap's Corral in Lakeview Terrace. This is where he met Dwight Yoakam in 1983, introduced by a mutual friend who played steel guitar with Dwight. Onstage, for fifty dollars a man per night, they played Yoakam's homages to Haggard and Owens, but in between cover songs they also worked in Yoakam's originals, such as "Miner's Prayer," which Anderson says kept getting them fired by club owners who wanted to hear Alabama songs.

In Los Angeles in the mid-1980s, cowpunk, a blend of country lyrical sentiments and musical nihilism heavily influenced by punk was taking shape in clubs on Sunset Strip. Anderson eased Yoakam into those clubs, forgoing the money that the honky-tonks paid and playing for next to nothing but gaining exposure for Yoakam among the local music journalists that were eyeing cowpunk as an emerging pop music trend. At the same time, Anderson convinced a friend to lend them $5,000 from a credit card cash advance to make a six-song EP. "I had told him about Dwight and he agreed to come down to the Palomino to see him," Anderson remembers. "The club was too crowded for him to get into and he thought the crowd was there to see Dwight. Actually, they were there to see Lone Justice, who we were opening for." Anderson did little to correct his friend's perception. This act of omission helped clinch the deal. The EP was released in the summer of 1985 and was distributed through an independent music distribution network that packed Yoakam in with alternative music acts such as Butthole Surfers and Suicidal Tendencies. Rather than hurt Yoakam, the contrast helped the record stand out to reviewers and produced reams of good press. A trip to New York to open for The Blasters brought Yoakam to the attention of Miles Copeland, the head of IRS Records, and he offered Yoakam a record deal. Anderson counseled Yoakam to turn it down. "I knew we needed a Nashville label," he says.

Yoakam came to the attention of Paige Levy, then director of A&R at Warner Brothers Records in Nashville, that same year. Levy, who had run Jim Ed Norman's production company in Los Angeles before coming to Nashville in 1983, flew down to see him perform at the Opry House in Austin, Texas, and offered Yoakam what Anderson had been holding out for: a Nashville record contract, with Warner's affiliated label Reprise Records.

Anderson had his stipulations, and they all ran counter to the Nashville way. "I told Warner's that Dwight doesn't cowrite; we use the EP as part of the Warner's record; that I produce his record; that we keep the EP artwork; that we do the records in Los Angeles," says Anderson. Levy agreed on Warner's behalf—as director of A&R she was able to sign an act without consulting company president Jim Ed Norman—but not without reservations. "We definitely had concerns about the sound that Pete had on the record, and about the lyrical content of the songs," Levy recalls. "They weren't structured the way Nashville was used to them, and we were concerned about how radio would react. Traditional country music was just starting to come back, but it wasn't the twangy country that Dwight sounded like. We were definitely concerned about the twang factor." Nonetheless, Levy says that Yoakam and Anderson exuded a confidence that overcame her concerns. The EP became the basis for 1986's *Guitars, Cadillacs, Etc. Etc.*, and it was destined to go platinum. "We took a flyer and it worked," Levy says happily. "It was a rare thing for Nashville at the time."

It still is. Independent record labels and releases—the way Dwight Yoakam got his start—have long been de facto extensions of A&R departments at major record labels on the pop side, a phenomenon that's accelerated in the last ten years. An industry that constantly needs the next big hit to survive increasingly looks to independents to function in the role of scouts, finding and developing artists regionally before the major labels move in and buy their contracts, and in some cases, the entire independent record company.

But in Nashville, a sharp distinction between major and independent record labels has developed. Artists on country independent labels rarely make the move over to larger labels. While there have been a number, including Ronnie Dunn, Linda Davis, Danny Shirley of Confederate Railroad, Collin Raye, Steve Earle, Mark Chesnutt, and Hal Ketchum, they're relatively few compared to the nearly 200 artists on major label rosters in Nashville. It is a fact that major country labels in Nashville have traditionally taken a far more activist approach in finding and developing new acts, whereas New York- and Los Angeles-based offices have been content to partially keep acquisition of developing acts as a function of funding hundreds of independent producers and scores of custom labels—which act as ad hoc A&R operations for them—in most other genres of music.

"Moving from an independent to a major label used to be far more common even ten years ago than it is today," observes Robert Oermann, a former staff feature writer for the Nashville *Tennessean* and an author of several books on country music. "That's because of the reliance country now has on new acts." One would then expect that such a reliance would foster the same need for independent and custom-label-based A&R activity. However, says Oermann, country

music has yet to have as broad and deep a base of independent labels to support such a phenomenon. Labels such as
Flying Fish, Rounder, Sugar Hill, and Nashville's Step One
Records, have diluted rosters when it comes to country—with
jazz, folk, and eclectic artists mixed in with the country acts.
"And the majors have a stranglehold on [what gets played
on] radio," Oermann adds. "It truly is a business of haves
and have-nots."

More independent record labels have surfaced in
Nashville, many within the last two years, such as River
North Records, Oh Boy Records, D'Ville Records, Winter
Harvest Records, E-2 Records, Imprint Records, Magnatone
Records, and Rising Tide Records. They are diverse in the
philosophies that determine their rosters and are funded in
an equally diverse variety of ways. Funding comes from
private venture capital and major-label capital to a public
stock offering (Imprint Records raised $7 million in a 1995
IPO), and, in the case of Dead Reckoning Records, capital
from the label's own artists—Kieran Kane, Mike Henderson,
Tammy Rogers, Kevin Welch, and Harry Stinson. And while it
is not based in Nashville, Pete Anderson now has his own
independent record label, Little Dog Records, whose roster
includes former major label Nashville artists Jaime Hartford
and Joy Lynn White.

Pete Anderson knew little about the inner workings of
Nashville, but he had seen enough from his perch in Los
Angeles to know that dealing with Nashville would be different. "I knew that Vince Gill had sung a number-one hit
[as lead singer] for Pure Prairie League and spent five years
trying to get a solo deal from a Nashville label," he says. "That
made me scratch my head. You sing a number-one pop record
and Nashville basically told him to take a number, we'll get to
you." Rather than get frustrated, Anderson rationalized
Nashville's approach based on his own past in Michigan. "It
was like building cars in Detroit in the nineteen fifties. It's not
a conspiracy. This is how it works and when you go outside the
system, it doesn't work."

Nonetheless, Yoakam and Anderson had gone outside the

system, becoming one of the relatively few success stories to do so. Since then, Anderson has continued to limit his interaction with Nashville. In the wake of Yoakam's success, Anderson was courted by Nashville labels, which viewed him as someone who could take marginally country acts and duplicate Yoakam's success with them. In addition to doing a solo record of his own, he produced songwriter Rosie Flores, whose critically well-received but underpromoted *Rockabilly Filly* on Hightone Records in 1995 sold poorly. He produced songwriter Jim Lauderdale's record for CBS/Sony. Aside from an initial single, it was never released. "That's when I said, enough," he says. "I never got the sense that I wasn't welcome there, but I probably wasn't. There's a machine in every kind of music and there's one in Nashville, too. They make records for radio instead of letting someone make a record and then being there as the promotional entity. Personally, I don't care. I live in L.A. And even though it seems like everyone from here is going to Nashville to find a better lifestyle, I'm not joining them. I don't worry about the gangs. Compared to Detroit, L.A. is a picnic."

The producer remains the linchpin to the Nashville country music community. And the considerable range of power that country music producers wield will only grow wider as younger ones who have grown up comfortable with computers and the music technology that accompanies them come of age. The addition of more engineers to the producers' pool in Nashville will complement the musicians who have historically made up their ranks. Both are children of the digital audio revolution, which proffers the ability to create records more and more autonomously.

Country's homogeneity as an art form has been, in large part, due to its continued residence in a single place—Nashville. By the same token, that coherence also rests significantly upon the fact that producers—activist producers who are as involved in artist development as they are in the daily operations of their companies—run the major record labels in Nashville. The Beatles and their producer, George

Martin, set the tone for twenty-five years of productions in pop music: the artist as the overall creative force, channeled by the producer. In country, the producer—with the decision-making power over songs, recording environment, musicians, and with considerable after-project input regarding marketing and other business support services—has retained far more authority over the record-making process. And the Nashville producers have learned their roles through an apprenticeship that is rarely seen in other music genres.

Will technology and changes in the larger entertainment industry tear holes in the apprenticeship scenario that has existed for so long in Nashville and in country music? It's too soon to tell, but some indications point that way. There are many nonproducers as producers running the increasing number of independent labels in Nashville, and while these labels have yet to have a significant effect on country music's larger picture, they could do so in coming years.

It is the producers of country, with their combined capacities to develop talent and to give their finds the highly organized, well-funded platform that is the Nashville music industry, who will most determine what country sounds like in the future. And if they are writing and producing in closed environments in home studios, they will have an even higher concentration of those powers and less connection to one another and the other elements that make up the Nashville music industry. If new forms of country music arise in these more isolated creative contexts, will they at some point mutate to where they can no longer be considered country? What would country be like without the constant interaction of producers with other producers, songwriters, and musicians? Would simply having the producers remain in Nashville, linked to their offices and each other via modems, be enough to maintain country as a distinguishable form of music?

In an age when recording artists routinely phone in their contributions to records over remote digital telephone patches, allowing them to sing or play from home even as the recording session goes on in a studio thousands of miles away,

Nashville remains a real place, a physical location in an increasingly virtual world. And the physical interaction that accompanies that—the ability to meet someone at a football game or on a street corner and hand over a tape—has been what Nashville has been all about for decades. The perception of Nashville among many producers, musicians, and recording artists in recent years has been that of a place that is an oasis where records are recorded by live human beings rather than by machines. The potential for technology to remove the producer from that environment constitutes a potential disruption in the way country has developed for the past half-century.

On the other hand, Nashville and country music have preserved the model of the record producer—a musical (as opposed to solely corporate) individual who serves as a link between the creative and the business sides of the music business. And Nashville has maintained that model not in any museumlike sense, but in a very robust one. Viewed from that perspective, it's equally possible that changes in technology and in the larger entertainment industry could dovetail with the apprenticeship-based curricula of country music in Nashville. It could be that individuals as adept at business as they are at the technical process of creativity would not be regarded as quaint by a changing entertainment industry, but rather as a rare resource. It's possible that Nashville's widely known ability to churn out productions in a factorylike fashion—a process supervised by Nashville's producers—could be just what a 500-channel, content-hungry entertainment complex needs.

The Songwriters

O N A DAMP, WARM NIGHT in mid-October 1993, Giant Records hosted a number-one party for one of its artists and for itself. Clay Walker's "What's It To You" had hit the top of the *Billboard* country chart on October 16. A few days after the issue hit the streets, a couple hundred people were milling in the cavernous space of video production company Scene Three's soundstage, a former movie theater on Twelfth Avenue South that was rented by Giant for the gala. Roast beef and salmon were served, and black-and-white balloons dropped from the ceiling. This was not only Walker's first number-one record; it was his label's first chart-topper, as well. The then-president of Giant's Nashville office, James Stroud, who also produced Walker's debut record, asked an aide to crank up the music—Walker's record was being pumped through huge theater speakers into the room, providing a score for the video clip of Walker on the massive monitor that dominated one wall. It produced the desired effect—all eyes turned toward the small raised platform in front of the monitor.

Stroud introduced Walker, a diminutive, energetic Beaumont, Texas, kid who wore a large black cowboy hat that dwarfed his small, lanky frame. Any nervousness that Walker, who would go on to have three more number-one singles within a year's time, might have felt at that moment was overcome by his eagerness to enjoy this limelight. His Nashville debut performance, at 1993's Fan Fair festival, had been electrifying, and the innocent, raw edges of Walker's talent were still sharp on this evening. His staccato tone at the microphone was in sharp contrast to Stroud's smooth, easy delivery.

Walker produced a slip of paper and began thanking those people he said were also responsible for the record's success. When he got to the songwriters, he mentioned an exchange with Kim Williams, with whom he had at least one cowriting session for the record. At the end of the writing session, Williams wished Walker success by saying he hoped his record charted well. "I said, 'Why's that?'" Walker said from the stage. "He said, 'Because if it doesn't, I'm not writing with you again.'"

The crowd laughed, with a smattering of applause.

Walker continued, "I thought he was joking and I looked at him and he didn't laugh. He said, 'I'm in this for the money. We're gonna write with singers that have hits.'"

The assembled crowd laughed at this line, too, but it drew knowing looks among some in the audience. What had been a cliché-like industry punch line had been amended by a coda that contained far too much raw truth to be funny. It was a reminder of the way Nashville's once familial community of songwriters had become a mirror image of the corporate environment that had overtaken Music Row in the last decade. And Walker's statement about the commercial side of what is an intimate emotional exercise, was all the more poignant for its ingenuous delivery.

Williams, whose credentials include five cuts on Garth Brooks records—two of them number-one hits—later recalls the exchange as mostly a joke. "But sometimes what we say in jest has a smattering of truth in it," he says. "I came to [songwriting] for the fun and the art of it, and I spent the first five years in Nashville starving. So I'm not ashamed of the commercial side of it."

Since Nashville is the single geographical center of the country music business, the competition among songwriters in Nashville is fierce. The Nashville Songwriters Association International (NSAI) lists 4,000 members nationally, more than half of them in Nashville and about a quarter of that portion are listed as professional members, meaning they make the bulk of their income from songwriting. Those numbers are dwarfed, though, by the Nashville-area membership affiliations of the three performing rights organizations; BMI, ASCAP, and SESAC (Society of European Stage Authors and Composers). They cumulatively represent an estimated 20,000 songwriters in Nashville and its suburbs alone. A BMI executive estimates that there are approximately 115 publishing companies in Nashville that have a total of over 1,000 staff writers signed to them. Other sources, such as the local industry trade publication *Music Row*, assert that number to be 10 to 20 percent higher.

Songwriters are making varied amounts of money: new writers in the first term of the usual three-year contract will draw an advance against future royalties of anywhere between $900 and $1,500 per month, for which they hand over all of their song publishing rights to the publisher. Periodic downsizing of these staffs leads to an annual game of real-life musical chairs in which a writer's performance is reviewed at contract option time and the numbers usually determine a writer's future.

On the other hand, some publishers now complain that the deals being made with the upper stratum of songwriters in Nashville are becoming financially unrealistic, with some deals approaching copublishing arrangements worth as much as a half-million dollars annually to the writer. In addition, publishers feel more pressure to acquiesce to demands such as nonrecoupable signing bonuses for writers with a proven track record of hits; while a signing bonus might often be between $5,000 and $10,000, they have on occasion hit astronomical heights of as much as $50,000. And more writers are demanding what is known as reversion clauses—contractual mechanisms that return the copyrights of unrecorded songs to the writer after a specified period of time. A reversion clause, which has been a routine part of many pop music publishing contracts for years, is anathema to Nashville publishers who know that it sometimes takes years to get a song cut, and due to the homogeneous nature of country music, a well-written country song can remain viable for years. A country song is not rendered obsolescent by quickly changing fads as regularly as it happens in pop music.

But Nashville's songwriters also have the specter of the end of the boom cycle shadowing them. As country music's sales began to drop off in late 1996, the genre's publisher's were already paring staffs in anticipation of lowered revenues in 1998. (There is a nine-month lapse between radio play and payment of airplay royalties, and closer to a year for payment of mechanical royalties from sales.) And even though country songs tend to have longer "shelf life," the devaluation of older copyrights has accelerated in recent years as country radio had tightened its playlists, excluding older songs from its programming.

The changing nature of the writer-publisher relationship in country music, the greater disparity of the financial aspects of those relationships, and the growing number of writers in Nashville have rendered the songwriting landscape in Nashville quite different from what it was like two or three decades ago.

"Before I Got To Nashville, I Was Always The Different One"

In the 1950s and 1960s there were as few songwriters as there were producers, publishers, or musicians. The scale of the industry was still relatively tiny compared to pop music. The repeat winners such as Harlan Howard, Curley Putman, Bill Anderson, Hank Cochran, and a few others dominated the parentheses underneath the song titles on records.

When Hollis Rudolph DeLaughter, of Bogalusa, Louisiana, came to Nashville in 1964, he was already twenty-five years old and was led into and through town by Justin Tubb, the son of Ernest and a writer and performer in his own right. By then, Hollis had become Red Lane, an easier stage name by which to pursue a country record deal—both then and now.

His first career as a recording artist was relatively brief, and a second time around after signing to RCA in 1970, proved just as fleeting; however, his career as a successful songwriter has been considerably longer. Justin Tubb had sent a tape of Lane's songs to Buddy Killen, who was then running Tree Publishing and who would later come to own it before selling it to Sony. In that office in 1964, just after Lane signed with Tree, Faron Young walked in and Killen suggested that Lane play him a couple of songs. One, "My Friend On The Right," became a hit for Young and the first successful single for Lane. By 1968 he was making a good living from his songwriter's royalties. It sounds like a simple scenario, and it was. And that was how simple it was back then.

Lane has found that simplicity appealing. Thirty years later, he is still with Tree, and he still has a deal remarkably similar to the one he signed with Killen three decades earlier: 100 percent of the publisher's share of his songs is with Tree; Lane keeps his writer's share of the royalties. He only recently considered a copublishing deal that would give him half—an arrangement that most writers of his stature would have demanded years earlier. Considering how many hits he's had during the time, from "Country Girl" with Dottie West, "Walk Out On My Mind" for Waylon Jennings, "They Don't Make Love Like They Used To" for Tammy Wynette to cuts on Doug Stone's 1994 release, Lane's reluctance to take a larger piece of his own pie seems peculiar. But he shrugs it off by saying, "It was just less hassle for me to mess with."

Lane arrived in Nashville before the big money did, when a hit song sold 50,000 copies at a two-cent royalty to the writer. It was a time when most composers wrote alone; cowriting as an innovation was ten years away and as a convention it was fifteen years down the road. The closest Nashville songwriters came to cowriting was playing their songs to one another at the Boar's Nest, a house on Music

Row that no one seemed to know who owned but which was readily available to writers and musicians as a hangout in the days before publishing companies had writers' rooms.

"Mel Tillis and I would sit around there at night—everything closed up at nine o'clock and there was nowhere else to go—and he'd play a song he had just wrote and I'd say maybe you should try this word there instead and he'd do the same for me and my songs," Lane remembers. "Things like that. We never thought of asking for a writing credit. The thing was, I was just happy to be around a bunch of people who were like me. Before I got to Nashville, I was always the different one." Lane ends with apt advice for the country song-writer: "The rule of thumb I've found all this time is that, keep writing the way you write. Whatever the music is doing, it won't be long before it swings back to that."

"I Didn't Really Get It Like I Got Country That Night"

It is five-thirty, already dark, and Bob McDill is ready to close up his office and go home. Gray hair, silver-rimmed glasses, and a tweed jacket, he looks like a college English professor tired from an afternoon of grading Lit. 101 essays. But the lacquered sheepskins that panel his office at PolyGram Music Publishing detail a different kind of literary accomplishment. McDill has written twenty-eight number-one country songs over a twenty-three-year career in Nashville, with the awards from BMI and the Nashville Songwriters Association to go with them. They include "You Never Miss A Good Thing" (Crystal Gayle), "Nobody Likes Sad Songs" (Ronnie Milsap), "Don't Close Your Eyes" (Keith Whitley), and "On The Road" (Lee Roy Parnell). But his earlier covers include songs written while he still lived in Beaumont, Texas: "Happy Man" recorded by Perry Como, and Sam The Sham and The Pharaohs's "Black Sheep." Ray Charles, Jerry Garcia, and Chubby Checker are among the pop artists who've covered McDill's tunes. And they've pretty much all been written on the nine-to-five schedule that McDill has kept most of his professional career.

In Texas, McDill was involved in the blues and folk music scene that thrived in Beaumont near the Louisiana border in the mid-1960. It was centered around a club at a local hotel bar and at Gulf Coast Recording Studios next door, owned by future Nashville producer, composer, publisher, and studio owner Jack Clement and Atlanta music publishing magnate Bill Hall. It was there he met the group with whom he would move to Nashville.

McDill had signed a deal with Allen Reynolds (now Garth Brooks's producer) and Dicky Lee's small publishing company. Clement bought the company and, with it, McDill's contract, bringing him to Nashville in 1970. "They didn't know what to do with me," he says. "I literally starved for a couple of years. I thought I was going to write rock and roll songs, but there was no one to record them then in Nashville. I was always around country music so much in Texas, I figured I could do that, too. But I tell you, I didn't really get what country was really about until one night I was riding around in [song-writer] Vince Mathews's Cadillac. It had a great stereo system in it and he put on a George Jones tape and the song 'It's Been A Good Year For The Roses' came on."

McDill quietly sings a line, then resumes the story. "Listening to that song, it hit me then and there like a ton of bricks what country was all about. How you do it, what it says. It's painful, it's singular, it's about loss and hurt. It's not so much about music or beat or groove. It never clicked for me like that with pop. Maybe I didn't really get it like I got country that night."

The rules were changing in the early and mid-'70s for songwriters. Copublishing and cowriting were becoming issues. McDill had cowritten with Dicky Lee even before he got to Nashville, and while he has done it regularly through-out his career, most of his biggest hits, like many writers of earlier country music generations, have been penned solely by him. "I was outside a lot of what was going on here at the time, and I still feel like I'm on the edges of it sometimes. We were way down the other end of Sixteenth Avenue, away from the power stuff. We had a crazy little community down there with Clement and [songwriter] Wayland Holyfield and [producer] Allen Reynolds. We were all folkies and none of us had really completely understood the way Nashville worked yet."

McDill remembered how he learned some of the finer points about what could and couldn't be said easily in a country song. "Wayland [Holyfield] and I wrote 'Red Necks, White Socks And Blue Ribbon Beer' together. It prompted a mini-scandal around town because you weren't supposed to use the word 'redneck.' It was considered a derogatory term, like 'cracker.' I didn't know that. And in the song 'Amanda' that Don Williams had a number one with, the term 'hillbilly' [was used in the lyrics, changed by artist Don Williams from the original "rock and roll band"[1]]. Some guys over at RCA [studios] backed me up against a wall in the rest room like they were going to whip me and said we've been trying to get rid of that word for decades and here you go putting it in a song."

Country music has policed itself lyrically throughout its history. There are numerous instances in which lyrics—and sometime the titles—of songs have been changed to accommodate the timidity of radio programmers and, more recently, their consultants. For instance, the title of Lorrie Morgan's 1996 release was *The Best Damn Thing*, but the single released to radio was edited to "The Best Thing." MCA had Steve Earle change the line in his signature song "Guitar Town" from "I've got a two-pack habit and a Jap guitar" to "a two-pack habit and a cheap guitar." The last verse of Garth Brooks's "Friends In Low Places" was excluded from the record (but not from live performances) thanks to the phrase "kiss my ass." And Alan Jackson's "I'll Try" saw the line "we both know damn well" changed to "we both know too well."

McDill learned to tread cautiously from the experience. Aside from the simple melody and harmony, he told an interviewer that, as far as subject matter went, "Breaking up's still fine, but there shouldn't be any children mentioned."[2]

---

1. *Music Row* interview, May 8, 1993
2. *Adam Smith's Money World*, PBS, broadcast June 21, 1991

Some of McDill's protocol gaffes were funnier, like the time he met singer Tompall Glaser, one of the seminal writers and performers of country music's outlaw period in the mid-1970s, as the singer was riding a big hit. "I asked him what he did for a living. There was this long silence. Then he kind of chuckled and said, 'Well, some people think I'm a goddamn star.' What I learned was, you had to learn the rules to get your songs recorded. Not just the politics but what you could and couldn't say in a song. You could talk about black people but only in an avuncular way. Women could not drink in a country song; the man drank—the woman waited at home while the man drank. There were stereotypes you had to adhere to. You couldn't take them out of character too much."

While McDill was already making a decent income from songwriting in the late 1970s by skirting the songwriting conventions of Nashville, he was just as willing to learn the rules to make even more money. "You know that you can follow the rules and stay within the boundaries and write something that will be recorded and make you a lot of money. And if you reach beyond the boundaries and try to write something that New York or L.A. might like, then you got to know that your chances are one in a million, so why bother? What I do is try to stay at the front edge of wherever the boundaries are. I guess I had an idealized idea of what country music was supposed to be. Hell, 'Amanda' wasn't a country song. None of the stuff I did with Don Williams was. It was folk music, where you could say a little more. So you try to find a way to stay within the rules and still get out what you want to say. That's the balancing act of country. That's why I loved Don Williams so much. I never had to pull anything back with him, and I was blessed with that guy for twenty years."

The dreams of country songs crossing over on to the pop charts that McDill and other writers had in the 1970s and 1980s as they watched mainstream pop and country music periodically intertwine, such as during the *Urban Cowboy* craze, faded as his success in and his familiarity with country music grew. And as country grew in sales and stature in the 1990s, the whole notion of crossing over became irrelevant to

McDill. "Who cares now about crossovers?" he asks rhetorically. "We're selling more than pop anyway." The diversity of country's styles and lyrical content has been a good thing for the business, he says. "It's more fun than it used to be. In fact, I'd probably be retired now if I still had to write nothing but three-chord ballads. Now, you can do damn near anything as long as its good and it doesn't insult anybody and it's mainstream-sounding. I like the rock and roll influence."

McDill has slightly increased the amount of cowriting he does to accommodate the wider range of styles, and the mercurial desires of the industry from week to week. "When everybody in town says 'up-tempo,' yeah, I'll go and write up-tempo. Or if everybody wants something that sounds like so-and-so, I can put myself there. That's the craft part that really takes over after a while. But I can still get excited about it."

It's six-thirty now, and the street lamps along Sixteenth Avenue are buzzing with a high-pitched warble. It's time to turn the office lights off and say good-bye to whoever's left roaming the corridors of the building. Bob McDill has stayed after hours, and he wants to get home. But at the same time, he's not disturbed that he's broken his own rules. He does that every now and then, just to stay in character.

LIKE FATHER, LIKE SON

Country music has always been a family business in Nashville. In addition to the dynastic Bradleys, any number of artists, producers, musicians, and publishers have handed their businesses and accumulated wisdom down to their own progeny entering the country music business. But as the influx of people from other music fields continues to change the landscape of the Nashville music industry, it's among the writing community that an abiding continuity still resides in creative escrow.

Max D. Barnes was born in 1936 in Hardscratch, Iowa; his son, Max T. Barnes, was born in 1962. Through the 1970s and '80s, Max D. Barnes racked up an impressive catalog of hits, including the Conway Twitty/Loretta Lynn 1977 duet "I Can't Love You Enough" and The Kendalls's "Thank God For The Radio" in 1984. As these hits amassed, Max T. Barnes was listening, watching his father work, and in 1983 they wrote together, creating "Way Down Deep," a Vern Gosdin hit that may have been the first Top-Ten father/son collaboration. However, it took a while before they managed to work together in the family business.

"He was going to be a guitar player, and I told him there's nine million guitar players in Nashville," says Max D. with a note of paternal concern in his voice. "But he became one anyway and a very good one, at that. Played with a lot of people and toured all over the world." To which Max T. notes, "Dad didn't write with me until I was about eighteen or so. Until he figured I was really serious about songwriting. I had written songs since I was a kid, and writing with him was something I always thought about. We used to play our guitars together, and one day we were playing and it just sort of happened. We started writing a song. That was the first time."

The time and generations spanned between the two— and the notion that a good song is timeless—was nicely illustrated at the 1992 CMA Awards where father was up against son for Song of the Year honors. Max D. took the award for "Look At Us" a hit for and coauthored by Vince Gill, beating out Max T.'s "Love Me," recorded by Colin Raye.

But they do not feel competitive with each other; there is enough of that to go around in Nashville. Instead, Max D. makes the most emotionally generous observation that a father could ever make of a son. After Max T. tells about how as a child he would listen to his father write songs and how he learned from that, Max D. interjects, "I probably learned as much about life in general from him as he learned from me."

"Nashville Is Pretty Obsessed With Image"

Gretchen Peters is standing in the hallway of Sony/Tree's headquarters on Music Row. She is talking with composer

Gary Nicholson, formerly a Tree writer and who has written and cowritten a long string of hits including "One More Last Chance" (Vince Gill) and "Giving Water To A Drowning Man" (Lee Roy Parnell). They are discussing songs, but in a context different from that of earlier generations: today they are conferring on what types of computer software best help them keep track of their song pitches and cuts, and which songs fall under which of their previous publishing deals.

Peters has had much to keep track of in the years since she arrived in Nashville from her home in Boulder, Colorado. In the first year of her first publishing deal, she scored a cover with "Traveler's Prayer" with George Jones. The second year saw the title cuts to Highway 101's "I'll Paint The Town," George Strait's "Chill Of An Early Fall," and Randy Travis's "High Lonesome." Then came high-charting songs for Pam Tillis with "Let That Pony Run" and Martina McBride's "My Baby Loves Me" and her controversial—and Grammy-nominated—"Independence Day" in 1994. In 1996, Peters was again nominated for a Grammy Award for "You Don't Even Know Who I Am," recorded and taken to number one by Patty Loveless. That same year, Peters attained what she said had been her goal from the beginning: she signed with independent label Imprint Records, which released her album *The Secret Of Life*.

Peters is not the only writer who hides her observations about Nashville in her songs, but she's one of the few who will openly discuss them. She came to Nashville in a quaintly traditional manner—by truck, with her husband Green Daniel (with whom she wrote "Chill Of An Early Fall" and who would later produce her first album as an artist) and a three-year-old daughter in 1988. The road was paved several years before by previous visits to Nashville and an introduction by Tony Brown to her first publisher, Noel Fox at Silverline Music, where she got a $14,000-a-year "subsistence level" publishing deal.

After the first few hits had come and her Silverline deal had run its three-year course (during which she followed her contract through corporate acquisitions first by Lorimar

Music and then Warner-Chappell Music), she was courted by Sony/Tree and its then-vice president of creative services (and now head of Sony Records), Paul Worley. "They told me they wanted a strong female writer," she recalls, her legs tucked under her on a writers' room couch at Sony/Tree's office. "I thought that was odd. Why not just a strong writer, period? I mean, maybe Tree was still trying to shake the image of a good old boy publisher, even though they haven't deserved it for some time. Nashville is pretty obsessed with image."

This is why Peters stands out at a time when substance in country music has slipped in its competition with style. "Souvenirs," cut by Suzy Bogguss, is more than an observation on tacky cultural icons; the lyrics impart a sense of loss and resentment about her present environment that are more trenchant and deeply felt than their images imply: "I been searching for the promised land / But it's just another neon, come-on one-night stand / Little tin toys that fall apart, that's all they got here / I come all this way to find my heart / All I get is souvenirs."

"It comes from anger at this tendency to trivialize everything here [in Nashville]. Because Garth [Brooks] got so big we all had to go out and find another Garth. We're always making copies of something instead of looking for the real thing," she says.

The same sentiments also rustle beneath the surface of "My Baby Loves Me," cut by Martina McBride. "[That song] is a sort of anti-what's-on-the-surface thing. It's a veiled observation about life and this microcosm we live in in Nashville. But it also has to do with . . . how women feel about being judged and how they're judged. 'Independence Day' came partially out of my own childhood; my parents divorced when I was eight and I've always been fascinated with the child's point of view on issues like that. That's part of it, but it's also some purer anger; I had quit smoking at the time and I was easily pissed off. I kept trying to change the ending, and I guess Nashville did get to me on that issue. I couldn't have her blow up the house with the husband in in it."

Reminded about Worley's desire to have a strong female point of view, Peters stops for a moment. "I didn't understand what he meant at the time. But, you know, it's like Green keeps telling me: It's not rocket science, but it ought to be."

PERFORMING RIGHTS ORGANIZATIONS

BMI and ASCAP face off from their respective new buildings on either side of Sixteenth Avenue South at the top of Music Row. The primary mission of BMI, ASCAP, and the smaller but quickly growing SESAC is to oversee the collection and distribution of performance royalties of their members' compositions. However, there is another, less-official function that they serve among Nashville's crowded community of songwriters: over the years they've taken on the role of referring new writers to local music publishers. Referring writers to one publisher or another has been stepped up in pace since the 1990s, and since virtually every publisher has both a BMI- and an ASCAP-affiliated company, an element of insider trading in songs and writers is common. Writers are usually referred to one of the performing rights organizations (PROs) by friends or other writers.

The methods by which each of the PROs evaluates the music markets differs, and as a result the payments to members of different organizations can vary. BMI tracks between 9,000 and 10,000 radio stations nationally, each of which is logged for a full week once a year, several hundred stations a week, by an accounting firm retained by BMI. The logs form the basis for an extrapolation of what songs earn on an annual basis. ASCAP uses a combination of tapes sent in by its reporting stations and station logs to accomplish the same thing. SESAC, with a relatively small percentage of the total number of composers and a heavy emphasis on gospel and Latin writers, pays solely on the basis of chart activity.

Jody Williams, formerly BMI's senior director of writer-publisher relations and now president of MCA

Music Publishing, Nashville, used to spend a good part of his day as a traffic cop between writers and publishers, seeking to make connections between them and the hundred-plus or so new writers who passed through BMI's doors each week. "I listened like a publisher," says Williams, who had worked for Screen Gems Music, Chappell Music, and Tree Music before coming to BMI. Of his time at BMI, Williams says, "I didn't care where the writer was recommended from. I didn't start opening doors to publishing companies until I hear what [the writer] had to offer. It has to be that way, because the number of writers just calling to try to get appointments here has quadrupled in the last few years. A pretty good song doesn't cut it around here anymore. The competition is fierce, so every song has to be a great song. And that's a lot of pressure for people to be under."

But there are other things to consider, as well. Williams was looking over the local paper, the Nashville *Tennessean*, a few years ago when it was announced that Liberty Records (now Capitol) would open a sister label, Patriot Records. Patriot and other expansion labels such as the reactivated Decca were part of a mid-1990s trend in the country music industry of diversification to accommodate larger and larger artist rosters at the main labels. "I don't know where they're all going to go when it comes to radio," he muses, echoing the concern that has covered Nashville's music industry like a blanket in recent years. "There's a ton of people coming here now, and a lot of them don't belong here. In this market we're fitting a box that has defined edges. There are rules here and you can't go outside them, even though the rules have stretched some. It's a lyric town. You can't be too esoteric or artsy." Although, he adds, that these days, "A good sound can mask less-than-great lyrics."

John Briggs handles writer-publisher relations at ASCAP. He and other counselors at ASCAP and BMI share both a friendly rivalry and a sense of being overwhelmed at the increase in calls looking for a connection in Nashville over the last four or five years. Briggs, who worked at EMI

Music and several other publishers before coming to ASCAP in 1985, says he's seen his calls more than double to over fifty per day since 1990. ASCAP has close to 55,000 members nationally, compared to about 100,000 writers and 50,000 publishers affiliated with BMI. Both organizations represent approximately two million copyrights each; the prolifagacy of BMI's country, blues, gospel, and R&B writers helped swell its copyright collections since its formation in 1940, twenty-six years after ASCAP. (SESAC has about 3 percent of the U.S. registered copyrights, with 5,000 affiliated writers and 160,000 works on file.) The membership of both BMI and ASCAP is broken down not by genre but by state, and Briggs agrees that "a good chunk of them" are living in and around Nashville. Many of the new calls these days come from transplanted Los Angeleans. "They're changing things here," he commented. "They're changing country. They grew up listening to the Eagles, just like I did."

Briggs and a small staff will screen calls. Writers unaffiliated with ASCAP are directed to the Nashville Songwriter's Association; he'll listen to the tapes of writers already affiliated with ASCAP, although wading through them all takes some time.

Briggs remembers that a former associate at ASCAP had left in 1988 to pursue management of a young artist. Bob Doyle sent a tape into Briggs of Garth Brooks singing "Too Young To Feel This Old," looking to place Brooks on a showcase that the Nashville Entertainment Association was doing at the Bluebird Cafe. "I thought he was a great writer but I told Bob there was one catch—there was an entry fee and they had to be a member of the NEA. Cost like around thirty-five dollars each. Bob said, 'I can't do that. I don't have the money.' I remember we talked on the phone three times before he said, 'Okay, I'll pay it.' Turns out that was the showcase where Lynn Shults from Capitol heard Garth and signed him." Stories like that are often what keeps the people in writer publisher relations listening to tapes long after the rest of the office has gone home.

THE HOLD

A hold takes place when an artist, producer, or A&R person finds what they think might be the right song for a record. Out of the hundreds of songs listened to for each country record, the final ten or twelve are chosen in several rounds, and in each round as many as a score of songs from various writers and publishers are placed on a reserve status known as a hold.

When the number of country releases increased dramatically in the early 1990s—with over twenty labels, the genre was seeing over 250 releases annually during the period—the number of holds skyrocketed. Compounding the situation was the labels' heightened concerns over profitability as rosters and releases grew in number—the necessity for more hit records became that much greater, and in the process of looking for the songs that would create those hits, the number and the length of holds increased. This limited the ability of publishers and writers to expose songs to other artists. In addition, the number of publishers in Nashville had proliferated; many of the newer ones were not familiar with the sort of handshake agreements that often regulate the hold practice. This gave rise in the early 1990s to the concept of the "second hold," in which an artist's representative (producer, manager, or A&R person) would request that his or her artist be given a hold on a song contingent upon the expiration of an existing hold. This put an additional lien on a song's ability to circulate.

Periodically, attempts were made by publishers and groups of publishers to establish some kind of guidelines as to how long a hold could last. These attempts at self-regulation were useful in that they raised the issue in a sort of collegial forum. However, the net result has been that, if a publisher feels that a cut is imminent, extensions on it are routinely granted.

While each hold represents a potential cut, it becomes quickly apparent that its primary value over time is a barometer—in its ability to encourage both the writer and the publisher. That encouragement, however, comes with the price of frustration when songs go on holds often but don't result in cuts. "I'm just glad they spelled my name right," says John Swaim, holding a copy of Alan Jackson's 1996 *Everything I Love* album, on which is a song Swaim wrote called "Walk On The Rocks." This is the first cut for Swaim, who came to Nashville seven years earlier to work as a strolling banjo player at the Opryland theme park. During the next few years he kept his job at Opryland and picked up live gigs along the way that formed the "day job" that writers need to survive. Even with an estimated 1,000 writers in Nashville employed by publishers be a staff deal is still a relatively rare commodity given the number of people vying for such positions. "I don't have a lot of money, but I live pretty frugally, so it's fine," says Swaim.

Swaim made the rounds of publishers over those seven years, cutting single-song consignment-type contracts with several of them—deals in which the publishers take the song for a specified period of time and work it around town. "Walk On The Rocks" made the rounds of publishers until Buzz Aldredge of Marledge Music, a small independent publisher, took it on consignment. Over the course of a couple of years it was on hold four times; first with Alan Jackson for his *Greatest Hits* record, then with Rhett Akins, Diamond Rio, and John Anderson. "Having all those holds not pan out was frustrating sometimes," he recalls. "But mostly it was encouraging. It told me that it was a good song. All I had to have was patience and continued trust in God that if it was meant to happen, it would."

Buzz Aldredge, Swaim's publisher on the song, shared the frustration. "That song had been all over and everyone loved it but I had nothing—a big zero—in terms of a cut," he says. "So I looked at the phone one day and said what have I got to lose? Let me give Keith [Stegall, Jackson's producer and Mercury label head] another call. I didn't even know he was cutting again with Alan. And he was pleasantly surprised that that song had not been cut yet and said, 'Send me two copies right over!'" The song went on hold again, but this time it also went on the record.

It took Swaim seven years to get his first cut, and there was no guarantee that it would become a single off the record, which would vastly increase the song's earning potential for airplay and sales. Getting the single is such a high priority that publishers and writers look for every omen they can find. For instance, "Walk On The Rocks" is the number-eight track on the Jackson CD; Aldredge, who used to produce records at PolyGram years ago, says singles are usually placed at the number one, five, six, and ten positions, a relic of the vinyl record days when singles were placed at either ends of both sides of a record. This was not a good omen. But, says Swaim, "I have to pull optimism out of everything I can. You need all you can get of that in this business. Just the song being on the record is a miracle for an unknown writer; it'll be another miracle if it becomes a single. But I tell you, right now, life's good for John Swaim."

COWRITING

Cowriting songs is nothing new to music, country, or otherwise. Professional collaboration has been a tradition in popular music since the nineteenth century. However, it's been elevated to the point of obsession in Nashville: over the last twenty years it's been viewed as a means for young writers to enhance their chances of getting a song recorded; a way for veteran writers to stay current; as an evil that dilutes copyright value by publishers; a productivity expander to meet the needs of a voracious genre; a way for recording artists to participate in the publishing revenue stream from their own recordings; and most recently, at a time when more recording artists write their own songs, as a way for publishers to sign prospective recording artists whose songwriting abilities may not yet be developed—or present at all—but who offer the potential for generating their own cuts if and when they make their own records. And in doing so, the publishers are encroaching upon the talent scouting and artists development turf that has historically been the purview of the record labels and producers.

Half the human activity of Music Row during the week can be attributed to writers crossing from one publisher's writers' rooms to the next on a schedule that rivals that of the city's studio musicians, and one just as rigid—writers can and do schedule and accomplish as many as three three-hour writing sessions a day, aside from the spontaneous ones that have been known to erupt in bars, laundromats, and at halftime at football games. A clinical laundry list of rationales for cowriting shouldn't obscure the fact that a lot of people cowrite because that's simply how they like to write songs. But purely artistic collaborations regularly compete with the more calculated ones, prearranged marriages between writers by publishers, managers, producers, and each other, looking for whatever the Nashville record machine wants that week. And its demands do change virtually on a weekly basis, partly because of coincidence—three balladeers might be looking to start records around the same time—but also because trends develop as certain songs or new artists become hits—from Kitty Wells's "It Wasn't God Who Made Honky-Tonk Angels" famous 1952 response to Hank Thompson's "The Wild Side Of Life," to the scramble for teenage-oriented performers in the wake of Mindy McCready's "Guys Do It All The Time" in 1996.

Chuck Neese, a publisher with The New Company, characterized the cowriting obsession of Nashville at the 1994 Music Row Summit, an industry symposium, as "an apprentice system." But, he added, "I think we've dropped the ball. We're chasing our tails, teaching them the same things over and over." Another panelist, Byron Hill of BNA Entertainment, countered that, "it's still a good system for learning."

Cowriting is the major network among Nashville composers. For many, the building of a network is as critical to success as the songs themselves. Like any organization, the country songwriting community is built like a pyramid, with a few dozen successful writers at the top and literally thousands below, with more arriving every week. Some come because they have a spiritual or emotional connection with country music; others come because Nashville has gained so much attention in recent years both from inside and from out-side the music industry in the United States. And some, like bank robber Willie Sutton, simply figure, "That's where the money is." All eventually learn—among other things—that cowriting is the *modus vivendi* for most songwriters here.

On a practical level, cowriting helps keep up output in this, the last outpost of some formal separation between song-writer and artist—the relationship that was the convention in most of popular music throughout its modern history. The Tin Pan Alley and Brill Building archetypes of the '30s, '40s, and '50s in New York City—densely packed spaces of composers and publishers—created structures for writers and publishers to feed the song needs of artists. The dominance of artist/composers in the 1960s rock & roll revolution diluted that relationship and the highly structured framework that traditional music publishers provided for their songwriters eventually withered everywhere but in Nashville. In pop, only a relative handful of journeymen composers are left who still operate on the principles of that era—composers such as Diane Warren and Desmond Child, all of whom had artist careers at some point in their careers but whose primary success has come as composers for other artists. (Although they, too, have learned that cowriting with pop artists has an economic incentive that can rival the artistic one; Desmond Child, for instance, has been a regular collaborator with Jon Bon Jovi. He has also made regular forays to Nashville to cowrite with composers there.)

Nashville is home to the kinds of writers, as well, who prefer to write by themselves. But the vast majority of songs on country records in the last twenty years have had more than one byline. However, cowriting is about more than the amount of output. It is simultaneously a search for entry into the music business and success in it. Writers with a hit, or even an album cut, are often deluged by calls from people they've never met suggesting that they write together. The introductions are made by publishers, managers, record label people, by friends, family, and on cocktail napkins passed across the bar. Cowriting thus serves a social function and as a networking and support device. The perspective on cowriting, though, varies according to where one is on the pyramid in Nashville. Those in entry-level positions scramble to make contact with those further up the line. For those in higher positions, the access gained by success becomes guarded to various degrees.

"It Makes Me Feel Like A Tailor"

"You talk about people trying to climb the songwriting pyramid here: Unless you have some sort of incredibly charismatic personality or have gotten someone to sort of mentor you as a writer in Nashville, the only way an untried writer generally gets to write with someone who's at the top of the pyramid is if they have a record deal," says songwriter, Bob DiPiero.

Bob DiPiero is talking on the phone from Studio 19, a recording studio on Music Row where he is overseeing the mixes on his latest batch of publishing demos. DiPiero came to Nashville in 1978 from his hometown of Youngstown, Ohio. He felt his early days in Nashville were somewhat charmed; within a year of coming to town he had secured a publishing deal at Combine Music. Within a few more months, he had his first hit with "I Can See Forever In Your Eyes," a Reba McEntire single that broke the Top-Twenty *Billboard* country chart in 1981. Two years later he had a number-one record with the Oak Ridge Boys's cover of his "American Made." More recently, DiPiero had number-one records with "Wink," recorded by Neal McCoy, Reba McEntire again with "Till You Love Me" (number one in January 1995), and "Take Me As I Am," also the title track of Faith Hill's debut recording.

DiPiero learned cowriting under the strictly enforced precepts of Bob Beckham, a very conservative, old-line Nashville publisher who consistently frowned on cowriting in general and grudgingly allowed it by his writers on the condition that they wrote only with other Combine writers. "It was the old school of cowriting," DiPiero remembers.

"The only hot writers you could be angling to get with were whoever was hot at Combine, like Bob Morrison. So there was not much in the way of Machiavellian maneuvering going on."

But as cowriting became the convention in Nashville, DiPiero, like others, did a lot more of it. And in the last several years he and his cohorts at the top of the pyramid have found themselves more and more in demand as guaranteed hit-makers for aspiring recording artists intent on both establishing themselves as writers and participating in the increasingly lucrative publishing royalties of country records.

The pursuit is a double-edged sword. In an industry in which ego is often the dominant motivating force, it can be the ultimate sort of flattery for the veteran, successful songwriter. But it also raises personal and professional issues that can drive a wedge between the art and the craft. "It can get to the point where you feel almost whorish," observes DiPiero. "Sometimes the artists they bring to you are good writers, maybe not with all the tools down and developed but with good ideas and a focus of what [they] want to write about. When that's the case, I'm there for the artist. But then there's the artists who aren't really writers and have not ever really written a good song. I've been in the room with a guy where he sits on his cellular phone and takes calls from his manager and now and then looks over to me and says, Yeah, I like that line or no, I don't like that one. It makes you feel like a tailor. If the guy is really a writer and wants to work at it, I'll be there for him whether it takes two hours or two days. But if he just wants his name on a song, then it's not fair, to me or my publisher."

What DiPiero describes would turn out to be a familiar refrain among many successful composers in Nashville. But what he finds even more annoying is a variation on the arranged marriage between tunesmith and new recording artist, in which a new recording artist wants to write with him ostensibly for his own record but in reality wants a song to pitch around to other recording artists by trading on DiPiero's or another established writer's name to get the song listened to and in doing so helping to position the new artist as a viable writer himself. "They want to get the whole double-dip," he says.

DiPiero says he's turning down more and more cowriting opportunities that are brought in by managers and A&R personnel. He now asks for tapes up front for evaluation before he'll commit to a writing session. And he relies more on the intimacy that the Nashville music community offers its tenured residents for straight answers from those who petition him. "Look," he says, "after being here for years you get to know most of the people in the business. Many become your friends and friends are supposed to be straight shooters. That's one of the rules. What I want to know in these situations is: is the guy really a writer? That's always the first question. Because I don't feel that at this point in my career that my job description is to be giving songwriting lessons to people. I do seminars on that for the NSAI [Nashville Songwriters Association International] and other groups. But it's not my job description to teach them and then give them fifty percent of the song."

Some of the twists that have come with the culture of cowriting have changed both the nature of the songwriting experience for DiPiero and the way he looks at the Nashville music industry in general. He says he's watched it change from a closely knit, kindred community into a more opportunistic society. One illustration comes to mind rather quickly: "I can remember about ten years ago where an artist had approached me and a cowriter and friend, John Scott Sherrill. I can't say the name of the song or the artist—both are still pretty well-known. The artist tells us he really likes the song but that he thinks it needs a bridge before he can get behind it and cut it. And then he says, I want to help you write it. Me and John Scott were still pretty young and new to it at the time and we agreed. [The artist] shows up and hums a pretty generic melody idea and then has nothing else. So John and I wrote the bridge and the artist got a third of the song. It's a favorite song of mine and I still believe it was just fine without a bridge. Now when I go out and perform that song,

I can never sing it without thinking of what that artist said to us that day: 'Why don't *we* write a bridge?'"

Gary Nicholson came to Nashville from Dallas in 1980 and was a staff writer at Sony/Tree for over a dozen years. In 1994 he had the number-one position with a cowrite with Vince Gill called "One More Last Chance." That and other cuts such as "Shadow Of Doubt" for Bonnie Raitt, Don Williams's cover of his "That's The Thing About Love" (also a number-one hit), and the Neville Brothers's "Fearless," have put Nicholson far along into the club. He's found that in recent years he is approached more by managers and A&R people suggesting he write with one or another new writer or artist.

"You wind up with a variety of experiences," he says. "I probably have wound up spreading myself too thin over the years doing it and I'd like to kind of wean myself off the cowriting merry-go-round. On the one hand, if someone is making a record and needs a particular type of song, there's an advantage to me in that that song will probably get recorded. And also there's the fact that someone in that position will bring a tremendous focus to the writing session that allows me to be something of a musical chameleon. And you get a very focused piece of work out of it.

"But on the other hand, it's very satisfying to be able to write something really good by yourself, as well as meaning more money for you as the only writer."

But as an established, hit-generating composer, Nicholson, like others of his status, is often approached by representatives of newly signed recording artists eager to participate in the publishing revenues generated by a record and to earn the additional notch of status that accompanies being an artist that writes—but not necessarily with the kind of songwriting abilities needed to get hits. Writers with track records such as Nicholson's are then sought out as writing partners.

"It's not often that the people contacting you will admit that a new artist isn't a great writer up front," says Nicholson. "Sometimes there will be the A&R man or manager that asks me to write with the new 'hunk in a hat.' And you don't always have a good feeling about it. But I never felt like anyone was using me or asking me to do something I don't want to do. If I don't want to do it, I don't. Obviously, it goes on. In my personal experience I haven't seen what I would call a lot of it. It's just part of the business. You write with a new artist and you're pretty certain of getting a song recorded. I make a living writing songs and it might sound like I'm prostituting myself and maybe I'm as guilty of it as the next guy. But I have a family to support. I've done it in the past and I'll probably do it again in the future. There's nothing wrong with it as long as the song is good."

However, Nicholson acknowledges that writing with artists whose songwriting skills are undeveloped or nonexistent can lead to some personal angst. "There are times when you wind up with songs [from a cowriting session] that I've actually written totally by myself at the end of the day. On the other hand, though, you have to tell yourself that you would never have written that song that way unless the other person was there. The worst case is when you get with someone who is not a writer, who has no ideas. Then you finally pull out one of your own ideas that you had been saving and write on that. But it doesn't usually come out as good as if you had written it yourself or with another pro. Then the song goes up to whoever is judging whether it goes on the record and it doesn't get recorded. Now your idea has been written and you can't go and take it back. It's happened to me."

Not all such experiences are problems; in fact, he says, most are positive. Nicholson cites cowriting sessions with Capitol Records recording artist George Dukas as among the most positive experiences. But that collaboration was one that came through less direct conduits than a contact by a label or a manager; writer and artist Radney Foster made the recommendation of Dukas to Nicholson.

Finally, there is always the possibility that one of those sessions with a new artist can turn out to be more successful than considered possible. "[Manager] Bob Doyle came to me at one point some years ago and said he had a new artist he wanted me to write with," Nicholson recalls. "He talked about putting me together with him but I never pursued it. Turns out that was Garth Brooks. Whenever a new artist or writer comes along that someone wants me to write with, I think about that. You never know where the next one's coming from."

Cowriting can often be simply a production mechanism, and many in Nashville will tell you the songs often sound like it. At times, though, two writers will produce a song that is more than the sum of their parts. These are magical occasions, and not always immediately apparent to their composers. Garth Fundis—a Nashville producer and the owner of recording studio Sound Emporium; producer of several major Nashville acts, most notably Trisha Yearwood; and a former vice president of A&R at RCA Records and now director of Nashville operations for Almo Sounds Records—recalls hearing "Walk Away Joe" for the first time. "That was more than a cowrite," says Fundis. "It was a moment in time. I'd been at a showcase for Patrick Joseph Music writers at the Bluebird Cafe in 1990. Greg Barnhill and Vince Melamed, the writers, performed it. Greg sat onstage and sang and Vince played piano. It just floored me. I went right over to [Patrick Joseph owner] Pat Higdon and said I want that song. He told me it was already on hold for the Judds."

Which it was, and would later be put on hold by Wynonna Judd for her first solo record. The song surfaced on Trisha Yearwood's second record, three years after it was written in 1990 by Melamed and Barnhill working off a Southern idiomatic term that Barnhill had often heard as a child in his native Louisiana. It was written in three hours. "We thought it was a cool song but the only thing that we really thought was significant about it was that it probably wouldn't be radio-friendly," recalls Vince Melamed. "We were pitching it to people like Bonnie Raitt because we never thought we'd get it cut in Nashville. I mean, [country] radio has its rules and things were really restrictive then. And here we had a song about a seventeen-year-old girl running off with a guy who robs gas stations. It was a pleasant surprise when it made radio."

"Walk Away Joe" did well, on both radio and on the charts,

after publisher Higdon reapproached Fundis with a demo of it for Yearwood's second record, *Hearts In Armor*. It reached number two on the *Billboard* country charts in 1994 and garnered a Grammy nomination for Best Country Song.

Many Nashville writers will say that cowriting is both productive and practical. When pressed, they will also acknowledge that it is also politically correct in the Nashville way of doing things, and that it's simply one more method of networking in an industry that is predicated on personal interactivity.

The esthetic implications are harder to assess. Using the reference of commercial success, cowriting hasn't seemed to hurt country sales; indeed, the process is almost transparent to consumers who seldom look at the names in parentheses below song titles and who even more rarely make purchasing decisions based on them.

But then there are the less tangible assessments—more difficult to make, but to many just as important. When you look at country as a music and not as an industry—a perspective that is less and less automatic for many in the business—the dominance of the song becomes immediately clear. Cowriting songs often comes about because the participants find a connection between themselves that has nothing to do with the business side of things. No appointments are made, no percentages are sorted out. It simply just happens. What's happened to that bucolic vision of collaboration in the 1980s and 1990s is the result of pressure to produce more and more hit songs in an ever-more competitive environment. The song itself has become a reason to put parts of a business equation into a room to produce a product instead of letting their individual muses bring them together. It has become, in many ways, like an artful dating service. Regulating and managing the creation of art is nothing new, but in Nashville the craft of doing so has become tantamount to the craft and art of songwriting itself.

The process has also arguably had its effect on country music's primary conduit to the world—country radio. With publishers' pitch sheets consistently referring to songs that were on the charts only weeks before as guides for what's wanted next, it's understandable that a committee process becomes an efficient manner in which to reproduce rather than to create songs. In this regard, cowriting is as much a marketing tactic as it is a way of writing songs.

Cowriting was resisted in the beginning by two generations of Nashville publishers not on esthetic grounds but on economic ones—it sliced their piece of the publishing revenue pie thinner. But perhaps those publishers intuitively knew that the practice could affect quality as well as their bottom line. "What cowriting does is it often pasteurizes the process," says Garth Fundis. "It's creativity by appointment, and I don't know how you can be brilliant by appointment with any consistency." As a producer, Fundis is a bit of a throwback in Nashville in that his most well-known production client, Trisha Yearwood, makes a point of making records that are filled with songs she had no hand in writing. Lyrical interpreters such as Yearwood, originally the paradigm in Nashville, have become increasingly scarce there in recent years. "I've seen people walk up on stage at award shows and you know they're feeling embarrassed about collecting an award for a song they didn't really write because the pro they wrote with did the real work," he says. "It works because radio likes it, and guys in radio don't like to take chances; they operate not on creativity but on the bottom line of selling advertising, and they need guaranteed hits to do that. But [cowriting] has more often than not diluted the process of songwriting and increased the flow of mediocrity out of Nashville. And it's just a matter of time before the listener will come around to the same viewpoint and it turns around and bites Nashville on the ass." He pauses for a moment and continues, "And I think it already has."

"It's A Flavor-Of-The-Week Kind Of Town Now"

Fred Koller meets you in the Chinese restaurant in the Bellevue neighborhood on Nashville's west side and says,

"The soup's all right; everything else, you're on your own." The Chicago native's gruff voice is sometimes hard to understand against background noise. It's as quirky as Koller's writing; songs such as "Let's Talk Dirty In Hawaiian" have earned him a cult following for both his compositions and his live performances, that sometimes show at the dozen or so songwriting seminars he does each year. His strictly country credentials include "Going Gone" and "Life As We Knew It," both recorded by Kathy Mattea; his pop credits include Jeff Healy's recording of "Angel Eyes," which Koller cowrote with John Hiatt.

Koller's voice is why he generally gets others to sing his songs for demos. Some of his vocal stand-ins for publishing demos of his songs were for Kix Brooks and the late Keith Whitley. And having a future well-known country recording artist sing your demos, he acknowledges, is not a bad way to get songs around, either. "The trick is, you gotta pick 'em before someone like Tony Brown or Scott Hendricks finds 'em," he adds. "And if it were that easy to do then I might be doing something other than writing songs."

Koller came to Nashville in 1972 after spending some time in the folk milieu that blossomed in and around Saratoga Springs, New York, in the late 1960s. Coffeehouses such as Lena's Cafe had the kind of cultural magnetism then that Nashville's Bluebird Cafe has now but had no music business infrastructure around them—which Koller and others believe was part of their charm. Koller arrived in Nashville with the first wave of singer-songwriters in the early 1970s, and he regularly crossed paths and wrote with equally quirky writer/performers such as John Hiatt and Shel Silverstein. The idea of performing songs was very much intertwined with writing them for this generation of country composers. He learned the craft of the three-minute country song by voraciously reading short stories and by passing through the series of music publishers that most long-time Nashville writers will accumulate. Koller started with the British-owned ATV, then went on to Loretta Lynn's Coal Miner's Music, Terrace Music, and Don Gant's Old Friends Music before landing at a deal with PolyGram's publishing company, with periods in between—including the present—when he acts as his own publisher.

"I came here not knowing anything except what I thought country was," recalls Koller. "So I got cuts with people like The Sons Of The Pioneers and Rosemary Clooney. At that time the publishing companies were being run—not owned, but run—by [musicians] who had turned into writers and then turned into publishers. The music business was run out of itty-bitty houses on Music Row, which was still more than half residential at the time. People could still live on the Row. [A zoning petition up for review in late 1996 would allow residential houses on the lower parts of Sixteenth and Seventeenth avenues—Music Row—to be used for commercial purposes, thus extending the reach of the Row.] My first apartment there cost me forty dollars a month. And you spent every day in those little houses, learning the lingo, learning to write. Learning things like, don't write down to people, don't overproduce your demos. The little rules that make up the music business here and that take years to learn.

"Now a lot of that's all changed. The songs are getting predictable, they're a real setup. It's a flavor-of-the-week kind of town now. There are no honky-tonks anymore; video's changed all that. You have acts like Faith Hill that look and act country but are actually rock acts. And people like Garth—the great chameleon—who records Kiss songs. The songs aren't theme-driven anymore; the marketing is. Like the Eagles *Common Thread* thing. I keep waiting for the Monkees tribute record to come out of here."

Koller's humor is acerbic and ironic; a Beatles tribute by country artists was in the works as he spoke and came out in 1995. And, as he spoke, it was only three weeks after Tommy Boyce, who with partner Bobby Hart wrote many of the Monkees records, committed suicide in Nashville. But the pithy remark also underscores a transitional mentality in Nashville's songwriting community: a sarcastic surveying of a contemporary scene that, in Koller's view, has relegated the lyrical narratives he treasures to a backseat behind a marketing-based pop music approach to record-making. His is a sense of humor made a bit edgier by the fact that he is in "a cool period" of his songwriting success. But then there are the verities of Nashville, the ones that persist and endure and provide the magnetic force that keep people in this orbit: the craft-driven work ethic that tells you to keep writing, no matter what, and that tells you intuitively when you are on the right track. But, it is one that reminds you that, even if you're not crazy about what's coming out of the studios and on the charts, if you can write one, you do it anyway. Ultimately, no matter how long you've been here or how much you've written, you're waiting for lightning to strike. "It's all I've ever done," he says. "And I've been struck by lightning four or five times now. It could happen again."

AS GOOD AS YOUR NEXT HIT

There is a long-standing punch line in the songwriting business that goes, "You're only as good as your last hit." To Dave Gibson and many other Nashville songwriters who have watched as the comfortable nature of the songwriting business of country music has changed, the refrain has become, "You're only as good as your *next* hit."

Arkansas native Gibson was one-half, with Blue Miller, of the Gibson-Miller Band, which recorded for Epic Records from 1991 to 1994. The band was a longtime dream for Gibson, who moved to Nashville in 1982. He came close to having his own record deal that year when producer Tony Brown, then an A&R man at RCA Records, recorded some sides with him in the studio as a prelude to a possible artist deal. But RCA passed on Gibson as a recording artist. However, in the process, Gibson found his lyrical voice as a songwriter, and through the 1980s penned a string of hits, such as "Midnight Fire" for Steve Wariner (his first hit in 1983 and an outgrowth of his association with Brown), a number-one record, "If It Don't Come Easy," for Tanya Tucker in 1985, and "Ships That Don't Come In" for Joe Diffie.

But Gibson never lost the desire for the band experience,

and when Epic signed Gibson-Miller in 1991, Gibson was ready to tour to support the record. What he wasn't ready for was, in a town that prides itself on nurturing the memories of some of its most obscure talents, how fast a writer can be forgotten in Nashville in a year. "I came back and I was out of the loop completely," he recalls. "I was signed to Sony/Tree Publishing before the second record was done, and when I came back off the road the town had completely changed: new people at the publishing company, new writers in town, new artists, new labels. I realized that if you're not in that office every day, reminding people you exist, then your songs don't get pitched. That's the way Music Row is: music people playing musical chairs."

Gibson had to buckle down and not only remind Music Row he still existed, but he had to change his writing emphasis from composing for his own project back to writing with specific recording artists in mind. "I mean, I know it's the nature of the business," he says. "But more so than anywhere else, a songwriter in Nashville has to be his own song plugger, even if he's with a publishing company. Especially if he's at a big company. That's where you really become a number instead of a name."

Gibson is writing with a copublishing arrangement with Maverick Music, the publishing company owned by pop music performer, writer, and producer Madonna, which opened an office in Nashville in 1994. Gibson says he likes the attention he gets from a smaller company, but his experience in the wake of Gibson-Miller will remain with him. "Nashville is a great place for writers and the people who are really your friends will always accept you back," he says. "But Nashville can make you kind of desperate. Even when you have hits, you're always worried about where the next hit is gonna come from. Nashville changed when all the new money and people came in a few years back. It's more money-oriented now. But you can't get bitter about it. A writer's life is a roller coaster, and when it gets to the bottom you have to work as hard as you can and believe it's going up again."

What Do You Mean, He Can Write?

One of the long-standing requirements for a publishing contract was the ability to write. That statement is not as facetious as it may at first seem. New artists are routinely signed to publishing agreements with their record labels, or with other publishers—particularly if that publisher saw more recording artist potential in the person than writing potential. A recording artist who writes provides the label and the publisher with up to a dozen slots per record, and publishing revenues often exceed mechanical (sales) ones. So even the hint of writing ability becomes grounds for a publishing deal, as long as the writer has a good shot at becoming a recording artist. Nashville's large pool of established writers then becomes a resource with which to pair new artists and, at best, hope to hone and develop their writing abilities—at least, to write the songs and give the artist cowriting credit.

"If you asked me eight years ago what it means to be a songwriter, I'd have told you it was a means to an end," says Jeff Wood, a twenty-eight-year-old composer and an artist on Imprint Records, a publicly traded independent label that has only charted one artist—Gretchen Peters—but is run by Roy Wunsch, the savvy, longtime head of CBS/Sony Records. "That end was to be a recording artist. But as I slowly learned the craft [of songwriting], I found that it became a passion. I am a recording artist, but I find that songwriting is what stays on my mind."

Wood came to Nashville twice from his native Oklahoma, in 1989 and 1993; the second time took. He was signed to Capitol Records (then known as Liberty) by then-president Jimmy Bowen, and to Bowen's joint publishing venture with EMI Music, Tower Street Music. Wood was signed primarily as a recording artist; his songwriting skills were self-admittedly still formative. Bowen and EMI Music were betting on him mainly as an artist who would then cowrite much of his own material, giving them additional revenue from his publishing. The plan was to match Wood with a number of cowriters to build material for a strong record.

Something went wrong. Unlike a number of artists in that position, Wood confounded everyone by turning out to have the instincts necessary to make a good country songwriter on his own. The former law school student refused to turn into a grinning hunk with a hat. He and Bill Douglas wrote "Cowboy Love," his first song under the Tower Street deal, which went to number three on the *Billboard* country chart in 1996 for John Michael Montgomery. "The label had told me, don't pitch your songs to other artists, keep them for your record," recalls Wood, whose album *Between The Earth And The Stars* was released on Imprint in 1996. "But the secretary at EMI didn't know that and she sent the demo tape to John Michael's guy when he heard it playing up at the office. It just happened."

Wood's record contains the fruits of cowriting sessions with hit composers such as Gary Burr, Verlon Thompson, and John Scott Sherrill; it has non-Wood compositions, as well, reflecting Wood's demands on himself that his own record contain the strongest material regardless of who the composer is. And he is starkly aware that his talent as a performer led to his writing success, not the other way around. "Let's be realistic," he says. "A lot of the opportunities I've had as a writer—the cowrites in Nashville, the John Michael cover, the trip to France to write at Miles Copeland's castle with other great writers [Copeland, IRS Records founder and manager of Sting, hosts an annual songwriter's retreat at his French estate, to which many of Nashville's writers are invited]—came from the fact that I had a record deal. It's a game you have to play. But I want to play it fairly. I don't want to be one of those first-record artists who the publisher puts together with great writers and who comes into the room 'with an idea and a cold beer,' as they say here, then sits around while the other writer does his stuff. The pressure is always there to produce a song. But as an artist, the pressure is less on me to write a lot of songs than it is on a writer who doesn't have a record deal. That writer has to go out and get cuts. It's not fair, but that's the way it is."

"That's How You Paint Pictures"

David Olney came to Nashville in 1973 from Rhode Island via North Carolina and Atlanta. He is a songwriter. That, to his way of thinking, is distinct from being a country songwriter, and which to others is distinct again from being a Nashville songwriter. It's a mind-set that does not conform to what's expected in Nashville, and there are prices to be paid for not conforming.

"Nashville is a good town for someone who will toe the line," says Olney, with a Southern accent acquired during his travels. "I don't mean that negatively. But the way I look at it, painting could either mean painting houses or pictures. Painting houses is a matter of quantity, and that shows up here in the cowriting. You get some good songs out of writing with as many people as possible, but it's mostly just a steady stream of songs. Writing by yourself is a slower process. But that's how you paint pictures."

Olney wrote mostly by himself, songs that didn't often conform to the Nashville rules of content or structure. They're folky, rambling stories whose points are sometimes murky and often unresolved. In twenty years he achieved most of his cuts himself, on three records of his own released on Boston-based independent label Rounder Records. Despite several publishing deals, it was one of his own recordings off his 1988 *Deeper Well* album on Rounder that found its way to Emmylou Harris for her 1993 *Cowgirl's Prayer* record. "Jerusalem Tomorrow" is about a religious huckster dealing with a rival, and during the course of the rambling talking verse the listener finds out that his competitor is some guy named Jesus. Olney believes that his publisher at the time would not have had the imagination to have connected a song like that with Harris—or any other country artist.

"I don't think you choose to follow the rules or not," Olney says. "I think you are who you are and that makes the choice for you. No one's been a crook or bad when it comes to my publishing experiences. But you give someone your songs and if they don't fit the mold, the [the songs] are trapped. They won't get pitched."

That is the ultimate conundrum for a Nashville song-writer, and the chute through which those who do conform best are routed. It is an approach that generally favors and rewards craft over inspiration. It is left over from a time when writers wrote and singers sang and a distinct separation of roles was the order of the day. Cowriting increases one's output but not necessarily one's changes of success at a time when more artists are writing for themselves or seeking one-shot alliances with the cream of the writers' crop. Independent labels and niche markets have provided such as Olney an outlet. Not a lucrative one, but something. "Being in a place with rules like these has been good in a way, and it's also been frustrating. If I measure myself by how many cuts I've had and how much money I've made, I might as well slit my wrists now. But looking back at my work over the last twenty years, I find I'm pleased with it. And that's been enough for me."

"This Will Take Time. Lots Of Time"

Songwriting success is measured in many ways. It is incre-mental. At one stage, it is getting the single onto an album. Before that, it's getting on the album at all. Before that, it's getting anywhere at all, which constitutes the bulk of the universe for most Nashville songwriters. Bruce Miller is somewhere in the anywhere-at-all stage. At the moment, it is the low stage of the Bluebird Cafe on Hillsboro Road, a sprawling lane of upscale strip malls. The Bluebird has trans-formed itself from the unofficial home of up-and-coming composers to the status of semiofficial shrine for composers and would-be composers from around the country. The writers-in-the-round performances that have become some-thing of an industry cliché started there by Fred Knobloch, Thom Schuyler, Paul Overstreet, and Don Schlitz in 1986, four years after owner Amy Kurland opened the club. The Bluebird is the spiritual descendant of a series of Nashville writers' hangouts, from the Boar's Nest in the 1950s to Bishop's Pub, a bar in the Vanderbilt University neighbor-hood, which in the early to mid-1970s gave writers a first-come, first-served venue of half-hour performance sets while providing them with free beer and hamburgers. After Bishop's came Mississippi Whiskers and the Red Dog Saloon in the 1980s. The Bluebird has fared better than the 1993 film, *A Thing Called Love*, which used a mockup of it as a location. Due to the small size of the real one, the Bluebird was recon-structed on a Hollywood set, although not terribly accurately. The eight-by-ten glossies of writers that paper the blue walls were replaced on screen by green walls covered with posters of Garth Brooks and Tanya Tucker. "They made it a little more country," Kurland observes, slightly sarcastically. The Peter Bogdanovich film went into limited release, scoring less than a half-million dollars on its opening weekend. *Billboard*'s review asked, "Are consumers, despite their hunger for country music, just not interested in the lives of aspiring writers and singers? Not necessarily. Instead, it seems the movie just wasn't very good."[3]

Kurland works just as hard to get good box office, and has succeeded far more consistently. The club's stature within the songwriting community has evolved to the point where an assembly line of composers manqué make their applications to perform on rather detailed preprinted forms. If they live more than 100 miles away, they can audition by tape; more proximal hopefuls must come in person, and the club's quar-terly annual auditions usually find close to a hundred prereg-istered songwriting hopefuls, each of whom had to call six weeks in advance just to get a slot to audition and to wait outside the club's doors. The Bluebird's management fields

---

3. September 18, 1993

as many as thirty tapes a week and fifteen phone inquiries a day. On a Sunday night, eight or so of these writers get to do three songs each, serving as a minion of support acts for a headlining writer.

On this night, Bruce Miller does his three songs, some cowritten with Los Angeles writers. His pilgrimage to the Bluebird was afforded him by spring break at the Los Angeles Wildwood Elementary School where he teaches fifth-graders. "The Rag And Bone Shop Of The Heart" has its autobiographical genesis out in front, but "Something Wild" and "There Goes The Bride" evidence both an internal spark and the acquired calculatedness that are fundamental elements of contemporary country writers.

Out in front of the characteristically quiet Bluebird crowd, the songs seem to have a lot of potential. They have not yet skidded on the rougher streets of Music Row. Their fate there will be for someone else to decide. The protectiveness that successful writers in Nashville cloak themselves in is a thin film compared to the emotional armor that new entrants require to deal with a town with more writers and fewer possibilities than ever before. Miller knows something of the music business. Before he turned to teaching, he toured with pop singer Laura Branigan as a guitarist, and wrote pop and R&B songs. His first encounter with a music publisher in the mid-1980s in Los Angeles left him devastated and he put the pen and paper away for six years. A combination of country's resurgence and some friends who moved to Nashville inspired him once more as a composer. He started making trips to Nashville in 1993, and found, as do most, that an occasional presence is not enough. "The publishers that I went to see here all told me that I should relocate, start building the relationships that this town works on," he says. With a baby on the way, that creates a conflict. "I'm in this for the long run," he stresses. "But you wind up being torn between the urgency to get a cut, some kind of cut—that if it doesn't happen now it'll never happen—and the understanding that this will take time. Lots of time."

Everyone has been nice to Bruce Miller. That's just the

way Nashville is. It makes things easier to deal with, like the fact that publishers tell him that they're not looking for material, that they're swamped with their own writers' output, that they're more interested in hooking their writers up with people who have record deals, or signing people who have record deals. Or signing people who *had* record deals, because a track record, no matter how thin or frayed by time, is as much of a commodity as a hold on a song. And holds—which translates to "maybe this song is what we want and maybe it's not"—are as plentiful in Nashville as mosquitoes in July.

"The gatekeepers are tightening up at the gates," Miller says. "It's harder to get through. That happens when there's a lot of money being made. It reminds me of Los Angeles in the nineteen-seventies. The game is to get around the gatekeepers." He pauses, and adds: "In a perfect world, talent would be all you need. But like any other business, there's politics to consider. If I had to always deal with the realities of it, I might not do it. But you could say that about life, too, I suppose. So you look around at the people who are doing well and you tell yourself you can do that, too. Maybe you're fooling yourself, but that's life."

The Publishers

I think bigness is the antithesis of creativity.
—JOHN MALONE, *founder of TCI and Liberty Media.*[1]

HE SONG IS THE ultimate commodity in Nashville. Unlike other scenarios of supply and demand, the cassettes containing them circulate through the city in the tens of thousands, each representing either one of thousands of newly minted compositions or one of a million-plus sitting in catalogs, some buried four and five layers deep beneath sales and acquisitions of publishing houses that have taken place over the last fifteen years. Each one could be worth a million dollars; the vast majority will be worth little if anything. Nonetheless, the publishers and song pluggers who carry them around from office to office know that behind every door there could be a big score if you have the right song at the right time.

The management of this slew of songs is handled in any number of ways, from computerized databases to scraps of paper to mental lists carried in the voluminous and intuitive memories that are characteristic of the best Nashville publishers. A start-up company, Nashville Online, began offering song-pitching services via computer in late 1994. It was charging $80 for songwriters and publishers to have a writer's

---

1. *Business Week*, November 1, 1993

bio and a thirty-second clip of a song available for down-
loading by other network users, or $250 for the full song and
a digitized photo of the writer. In the search for other areas of
song placement, Nashville has reintensified its efforts to
bring its catalogs to Hollywood, and the attempt to become
more of a player in the film industry has also lent itself to
computerization—BMG Music, the music publishing division
of RCA Records and its affiliated labels, not only has a film
and television department in Nashville, but has also implemented a database of its catalog, allowing prospective music
users to choose potential titles by entering various criteria.
For instance, an up-tempo country song about drinking or
cheating will pull up several possible titles, after which a toll-
free number can be dialed which, after several user prompts,
will allow the song to be auditioned over the phone. If the
song works, the same program can be used to page a creative
manager at the publishing company's Los Angeles office who
will then take care of the details of the licensing.

But for all the technology being brought to placing a song,
more often than not, the songs are still carried around on
cassettes that reside in briefcases, jacket pockets, backseats of
cars, and in guitar cases—making the rounds of Nashville on
journeys that can last years.

"Let's Talk"

It is three o'clock in the afternoon and Troy Tomlinson is
waving through his sealed third-floor office window at
Opryland Music Group, trying to get the attention of someone
who left a tape holding songs chosen in a just-finished song-
pitching session. Whoever it is doesn't hear him or see the
jiggling cassette tape and drives off. "I'll get it to him one of
these days," laughs Tomlinson, mocking the urgency that
often accompanies song searches for records.

Tomlinson had been with Opryland Music Group for eight
years as of June 1996, five years short of the date when
Opryland acquired Acuff-Rose Music. With over 50,000 titles

in its catalog, it doesn't make Opryland Music one of the largest of the 100-plus publishing companies in Nashville—the number will vary annually based on new start-ups and sales of existing companies—but the acquisition gave Opryland's parent company, Gaylord Entertainment, which also owns the Grand Ole Opry, a renewed presence on Music Row. Gaylord reinforced its presence in late 1996 with the purchase of Christian label Word Records for $110 million, which marked Gaylord's reentry into the record business.

Tomlinson drives forty-one miles each way, each day, on I-65 from his ranch-style home in Portland, Tennessee, to Opryland Music's imperious-looking headquarters on Music Square West. The entrance to the red brick building is set back from Seventeenth Avenue, and cars negotiate a short but steep grade to make it into the parking lot. In his midthirties, Tomlinson looks a bit like Ricky Skaggs, with swept blond hair and a wide smile. His polo shirt bears the Opryland logo, the equivalent of an Oxford shirt and rep tie at this conservative company. He learned the basics of publishing from the legendary producer and publisher Rick Hall—unofficially dubbed the "Father of Muscle Shoals Music"—whom he worked for in Muscle Shoals, Alabama, after Tomlinson finished high school.

The computer on the desk holds a program that Opryland Music developed to more efficiently track and collect foreign royalties from the Acuff-Rose catalog. The company's publishing operations have been slower-paced than others as the company focused on extracting more from existing titles. (Opryland also launched a record label, Sixteenth Avenue Records, in 1986, which folded four years later.) With eighteen writers (writing country songs; the company also has five Christian music staff writers), Opryland has an average-size roster of writers. The first writer signed, in 1986, was Skip Ewing. Ewing's artist career was relatively lackluster, but he remains one of Opryland Music's—and Nashville's—most successful songwriters, with cuts that include "Love Me" (Colin Raye), "Little Houses" (Doug Stone), "It Wasn't His Child" (Trisha Yearwood), and "Someone Else's Star" (Bryan White).

Another signing was Aaron Tippin, whose own successful recording career was propelled by Opryland Music. "We signed him as a writer, and on the first demo session I asked him who he wanted to sing them, and he said, 'I'd like to,'" Tomlinson recalls. "I'd heard him sing around the office and it wasn't pretty singing at all but there was an attitude there. Halfway through the session the engineer looks over at me and says there's something here. I took the tape over to [then A&R director] Mary Martin at RCA and she called back and said, 'Let's talk.'"

Tomlinson was awaiting the arrival of Mark Brown, vice president of A&R for Capitol Nashville [Records]. The two would sit down and go through a pitch session, a procedure that has changed little in the last forty years. Thirty years ago, Tomlinson would likely have been sitting in the office with the producer and possibly the artist and the writers. The schedule of success has changed that, and as Tomlinson filters the catalog from his end, Brown, a former song plugger at Warner Chappell Music, will take the sum of conversations and meetings with the artists' producers regarding the direction of the projects and use that to make his choices for those artists. "I'd love to have the artist or producers here," Tomlinson says. "With the A&R guy I'm getting one step further removed."

The songs still get directly to the artist on occasion, and the personal connections that have wired Nashville's publishing industry since its inception are still very much present and an active component of its day-to-day operations. Opryland Music has had a cut on every George Strait record, thanks to Jim Vienneau, Conway Twitty's former producer who now plugs songs for the publisher, and his friendship with Erv Woolsey, Strait's manager. Vienneau is something of a legend in Opryland Music's halls, although he claims not to remember much of what makes him so. "I had the tape copy guy come into my office here once and said there's something you got to hear," Tomlinson recalls. "He plays this old reel-to-reel tape and there's this voice that says, '"Teen Angel," take one.' It's Vienneau; he produced that record." Even as Music Row moves further into the computer age to manage its huge database of songs, personal relationships still account for many connections made between song and artist.

A phone call several days earlier had prepped Tomlinson as to what Brown was looking for: specifically, he wanted songs for upcoming Suzy Bogguss and Tanya Tucker records. He started by checking off a computer printout of the previous pitches from other pluggers at Opryland Music. Acronyms next to the song titles indicate whether the listener had passed (P) or took a tape copy (TC), one step short of a "hold." "If a year from now Suzy's coming up again I'll see that there was something they liked and I'll play it again," he explains. "There's songs on this list I've been pitching ever since I've been here." The most desirable acronym that can come up next to a song is "R," for "recorded."

Mark Brown walked in and got Tomlinson's attention immediately with the comment that "the scope of the Suzy project has changed." The scheduling for a duet record with Chet Atkins, *Sympatico*, has been moved up and that her own record has been pushed back from fall to a winter 1995 release. Atkins and Bogguss would cut four old songs, four new songs, and two that they will presumably write together. One of the older cuts has been decided upon, an Elton John song whose title Brown can't remember. "Another one's called 'Wives Don't Like Old Girlfriends' and the other one I can't remember but it's that kind of 'I'm-out-of-here-kiss-my-ass-I'm-gone' kind of thing. That should give you a clue."

Brown already had about twenty songs on hold for Tanya Tucker's next record, which would eventually become 1995's *Fire To Fire*. "Some of the things that [producer Jerry] Crutchfield are putting on hold are a little more sophisticated, like 'Two Sparrows In A Hurricane' instead of like 'If Your Heart Ain't Busy Tonight,'" he tells Tomlinson. "That kind of thing. But he's also been putting some typical Tanya stuff on hold around the Row. Crutch has said he's looking for a change in direction." For Bogguss, who had begun coproducing her records with Jimmy Bowen, Brown dealt with her as he would the producer. "She's looking for a little more intellectual type of song. Like 'Hey, Cinderella.' I'm assuming that Suzy and her husband Doug [Crider] are writing a lot of what will be on this record."

That statement perked up Tomlinson, who had been quietly listening and processing all this new information and mentally comparing it to his prepared list of pitches. Brown notices and adds, "But if I found something a little different, something with a little tempo, I think she'd be interested. Me and the label A&R staff went out with a sack of songs and listened and they were all introspective, heavy ballads about middle-aged women in search of their identity and thought to ourselves, holy cow, anybody got anything with some tempo in it?"

Tomlinson says Brown's comments didn't change his pitch plans. "But what he said about the Chet and Suzy project reminded me that there was a song I was playing for Scott Hendricks and Larry Stewart the other day and Scott said he heard that Chet and [Mark] Knopfler were gonna do another project together and would be looking for those kind of light-hearted songs that Chet can play. It's a song called 'Miss You Missing Me' by one of my writers Tommy Polk, and I'm gonna play that, too."

That was the first song Tomlinson played. Brown stayed with it for two verses and choruses, twice as long as most songs get in similar situations. He asked for a copy. The next several were rough versions of Skip Ewing cowrites. Referring to the lack of harmonies on the demo mixes, Tomlinson adds, "They all need voices," a way of saying to Brown, 'Try to imagine the harmonies.'" "Our Love" drew a wordless pass after the first chorus. "Long As I Got You" was set up by Tomlinson with the comment, "I don't know if this is right but it's a hit for somebody." After hearing it, Brown says, "Gimme a copy for Chet and Suzy. It might work for one of those radio things for Tanya, too."

"He wrote 'If I Didn't Have You' for Randy Travis. It's right in that bag. It's nonoffensive for radio," Tomlinson adds as the hopeful deal-closer.

The caveat on "Just Another Heart," written by Ewing and Tim Johnson, was that it was on hold for the week for Clay Walker. "It don't sound like Clay but [producer James] Stroud is just in love with the song and they're gonna try to track it this week. It's kind of an introspective thing, kind of a Wynonna," opines Tomlinson, using reverse sales psychology by putting the song out of reach. It was the only song in the session Brown listened to all the way through. "Can I have a hold on it for Tanya when it comes off Clay Walker?" he asks. "Just put me in line."

The comments throughout the session dealt with the songs simultaneously on two levels—as works of art and as products. "What Am I Gonna Do," by Richard Ross and Donny Keys, precipitates a discussion about whether it was a better pitch for a male or female singer before Brown lets it go with the comment, "I may need to hear that again. Someday." The striking "Just Another Heart" was followed by a pause from both Brown and Tomlinson, a sense of unspoken appreciation apparent between them.

After a few more songs went by, Brown observes that, "When I was at Warner Chappell pitching songs I used to have my favorites and wondered why the hell isn't anyone cutting these? And now that I'm on this end of it I know why—because there's twenty-five songs just like it out there. And you got to find the one that's just like all the others but just has something a little bit special about it."

"Yeah, you want the great song," Tomlinson chimed in. "Don Gant once said, 'That's a good song, but if I want to cut good songs, I'll cut 'em out of my own catalog.' You always want the great song."

Brown left the office an hour after he arrived. Pitch sessions have a tempo all their own, but while the level of true affinity and affection for music is high among people who have found their true vocations in music publishing, an hour seems to be an average amount of time two people can spend listening to songs when the business of music adds its own special intensity to the process.

Tomlinson saw Brown out with a handshake and a promise that a tape with the songs he chose for consideration would be delivered to his office at Capitol Records the next day. After he closed the door, he says, "This is tough enough, but I don't think it's harder than having to run around to every publisher in town and listen to twenty songs a day. 'Cause he's got to go on and pitch them all over again to the producer and the artist. It's fun, until you've heard your five hundredth song of the week. I don't know how we do it. Just love it, I guess."

The standard analog compact cassette that Brown will get on his desk will join the scores already there, along with the DATs—the small digital audio tape format that has become just as popular as much for its two-hour capacity as for its cleaner sound—as well as the odd open-reel tapes that are still circulating in Nashville, and, increasingly, the CD-R disc, a CD format that adds recording capability to the CD. The catch is, you can only record each CD-R once. But the benefit is that you get the random access to tracks; no waiting as the tape fast-forwards to the next song. It gets you to that five hundredth song that much faster.

This feature will make life a lot easier for the hundreds of staff and independent song pluggers of Nashville who start out each day looking over the pitch sheets compiled by the publishing house outlining which artists are gearing up to record, when, they are going to record on which label, with which producer(s), and what they're looking for. This is a portion of a typical pitch sheet, issued by a Nashville publisher in November, 1996:

Label	Artist	Producer/Contact	Date	Comments
Arista	Diamond Rio	Mike Clute	Dec.	Great songs
Atlantic	Confederate Railroad	Csaba Petocz	Mid. Jan.	Railroad unleashed
BNA	Kenny Chesney	Wilson/Cannon	Jan.	Country songs
BNA	Lonestar	Wilson/Cook	Dec. 16	Up-tempos only
Cap Nash	Billy Dean	Shapiro	Late Jan.	Energy, cool grooves, soulful, rangy
Cap Nash	Chris LeDoux	Gregg Brown	Dec.	Same as current record
Cap Nash	Garth Brooks	A. Reynolds	Fall	Looking for all tempos, all types of songs
Cap Nash	Trace Adkins	Hendricks	Jan. 27	Up-tempos with integrity and ballads à la Light In The "Every House"
Curb	JoDee Messina	Gallimore/McGraw	Dec./Jan.	Progressive country
Curb	Tim McGraw	Gallimore/Stroud	Nov./Dec.	Country with edge; mid- to up-tempos
Decca	Mark Chesnutt	M. Wright	TBA	Killer honest traditional country songs

The pitch sheets are casual, belying the urgency and intensity of the most critical part of a country record's production process—the choice of songs. The shorthand of pitch sheets also offers other kinds of insights into Nashville's music industry, providing a snapshot of the state of the music at the moment. For instance, the first two producer names on the sheet, Mike Clute and Csaba Petocz, are both engineers who have moved into production. Clute is also a studio owner and came to production prominence in Nashville as the producer of Blackhawk's first two records. He also produced Diamond Rio's previous record, which he recorded completely to a hard disk computer-based recording system, which is commonly used in pop record production, instead of the conventional tape-based system, making it the first major-label country release to have been recorded that way. Petocz, who was looking for songs for one of Nashville's more rock-influenced acts, Confederate Railroad, is an Australian engineer who ran the console on pop records there and in Los Angeles for such acts as Metallica, Stevie Nicks, and Concrete Blonde before coming to Nashville, where he engineered records for Lorrie Morgan, Blackhawk, and George Strait before making his first country record as a producer—John Michael Montgomery's *What I Do The Best*.

The comment "same as the current record" for Chris LeDoux represents the safe road that's often traveled in country productions, particularly if it comes on the heels of a successful previous record. The Trace Adkins comment referring to his most recent hit single is also an indication that producer Scott Hendricks wants to stay on a familiar path with the artist. The plaintive comment "Country songs" that accompanies Kenny Chesney's entry speaks reams about how broad the rubric of country music has become when a country artist on a country record label in Nashville has to specify that he is looking for "country" songs.

Several of the comments refer to tempos; a mix of various speeds of songs on a record—measured, like Dance and Urban records are, in beats-per-minute (BPM) and covering country ballads to danceable tracks—is particularly important in country records. "It's because there's such a mold here," says Peter Cronin, general manager of the Nashville office of Maverick Music Publishing, a division of pop star Madonna's Maverick Enterprises. "A country record has to have the right mix of tempos, attitudes, and themes. There's a lot of research that goes into that, looking for proven formulas which Nashville will always go to. In the pop music world there's not nearly such strict rules about things like that."

Finally, the reference to Garth Brooks would stand out dramatically to many publishers and writers—in Nashville or anywhere else—given his sixty-million-plus sales history. What's also interesting in this instance is that while most of the dates on the sheet—which refer to when production of the record will begin—are within two or three months of the date of the pitch sheet. Brooks's production schedule would not start for nearly another year, another reflection of how his career is closer to that of a pop performer's in nature, if not in content.

The tapes on publisher's desks are the work of anywhere from one to 100-plus staff writers that they have under contract at any given time, with as many as 1,000 staff writers working every day in Nashville. Their contracts generally run for one year and are renewable at the option of the publisher. Renewals are not rare, since any savvy publisher knows that developing a writer is a long-term investment, with a commitment to them averaging two to four years. The writer gets a draw against future royalty earnings, usually in the form of a weekly check that starts at about $250 but which can climb to six figures, disbursed quarterly. They also get a demo budget, which averages $300 per song and which is, like the advance, held against the writer's future earnings, called recoupment. Other perks include access to writers' rooms, which range from windowless cubbyholes in the basement of the publishing house to airy, sunlit spaces that were once bedrooms in the converted residences on Music Row. The writer also has a wider pool of cowriters with which to interact, which in a cowriting culture is critical.

In return, the writer is expected to turn in a specified number of songs, usually anywhere from twelve to twenty-four in a contract year. If a song is cowritten with another writer, it counts as a half of a song toward his or her contractual quota. If it's written with two other writers, as a third of a song, and so on; cowrites among as many as four writers are increasingly common. Some publishers, though, are more liberal in interpreting those fractions. The corresponding demo costs of cowritten songs are charged back to the publisher's signed writers and his or her cowriters or their publishers, if they have one. The bookkeeping of music publishing is a deep bog long before a song gets cut.

Once a song is cut, its revenues are applied back to the writer's account at the publishing house. Most of these revenues come from two basic sources: mechanical and performance royalties. Mechanical royalties result from sales of records; the present mechanical rate is $0.069 per unit sold, whether it be a single or an album cut. But from that seemingly small figure the numbers of publishing begin to take on a recognizable shape: with unit sales that hit the gold mark—500,000 or better—a copyright will earn $34,500; sales at the platinum level—1,000,000 units—earn nearly $70,000. Numerous country record releases in recent years have attained the multiplatinum mark, including Reba McEntire, John Michael Montgomery, Alan Jackson, Travis Tritt, Diamond Rio, and Brooks & Dunn. The multiplatinum country crowd used to be reserved for a few current artists and was made up mainly of catalog records through the mid-1980s. Now, according to *Billboard*, over 20 percent of records on its country charts sell to the two-million-or more level. Country's music's multiplatinum pack is led by Garth Brooks on the male side, with over sixty million records sold, and on the female side by Shania Twain, whose second record on Mercury Records—produced by husband and pop production legend Robert "Mutt" Lange, who also produced for multiplatinum pop act Def Leppard—had reached the eight-million mark by late 1996. With several hundred million country records sold annually, the $0.069 rate takes on more significance.

The Copyright Act of 1909, which first established publishing royalties, grew out of several Supreme Court actions that first denied, then affirmed, then reaffirmed the right of songwriters and publishers to be paid mechanical royalties. At the turn of the century, the main form of mechanical reproduction (as opposed to the passive reproduction format, sheet music) was music rolls for player pianos. Royalty payment based on their sales was an ongoing but, legally speaking, niche-level tug-of-war between publishers and manufacturers of the rolls. That is, until the advent of commercially released recordings heated the issue up in the late nineteenth century—if you could be paid royalties on piano rolls, by implication you could receive royalties on any other form of reproduction, and a lot of people began to see the potential for the Edison cylinder and the doors it would open for home entertainment. The opening waves of what would become the vast consumer music industry spawned by the invention of sound reproduction pushed the royalty issue in favor of music publishers.

In 1909 the statutory rate was set at two cents, and was applicable to any recording made under the compulsory mechanical license; that is, any song that has already been recorded in any manner may be recorded again by anyone else, as long as appropriate royalties are paid. This measure was aimed at breaking the monopoly held by some piano roll makers and ensuring that copyrights could be used by a variety of reproduction methods. The rate didn't change for the next sixty-seven years, until the Copyright Act of 1976 was implemented and created the Copyright Royalty Tribunal, which raised the rate to $0.0275 per unit sold and was empowered to raise rates periodically. Since then, the rate has risen to the current $0.069.

Other than by government fiat, the rate doesn't go up, but it can often effectively be reduced, via a mechanism known as the "controlled composition clause," that has become a fixture in virtually all new recording artists' contracts—country and otherwise. When implemented, it stipulates that songs written by the artist will be paid at a reduced royalty rate, generally three-quarters of the current statutory rate. The controlled composition clause has been a source of annoyance—outrage, in the words of one Nashville attorney who tries to negotiate the clause out of every contract she handles on her artist/clients' behalf—and significant lost potential earnings to writers and publishers since it became a widespread practice in the 1970s. To illustrate, a three-quarter rate applied to a platinum-selling song reduces its revenue potential from $69,000 to $51,750. The record labels' rationale for demanding the controlled composition clause is quintessentially a business one: a request for a volume discount. Since the labels feel they are already paying their artists a mechanical royalty, they feel it is reasonable to ask for a discount in other royalty areas. Beyond the resentment that this generates among artists and particularly the new ones who often lack the leverage to fight the imposition of the clause in first contracts, the impact of the clause ripples throughout Nashville because it includes all songs cowritten by recording artists subject to the clause, in effect applying it to writers for whom songwriting—not making records—is their main source of revenue. Many attorneys and managers regularly seek to eliminate the clause, or moderate it, with some negotiations producing controlled composition rates that move from 75 percent to 87.5 percent once the artist reaches gold sales levels (500,000 units) and eliminates it completely upon attaining platinum sales (one million units).

Another side effect of the wider implementation of the controlled composition clause has been publishers making a point of checking the status of the clause as it pertains to recording artists their writers may work with. It's not known for certain whether the controlled composition clause has ever prevented a pairing between writers in Nashville, but it has certainly become one more practical consideration that must be acknowledged before the creative process can proceed.

In Nashville, getting that process started and keeping it going is critical. Thanks to more accurate sales reporting via the bar code-scanning technology of SoundScan, a hit country song is worth more than it has ever been. However, the numbers need to be analyzed yet again to reflect how much a writer truly sees from a cut. Writers are statutorily entitled to half the gross publishing revenues from both sources, the other half going to the publisher. These are referred to as the "writer's share" and the "publisher's share" of the gross revenue of a song. At $0.069 per unit (album or single, any format) sold, the writer's share—half of the gross revenue total—of the mechanical royalty on a song that sells one million units is $34,500, divided between the number of writers involved. A three-way cowrite reduces each writer's share—assuming they do not retain any of the publisher's share—to $11,500.

Now, more country songwriters do retain a portion of the publisher's shares, thanks to copublishing deals. The default definition of a copublishing arrangement is one in which the writer retains half of his or her own publishing, which in the case of the three-way cowrite would add back nearly $4,000 to the writer. This copublishing arrangement would effectively give the writer 75 percent of all revenues generated by the copyright. (The split of publishing on a copublishing contract is not statutorily defined and is thus negotiable.) A fully self-published writer—which is rare in country music except at the very highest levels—would keep all revenues generated by the song.

Airplay royalty payments to writers and publishers is based on a more complicated formula than the straight-forward mechanical rate. Performing rights collection organization BMI, for instance, pays a base rate of twelve cents per play on its upper rate, called Radio 1 (large market stations as a percentage of their advertising revenues), and six cents per play on Radio 2 (smaller market stations). A radio hit commensurate to two million records in sales could generate about 125,000 plays on Radio 2, earning $7,500 (on its way up the charts) and 375,000 plays on Radio 1, earning an additional $45,000, for a total of $52,500. Of that amount, $26,250 would automatically go to the writer(s) or be credited to the writer(s) draw accounts at their publisher(s). Airplay bonuses—which kick after songs reach certain radio performance plateaus—could as much as double those figures. In a story in the January 1995, issue of the magazine *American Songwriter*, the three major performing rights organizations (PROs), BMI, ASCAP, and SESAC, revealed their respective estimated airplay earnings ranges for a number-one airplay record. They range from $112,942 to $194,230, just for the first year of play, during which they accumulate bonus monies from high rotation. Continued airplay over subsequent years earns the writers royalties at diminishing rates. ASCAP's reported average earnings level for a song that achieves number-one status over several years was $144,571; for BMI the average was $137,000; and for SESAC, the smallest of the PROs, $137,151.

Thus, a major hit in terms of both airplay and sales is worth close to $200,000 to the writer(s). On top of that, usages for television earn both performance royalties and flat usage fees, known as "synch" licenses, short for "synchronization"— any use of the song in conjunction with a moving picture. (Synch fees are negotiable between the publishers as writers' agent and the user, and can range anywhere between $500 to $500,000 for television and commercial performances, and $5,000 to $20,000 dollars for film usages.) Writers and publishers have also been able, in some cases, to negotiate financial participation in videocassette sales when songs are used in feature films. Other forms of revenues from songs include fees for commercial usages—anything from a broadcast advertising spot to a private corporate function and sheet music sales, which include songs that enter the "perennial" repertoire (songs played seasonally, such as "White Christmas," or at events such as weddings). "I Swear," made into a hit by John Michael Montgomery on the country charts and Boyz II Men on the pop charts, is one such song that has achieved the coveted perennial status.

The original major publishing companies in modern country music—Acuff-Rose Music, Tree Publishing, Cedarwood Music, and Combine Music—were the first to keep the revenues generated by country music in Nashville on a major scale.

Their main principals—respectively, producers Fred Rose and his son Wesley at Acuff-Rose, WSM executive Jack Stapp at Tree, ex-WSM employee Jim Denny (who ran the station's Artist Service Bureau which booked the Opry and who later managed it) and his partner country star Webb Pierce at Cedarwood, and Monument Records founder Fred Foster—established a way of doing business that was unique to country's needs and which persists to this day, even as the publishing landscape has changed dramatically. They signed writers and developed them, as well as developing some as recording artists. They established relationships with the PROs, using them as banks to further fund writer roster expansions. They sometimes made forays into production and record company ownership and executive management. Overall, they intertwined the publisher and the record label more tightly than ever before. That handful of publishers literally constituted the Big Four of the business into the 1970s, a golden age of Nashville ownership of the one thing that gave the industry its highest, most reliable return on investment: the song.

Some of Nashville's recording industry leaders in the 1950s, when these companies were still in their own developmental stages, thought that large publishing companies—even locally owned ones—would only get in the way of the songwriter/producer/artist relationships they had established. But country music was growing, as was the U.S. entertainment business in general in the postwar economy. However, the need to keep more of the money that country music was producing in Nashville overcame any unease.

Publishing was also the part of the business that was open to a wider range of entrepreneurs. Most of the metaphorical descendants of Fred Rose didn't come to Nashville to be publishers. They came to be artists, musicians, writers, or producers. They came to be anything but publishers because of the amorphous and transient nature of the concept: musicians have guitars, songwriters have their music, artists have their records, and producers have their studios and labels. There was something tangible in those pursuits that left the idea of trafficking in "intellectual properties" seem a little abstract and to some, distasteful. But that was only if you took the time to sit back and analyze it. And as country grew, no one in Nashville had that kind of time to waste.

Fred Rose (1897–1954) formed Acuff-Rose Music with Roy Acuff (1903–92) in 1943. Rose was an accomplished songwriter with an esthetic sense that straddled the line between country and pop. His own compositions, such as "Blue Eyes Crying In The Rain" (a hit for Willie Nelson and others) and "Take These Chains From My Heart," recorded by Ray Charles, had a polished simplicity about them that worked equally well with country and mainstream pop artists. His friendship with sing-along impresario Mitch Miller, then head of A&R for Columbia Records, provided a pop outlet for songs that Rose would either write or publish. It was those sensibilities that instinctively led him to sign Hank Williams in 1946.

Wesley, an accountant by trade, was brought to Nashville by his father the year before to straighten out the firm's books, and his talents initially lay in balance rather than pitch sheets. "He got more involved with the music as he went along," says Ronnie Gant, who with his brother Don worked for Wesley at Acuff-Rose when the younger Rose took over after his father's death in 1954. "The books were a mess and he straightened them out," recalls Gant, who began his publishing career as a part-time mail room manager and studio singer for Acuff-Rose demos, graduating to house recording engineer for the publishing company. "Fred was really the one who caused publishing to start and work in this town. Before him, the New York publishers were taking the money out of Nashville. Wesley got more involved with the music as he went along, but he was always more of businessman. But that was also something that made a difference for the future: the combination of song sense and business sense." That balance has characterized all the successful Nashville publishers since then.

As successful a writer, performer, and recording artist as the other half of Acuff-Rose was, Roy Acuff was relatively hands-off the business side of the publishing venture. "Roy was an artist and pretty much involved mainly in that part of his career," says Gant. "He was pretty much a silent partner in Acuff-Rose. Every now and then he and [his wife] Mildred would come out to the office and sign checks. We very seldom saw Roy."

Under Rose's guidance, Acuff-Rose became the home of a number of seminal songwriters of country's early modern age, including Williams and the Louvin Brothers, and later to acts such as the Everly Brothers and Roy Orbison. Acuff-Rose also owned Hickory Records, which helped keep a pop connection securely fastened to Nashville. Hickory had country artists like Don Gibson, but the label also did U.S. releases for several British pop acts in the early 1960s, including the New Beats and Donovan's "Universal Soldier."

Like many in country music in the 1950s, Jim Denny (1911–63) came into it through WSM and the Grand Ole Opry, becoming the director of talent there before leaving and starting Cedarwood Music in 1954. And like Fred Rose and others, his son, Bill, followed him into publishing, taking over its management in 1963.

Jack Stapp (1912–80) had a lifelong career in radio, including a long stint at CBS in New York starting in the 1930s. Upon his return to his birthplace, Nashville, he took over programming for WSM and, among his other achievements there, hired Owen Bradley's orchestra for the station. Stapp bought into a small publishing company started by musician Buddy Killen in 1953 that was funded by longtime friend and WSM executive Lou Cowan. This became Tree Music, which would go on to be the largest—and the most successful over the long term—of the four original companies.

Combined with Fred Foster's work that brought more pop artists to Nashville and enhanced the perception of the city as potentially more than a center for just country music, Rose, Stapp, Denny, and Foster laid the groundwork for a component of the business of country music that has undergone the most changes over the years.

"Back In Those Days, It Was Simplicity Itself"

Bob Beckham, an electrician by trade and a singer by ambi-tion, came to Nashville from Oklahoma in 1960 as a recording artist on signing to Decca Records. He won't make a point of it other than to say he had some initial success, but others will tell you about his first record, "Just As Much As Ever," produced by Owen Bradley, which made the *Billboard* Top-Twenty and stayed there for over thirty weeks. But one hit does not make a career, something Beckham and hundreds of others have found many times before and since. After his recording career faded, Beckham went to work for Atlanta publisher Bill Lowery, pitching songs by Jerry Lee Lewis, Joe South, and Ray Price. In 1963 he moved over to Shelby Singleton's Raleigh Music, one of the early small independent publishers, before starting with Combine Music in April 1965.

Beckham remained at Combine for the next twenty-seven years, through the bankruptcy liquidation of Combine and Monument, during which time he acquired a percentage of ownership in the publishing company. Part of his compensa-tion was also an ownership in the building itself that housed Combine, on Music Square East. (The building became the EMI Music headquarters after that company acquired Combine's catalog of songs in 1988.)

Beckham is one of the oldest of the active publishers from the era that saw Nashville's native publishing industry blossom. When he entered the field, the style and methods of doing business developed by Fred and Wesley Rose had become the way of the Row: the song was everything, as were personal relationships. "Back in those days, it was simplicity itself," Beckham says, sitting behind his desk at Hori-Pro Music, where he presides over two publishing companies. The desk is a bit of history, made from the walls of the writers' rooms at Combine and inlaid with carved graffiti. "There was Chet and Owen and Billy Sherrill and Jerry Kennedy running the labels and producing the records," he says in his pronounced drawl. "They were all music men; they based all their decisions on the song."

The rules were simple, too, and relatively altruistic. "I was a song plugger, and even if I heard a song that was with one of the other companies that was right for someone I was pitching to, I'd make sure they heard it. The thinking was, we have to keep these acts successful. I knew that the people at the other publishers would do the same for me, and they did. It doesn't work that way anymore. Not nearly. It's too competitive out there and it's too expensive to run the publishing company."

Beckham comes from an era when business based on a handshake and a promise worked. It was a time when, if a record sold 20,000 units, everyone was satisfied; if it sold 100,000 units, everyone was ecstatic.

But Beckham's principles were as much rooted in pragmatism and profit as in good sportsmanship. Unlike the current Nashville publishing reality of sophisticated and complex copublishing deals and researched, choreographed cowriting appointments, Beckham and his generation of publishers saw publishing revenues much more simply: they were distinctly divided between the writer's share and the publisher's share, period. The idea of a writer participating in the publisher's share was anathema. The same went for cowriting, another thing that would dilute revenues to publishers. "Bob was so adamant about not sharing copyrights through cowriting, he'd give up the song before he'd do it," comments one publisher who had once worked for him. "The idea flew in the face of everything he conceived publishing to be. He lost writers because of it when things began to change."

Beckham buttresses his stance in retrospect: "I didn't like the idea of splitting a copyright with a publisher I didn't know. When it comes time to try to help support a record with a split copyright on it, some copublishers would help out and others wouldn't."

By the same token, Beckham didn't tolerate a practice that still occurs on occasion in Nashville, as elsewhere in the music industry: producers who ask for a piece of the publishing in return for cutting the song. David Conrad, vice president of Irving Almo Music, in Nashville, the publishing arm of A&M Records, tells the story of one producer who tried to wheedle a percentage of a Combine copyright on a cut out of Beckham, who promptly returned the tape of the song with a pack of matches and a note that said, in effect, "Burn it, for all I care."

But Beckham's pragmatism and his realization of the changing realities over the years eventually overcame his ideological stance against copublishing. "Later on and now, some of my writers became copublishers with me," he says. "I have twenty writers now and maybe six are in a copublishing situation. It all depends upon their level of success. Once they get to a point where they're mature as writers and successful, and their contract comes up [for renewal], I'll start a company with them. I realized that I had better do something like that at some point, because it's gotten to the point in country music that, as you build a writer, you're also building your own future competition."

Beckham's adherence to a principle didn't get in the way of an ability to see over the horizon. He was one of the first in Nashville to anticipate the rise of the singer-songwriter, a publisher's dream: a writer who got signed to a deal had a tremendous incentive to record his or her own songs. It presaged the current phenomenon of recording artists who have become writers, looking to maximize the financial benefit to themselves from record sales. In the late 1960s Beckham signed a number of writers who would go on to sell a substantial number of records as artists, as well as garnering considerable covers of their songs by other artists.

"Beckham was the first to think of songwriter/artists," says another publisher. "He signed Kris Kristofferson, Billy Swann, Bob Galbraith, Thomas Kane, and Dennis Linde. They all got artist deals after they had signed as writers. Of course, most of them got their initial deals on Monument Records, which owned Combine. But that doesn't change the fact that Beckham saw the trend coming before almost anyone else. And at the same time, he was still very connected to the old Nashville of Owen and Chet. He really is a pivotal figure in publishing."

"To This Day, Bob Still Calls Me Alvin"

For years, it seemed as if no one ever got into music publishing on purpose. Today, Belmont University in Nashville and Middle Tennessee State University in nearby Murfreesboro both offer degrees in the music industry, including publishing as a career path. But for the class of the early 1970s, accident was the usual entrée. Apprenticeship was the pedagogy of the moment, and people such as Beckham were the headmasters.

Al Cooley, manager of A&R at Atlantic Records in Nashville, was a senior editor at *Zoo World* magazine, a now-defunct Florida rock journal he describes as *"Rolling Stone* without the politics." Atlantic's Nashville office was just starting to become successful in 1991, three years after the label opened its Nashville office for a second time (it had opened originally in 1972 and closed three years later). Cooley was feeling good about life in general, the memory of one six-month stretch without a gig in 1991 receding, although it made him realize, "When you're out of work in this town, it's a cold place."

When he was writing about music and not selling it, Cooley's journalistic beat covered Nashville, including a number of the songwriter/artists Beckham had signed to Combine. Meeting Beckham through stories he did on artists such as Swann and Kristofferson, Beckham suggested that Cooley move to Nashville. "I got the distinct impression he was saying he had a job for me," remembers Cooley. "So I came up to Nashville and—no job. Instead, he let me use the phone in the kitchen at Combine and that's where I did my interviews from, writing for any magazine I could sell something to. I don't think he really paid any attention to me up to that point. My name is Albert but I used the name Alvin Cooley as a writer's name. To this day, Bob still calls me Alvin.

"Anyway, within eight months I was broke, so Beckham

offered me a job doing publicity for Billy Swann and Dennis Linde three days a week. After three months Steve Singleton quit as general manager and Beckham walked up to me and said, 'Would you like to learn about publishing?' I said, 'When do I start?' I got a cut the first day on the job. I had written some stories about Dion [DiMucci] several years before for *Zoo World*. So I called him up and pitched him Thomas Caine's song 'I'll Give You All I've Got.'"

Cooley's first pitches were to pop artists, and Combine was one of the few publishers in Nashville that had enough credibility with the pop world at the time. While Nashville had many of its songs cut by pop artists over the years, overall those instances are still relatively few and far between, and as a result of the perceptual connotations with which the city has been long viewed, Nashville is not the first place that producers, artists, and labels in Los Angeles and New York look to for songs. But Cooley would also regularly accompany Beckham on his country music pitching rounds. "No one sits down and teaches you this business," Cooley states, his chair rocking faster now. "I don't think you can do that. You just go along and listen and soak it up. Beckham thought I had good instincts, so he would take me along to the producers' offices—to Billy Sherrill's office at Columbia and Owen Bradley's office at Decca. I just sat and listened while he pitched songs for their artists. Here's the rules you learn right from the start—never waste anyone's time, and always make a person feel comfortable when they turn you down. Don't argue. The real deal you're pitching is the ability to be able to walk back into the same office tomorrow with more songs."

Combine was small compared to Jack Stapp's Tree Music or Acuff-Rose, both in terms of the size of its song catalog and the number of its staff writers. But the depth was there, with writers such as Kristofferson, Dennis Linde, and Billy Swann, who were getting recording deals for themselves in the mid-1970s as well as getting covers of their songs on several charts. Swann hit number one with "I Can Help" on Monument in 1973. And Felton Jarvis, Elvis Presley's long-time producer, would use the Combine offices when he was in

Nashville, which along with Beckham garnered Combine eleven Elvis cuts. "Elvis was the only guy who could consistently give you big mechanical [royalties] in those days," recalls Cooley. "There were virtually no million-selling country acts. Beckham used to preach to me that we were not here for mechanicals; we were here to get airplay. A hot country record at the time would sell maybe eighty thousand units; today, if you don't sell a hundred thousand units you get dropped from the label. It was performance royalties that you made your money on. Back then, you made maybe thirty-five thousand dollars on a top-five country record. It's closer to a hundred thousand now."

Beckham, notorious in town for disliking copublishing and even cowriting if it did not occur between his own staff writers, was amenable to giving Elvis Presley 25 percent of mechanical royalties on a cut. Even that was less than what others were giving up for Presley cuts—usually a quarter of the entire copyright—half of that coming from the writer and publisher shares, including the airplay performance royalties. "Bob knew that when people came in asking for kickbacks, they almost always already had the song cut, so there was no reason to ever have to give it up," says Cooley. "There's no reason to give up anything on a good song. But you made an exception for Elvis Presley."

When Cooley came to Combine, he walked in on a group of writers that were as clannish as the other sectors of the music business in Nashville. Neither a musician nor a songwriter—pluggers were often writers themselves—Cooley was viewed suspiciously at first by Combine's staff tunesmiths, and their opinion was not softened by the fact that Cooley was a native New Yorker—a quintessential Yankee. And one of Beckham's rules was that you had to get the writers to respect you. "If you point out a weakness in a song to one of them, you'd better be right," warns Cooley. "You need to connect with them on a very personal and professional level, and the fact that I wasn't a writer was a problem with some of them back in those days."

Cooley decided in order to win their respect he would have

to cowrite with a few of them. He wrote one song each with Linde, Bob DiPiero, and Pat McManus. The songs were then sent through a screening process to determine which would get demoed and thus heavily pitched, a common practice with publishers then and now. "All the writers would put their songs into the pot and then Bob and [Combine vice president] John MacRae and me would go out to Bob's house one night and listen to them all and vote. You needed two out of three votes to get a go-ahead to make a demo, and if there were eighty songs in the pot, maybe fifteen would get demoed. The writers hated it, but it sharpened their skills and really helped them in the long run. DiPiero—the first several dozen songs he turned in were turned down in that process and he literally cried one day in my office. But he became a great writer, and I think that process may have had a lot to do with it." DiPiero, writer of numerous hits such as "American Made," a hit in 1983 for the Oak Ridge Boys and the basis of a commercial jingle for Miller beer shortly thereafter, remembers the incident and the pressure, recalling that, "I wanted to put my head in an oven . . . The committee met on Friday afternoons and we were like kids, sitting around waiting." In the screening session that took place after Cooley cowrote his three songs, he didn't tell Beckham and MacRae which ones they were and he stayed out of the voting process. One made the demo cut. "I did it to validate myself with the writers," he says. "It worked."

Cooley began signing his own staff writers in the early 1980s, including John Scott Sherrill and Mark Germino. This was just after *Urban Cowboy*—a record that Combine had participated in strongly, with cuts from staff writer Bob Morrison, who cowrote "Looking For Love In All The Wrong Places"—had raised and then dashed the town's hopes for a long, lucrative run for country music. "Beckham cured me of following trends, which is something I do more of now as a record guy," he said. "I always knew whether I liked a song or not; Beckham taught me to understand why I liked it and what made it good. And that's something about Nashville that I don't think happens anywhere else and what keeps things going here. There'll always be people who understand songs and understand why they understand them. And they pass that along."

"Everything's For Sale, At The Right Price"

Tom Collins looks like a caricaturist's delight, with a round face set off by steel-rimmed glasses and a thatch of straw-colored hair. His suspenders loosen as he rests a leg over the side of a Queen Anne chair in his Music Row office, a converted residence on Seventeenth Avenue. He gave up the idea of becoming a dentist after arriving in 1970 from Lenoir City in east Tennessee, where he was born in 1942. "I fell in love with Music Row," he says, and describes himself metaphorically as the youngest son of Wesley Rose—"Bob Beckham was the older son"—a reference to the time he spent hanging around Acuff-Rose picking up the publisher's trade.

Within a few months Collins had a full-time job, working for the only major black country music artist then or since, Charley Pride, and Pride's manager Jack D. Johnson, who jointly owned Pi-Gem Music. Pi-Gem had all of one song in its catalog, and a seasonal one to boot—"Christmas In My Home Town." This was not surprising since Pride was not truly a songwriter and this was a time in Nashville when staff positions at publishing companies were relatively rare. Collins noted that the fact that a recording artist was involved in publishing was unique at a time when Acuff-Rose, Cedarwood, Combine, and Tree were just about the only games in town, and it motivated him to look at other unconventional ways to approach publishing.

The Pi-Gem catalog grew, but not the small company's ledger books. "I had songs out all over town, but I wasn't getting any cuts," he recalls. He began looking for his own artists to cut them, and within two years had signed Ronnie Milsap, a Memphis rocker Collins convinced to go country, and country crooner Barbara Mandrell. Collins took Milsap, who had had minor releases on Scepter Records and Warner

Brothers, into a studio and played the tapes for RCA label head Jerry Bradley. "I think that was the moment I officially became a producer," he remembers. The 1973 release of Milsap's first RCA recording produced three top-ten country singles, "I Hate You," "Let's Fall Apart," and "That Girl Who Waits On Tables."

The avenue Collins chose was like most career moves in Nashville: born of necessity, urgency, and with very little planning. He said that it wasn't something many in Nashville's old guard regarded well, preferring to keep the same separation of roles that had worked for them. At the same time, Collins had plenty of role models to choose from. The most notable was Wesley Rose himself, who had Acuff-Rose-owned Hickory Records cutting plenty of its own copyrights and Fred Foster at Monument Records, which owned Combine Music. "People criticized it at the time, but me and Foster and Wesley were doing what I think they themselves wanted to do. If someone complains about a producer cutting his own songs but they don't have any hits themselves, they're wrong. The same goes for producers who cut their own songs but don't cut hits. That's wrong because that gets the producer and the artist nowhere. I mean, some people were taking an emotional attitude about the business, and that just doesn't work."

Collins and Pride bought out Johnston in 1978 and then sold the company to Welk Music three years later for over $4 million. Collins described the acquisition as one of the first that would stoke the selling of longtime independent music businesses during the 1980s, when Combine, Tree, and other major publishers became part of larger corporate entities. Collins recalls no terrible sense of emotion involved in that transaction, nor from any of the offers he receives regularly for his Tom Collins Music, the city's largest independent publishing company, which Collins founded in 1982. "Everything's for sale at the right price," he says. Collins himself made a bid on Acuff-Rose before Wesley's death. He also successfully bid on Tom T. Hall's Hallnote Music catalog in 1991.

Publishing is about money, as is any business. But Collins comes from a generation in Nashville that saw itself grow up as a financial and social stepchild to the other industries that have developed in Nashville. The local music industry of Collins's time wanted approval from both their peers in New York and Los Angeles, but just as much from their nonmusic industry neighbors in insurance and health care. Like many older Southern cities, Nashville has a plutocracy and a social pecking order that transcends occupation. "Nashville always ostracized the music industry here and laughed at it at cocktail parties," Collins says matter-of-factly. "What the music community here offered me was like nothing [nonmusic industry people] could. In fact, we got so taken with what we were doing that we eventually liked being ostracized. They let us develop and have our own little world, but now they and we realize that what we did is affecting the rest of the world, too."

However, even as Collins and his colleagues were changing the world, they wanted their little niche to remain somewhat changeless. Like other publishers who came into the business in the mid-1970s, Collins saw the rise in empowerment by songwriters during that period, with copublishing deals creeping into the industry fabric as threads that would change the pattern for the future. Like his cohorts from that pivotal time, Collins was and remains divided about the issue. "As country did better, so did the writers, and the ones who got hot were getting offers of copublishing deals from New York and Los Angeles publishers for more money than they could get in Nashville," he says. "Some of those deals are coming back to haunt them now, because many of them could never make back the advances. Now me, if I'm busting my butt to develop a writer, why would I want to offer him half his publishing back? But I'm not hypocritical; I'm against copublishing deals but I'll do one if I think it makes sense."

Collins's sentiments are now being echoed all over Music Row's publishing community, according to report in *Music Row* magazine.[2] Tim Wipperman, executive vice president of

2. *Music Row*, November 23, 1996

Warner Chappell Music, stated, "The deals are insane. They are one hundred percent over what they were . . . two or three years ago. And it's not just money, but the terms. . . ." Donna Hilley, president and CEO of Sony/Tree Music, added that she believed it was songwriters' lawyers who were upping the publishing ante in Nashville because of unreasonable expectations that country music's fortunes would continue to climb—a sentiment that has long run as an undercurrent among members of the city's music community who arrived here in the 1970s and earlier. "I think that the lawyers are trying to get more for the client . . . not [based] on reality, but [on] what they think is going to happen," said Hilley. "And attorneys are attorneys; they're not music people."

Speaking for their songwriting clientele, attorneys in the same article responded by asserting that not only are their clients worth the money, but that any bidding wars that have been going on in recent years are precipitated by the publishers themselves, not the songwriters and their attorneys. "To say that deals are ludicrous is not true," attorney John Mason was reported as saying. "There are deals being made from five hundred dollars per week to five-hundred-thousand dollars a year, and every one of those are based on a reasonable decision by both sides on what they think are the benefits and the risk of the deal."

Collins didn't even wince at the contradiction contained in his own statement that, while he may not like what's going on with large publishing deals, he'll still actively participate in them. To him, there is none. This is simply the way things are within an entrepreneurial culture that is still largely insulated—by design and by circumstance—from the larger, more corporate music industry but which is still very sensitive to how it is perceived by the rest of that industry. Collins's generation feels the isolation more sharply than those who came later. Just as well, since as the focus shifts steadily toward the way a record sounds at the expense of the quality of the song in country music, Collins and his contemporaries now see their long-held defensive attitudes as necessary to pull the music back toward the song—the core that kept country going throughout its history. There is an invisible yet very real line of demarcation between places such as Los Angeles and New York, where the record—the production—is what counts, and Nashville, where the song is king, Collins believes. That line is flexible, an adjustable rule when cuts like Restless Heart's "When She Cries" goes Top-Ten on *Billboard*'s Pop chart. Because, as Collins himself has said more than once in an interview, "Integrity is determined by whether you have hits."

"You Write 'Em, I Pitch 'Em, They'll Cut 'Em, We'll All Make A Few Bucks"

"The ethic here never really changed; copublishing didn't change it. It's always been purely pragmatic." David Conrad is sitting on the couch along the wall in his cluttered, casual office, worrying his neatly trimmed mustache and looking over the *Billboard* country chart for late September 1993. The soft-spoken Conrad is a late bloomer among this class. He spent eight years, until 1981, working at Pi-Gem, first with Tom Collins and then for him. After the sale of Pi-Gem that year to Welk Music, he became head of A&M's Almo Irving Music's publishing outpost in Nashville on a recommendation from BMI president and CEO Frances Preston. "It was a transitional time," says Conrad of those days. "When I got here, things were pretty well laid out. The publishing companies were taking advances from BMI and ASCAP, and writers [got] the writers' share and publishers got the publishers' share of copyrights. 'You write the song, I get the cut.' Why? 'I know Owen Bradley and you don't.'"

Conrad watched the rapid expansion of major publishing companies during his apprenticeship and as a result has kept Almo/Irving's staff relatively small—twenty-two writers in 1996—to counter what he saw as a potentially dangerous trend toward a publishing industry in Nashville that would not be able to adequately manage its resources. "The younger writers have suffered from a couple of things," he says. "First, there's the big deals that came in during the early nineteen-eighties in which successful writers were signed to large publishers for lots of money. That dilutes the amount of money you can devote to developing new writers. Secondly, the more writers you hire, the more thinly spread your pitching resources are." He continues to keep a wary eye on one publisher in particular—he is too politic or too polite to mention them by name. "They're going to be Publisher of the Year again because they control more of the chart because they have more songs because they have more writers," he says. "But I think it's physically impossible to service that many creative people. They're driven by market share. The old tradition was that market share never drove [country music]." He pauses and smiles wryly. "Of course, up till recently, we never had any market share."

Conrad's demeanor is calm and practical without any ideological ruffle. As he pores through that week's issue of *Billboard* spread open on a coffee table, he mentally computes the country chart. "Fifty-five percent," he concludes. "That's how much of this chart is available to me or any other publisher [this week] with a house full of journeyman writers after you take away the artists who write their own songs and the producers who write on records they produce. Five years ago the ratio was more like sixty percent." And within a couple of years more Conrad expects it will drop consistently below half the chart. "Once upon a time it was a hundred percent, Hank Williams notwithstanding," he laughs.

Conrad admitted that while his inclinations were toward the old school of publishing—"You write 'em, I pitch 'em, they'll cut 'em, we'll all make a few bucks," as he sums up that philosophy—he began following some of the evolving strategies in Nashville's publishing landscape, including the signing of writers he suspected had serious potential as viable recording artists. The first of these moves was Nancy Griffith in 1986, a very successful implementation of that strategy. Conrad also came to encourage cowriting between his staff writers and other composers, seeing both the practical aspects of it and accepting the fact that it would be the way of the future.

Conrad was also aware that the engines of country music had begun revving into higher gear in 1985 when the New Traditionalist artists such as Randy Travis helped reinvigorate country. While that was good news for a publisher, at the time before country record sales began to climb as they would in the early 1990s, the fact remained that airplay—not mechanical royalties—was still the big revenue producer for country music; the songs had to be radio hits to generate significant money. So Conrad began to scrutinize the cowritten material more than before. "Cowriting is sometimes viewed as a disease or an addiction around here," he says. "There's not a writer in this building that can't go home and write a hit song by himself and I try to help them maintain that. And when a writer disappears for a week or so, I understand."

Publishing was transforming itself from an intuitive, almost alchemic craft to more of a science as country changed during this period. Cowriting and copublishing was paving the way for record companies and their affiliated publishing divisions to jointly sign more and more artists who were also songwriters—or who at least had the potential to become writers. That, in turn, would open the gates to tactical pairings between artists and writers in a manner far more calculated than Nashville's songwriter community had ever seen.

"The lightbulb went on in everyone's head around that time to put the artists with the writers to help get cuts," Conrad explained. "Now, some of these artists couldn't write their way out of a paper bag and had no business even trying to write songs. But they knew enough—or their publishers did—to call up Don Schlitz or someone like that and say, 'Hey, can you help me write my record?' Record sales still weren't huge at that point, but by then everyone knew that copyright money was constant."

The increased levels of this activity evoked some of the same emotions in Conrad that are constant undercurrents in conversations of other publishers who were around in the mid-1980s. There was a guarded sense of hope and anticipation for the coming success of country, but one tempered with anxiety for the way in which that success could change country.

Having been through a couple of boom-and-bust popularity cycles of country music had already produced a defensive mind-set in publishers of Conrad's generation that is absent in their younger counterparts, who are more at ease with how quickly music and the world can change. The experience country had with the transient prominence that accompanied the film *Urban Cowboy* is indelibly etched into an older generation's memories and psyches. "It drove the business through the roof, then it collapsed," says Conrad, his eyes narrowing at the memory. "It was country, but it embraced the cosmetics, not the music . . . People got a false sense of security. But even more, it left a lasting mark on a lot of us. We had gotten a taste of big money. People were asking, 'When's the next movie going to get made?' 'How could we cash in on it?' We wanted our place in American pop music. No more second-class citizen."

Besides encouraging cowriting and signing artist/writers, there were other means of enhancing the environment for publishing. John Anderson broke on the country scene in 1983 with an unmistakably sonorous voice and a platinum-plus-selling single, "Swingin'." His first album spawned several other well-received singles, but his career seemed to slide downward within a few years of "Swingin'." Through the mideighties, Anderson shifted through three labels and as many producers looking for the right combination, becoming a victim of the same identity crisis that country itself was going though at the time. "I'd known John for years," says Conrad, who ran into him again in 1989. "He'd most recently extracted himself from a deal at Liberty [Records] with Jimmy Bowen. He figured, if all else failed, he could work the road the rest of his life and that would be enough to feed his family, which was the way the older country stars had done it when things like this happened. But John has such a great voice and the country sound was starting to get pretty homogenized at that point. You know who John is the minute he opens his mouth."

Conrad undertook the task of matching songs with Anderson's vocal prowess, but knew that, "to make a comeback, those songs would have to scream." Conrad signed

Anderson to a copublishing deal with Irving Almo and after a pitch of the new artistic package to BNA Records, Anderson was signed. *Seminole Wind*, coproduced by Anderson and James Stroud, saw four hit singles—"Straight Tequila Nights," "Seminole Wind," "When It Comes To You," and "Let Go Of The Stone"—and the recording had 1.7 million units in sales in 1993. Nashville regarded it as the comeback of the decade. Stroud acknowledged Conrad's role as both a publisher and as a broker who conceived a new unified vision of an artist and material in the process. "He's probably the reason why everything happened," Stroud says.

Conrad says that such a scenario could be regarded as a typical role that publishing has played occasionally and surreptitiously for some time in Nashville: a sort of surrogate A&R function, something that happens with far more frequency in recent years. "It's not unusual for publishers to be part of the deal brokering process anymore," he says. "If it ever was. But with so many types of country music—so many individual visions of what country was supposed to be from one minute to the next—clouding the horizon, matching artists like John Anderson to a wider range of writers and producers and guiding these combinations was becoming more complex."

"It Was An Enjoyable Isolation"

Tim Wipperman has a fish tank in a wall in the office from which he runs Warner-Chappell Music on Music Row East. The only goldfish in the tank are the ones brought in by an assistant each day that serve as dinner for the larger, more exotic ones—the Amazonian Red-Tailed Catfish, the Clown Knife, and the Arrawana—that dominate the aquarium. Wipperman regards the feeding process routinely and calmly. There was no sense of either the hunt going on in the tank or any sort of parallel to his own business as he watched larger fish gobble up smaller ones. He's seen too much of this scenario in both the fish tank and on Music Row.

Wipperman came to Nashville in 1972 from Wisconsin and he and David Conrad became best friends that first year in Nashville, sharing an apartment whose best piece of furniture was a Pirelli tire that served as a recliner.

They both got their first jobs working for a publishing company owned jointly by Chet Atkins and Jerry Reed for $62.50 per week. Wipperman left, first for a stint at Bill Denny's Cedarwood Music, then to Combine where he worked under Bob Beckham. He joined Warner Brothers music publishing house in 1975 and watched one of the first major acquisitions between publishers; in 1987, Warner purchased British-owned Chappell Music, creating the first multi-national publisher in Nashville and the world's largest music company.

Wipperman remembers the days at Combine with a "pink cloud around them," halcyon days when things were busy but considerably simpler and rules were learned by just hanging around. "We felt isolated. We were allowed to be part of the larger music business but were regarded as little red-haired stepchildren," he says. "But we didn't mind. We enjoyed our life and our lifestyle. It was an enjoyable isolation."

The publishing landscape was changing as the major labels were moving more of their publishing operations into Nashville, including RCA's Sunbury-Dundbar Music and Columbia's April Blackwood Music. Wipperman describes this period as an evolutionary rather than revolutionary time in publishing.

The revolution came in 1981. Performing rights organizations BMI and ASCAP had for many years helped capitalize new publishing ventures with advances against future performance royalty earnings throughout the industry, but were busier in Nashville than elsewhere due to Nashville's continuance of the separation between writer and artist—a relationship that had considerably eroded in pop music. In the early 1980s, however, litigation concerning performance fees brought about by television broadcasters against the PROs—known as the Buffalo Broadcasting case—caused the PROs to shut off the financial advance pipeline to publishers as a legal defensive maneuver. While both ASCAP and SESAC lowered their blanket licensing rates during their appeals, the opportunity to suspend advances to affiliated publishers was something that many publishers believe the PROs did with a considerable sense of relief since it unreproachably lifted from the PROs what had become a traditional burden. (The Buffalo Broadcasting Company's suit was ultimately rejected by the Supreme Court in February 1985.) With advances gone, the industry turned inward to finance itself, emulating the merger-rich environment of the 1980s that infected many other industries.

The trend started small but built rapidly. Cedarwood Music was bought by Mel Tillis's Musiplex Group in 1983—a catalog that included classic hits such as "Tobacco Road" and "Honky-Tonk Man," as well as eight Buddy Holly copyrights among its 10,000 titles. Around the same time, a pre-Sony CBS purchased United Artists Music for $69 million. CBS's own song catalogs were, in turn, purchased by SBK in 1986 for $125 million. Chappell became Warner-Chappell when Warner Communications, Inc. brought Chappell for $250 million in 1987, along with several other Nashville publishing properties, including Birch Tree Music in 1988 for between $17 and $25 million. Thorn/EMI, which had bought the Filmtrax U.K. catalog in 1990 for $115 million and brought its copyright base up to over 600,000 titles, acquired SBK Entertainment in 1989 for $337 million, which gave the company a net publisher's share of revenues of nearly $10 million that year.[3] In January of that same year, Sony Corp., in the wake of its 1988 acquisition of Columbia Records, bought Tree Publishing, the last remaining major independent publisher, for over $40 million. In October, PolyGram had acquired A&M Records for $500 million, a cash deal that included publishing division Irving Almo Music. PolyGram also bought Welk Music for $25 million that year.

"That was a line of demarcation in publishing," Wipperman said. "The power base shifted from a personality-

3. Ibid. January 14, 1989

driven one . . . to a corporate conglomerate one. All of a sudden, the publishers were their own bankers." While the loss of advances affected publishers nationally, the absence of those advances was especially felt in Nashville, where performance revenues had been estimated at more than twice the percentage of income from a record single as they are in pop music.

There was little warning that this was to occur, said Wipperman. "It was just like a big bombshell here. And because it takes three-quarters of a year for BMI and ASCAP to collect those advances and pay them to writers and publishers, you had three-quarters where people had no income. The advances stopped and the income streams didn't have a chance to catch up. There was absolutely a sense of panic among certain parties."

Wipperman and others who worked for major corporate publishers saw an opportunity, as did independent publishers. The letdown after *Urban Cowboy* and a general malaise in the music industry and the economy at large in 1979 had left county music sales depressed in the early and mid-1980s, creating a buyer's market for publishing properties with corporate buyers looking for bargains and independent publishers wanting to sell before reality caught up to the multiples[4] on which their catalogs' values were based.

The acquisition of independent publisher Bob Montgomery's House of Gold company by the much-larger Warner Music in 1983 mirrored both the economic Zeitgeist and foreshadowed an arrangement that was to become more common in Nashville in the next decade. "Everything that these [independent publishers] had built was threatened because of the cutoff of performance royalties compounded by the drop in sales," says Wipperman. "I don't think Bob

---

4. The multiple is based on approximately the number of years in which a buyer expects to recover the purchase price of a business. Historically for Nashville publishing companies, the range has been between four and twelve, with an average of five to eight. The multiple is figured based on a number of considerations including the number of successful writers under contract and the remaining terms of their contracts, and pending income from unreleased covers.

[Montgomery, a producer, composer, and one-time head of United Artists Records in Nashville] had to get out; I think he had enough cash flow to keep going. But he saw the potential for a big problem later in the year as the effect of the loss of advances became apparent and he was being pragmatic. Independent publishers could show these great multiples for the past five years or so because of the performance advances and they decided to sell based on those multiples rather than take a chance on what the next few years would bring."

The benefit to independent publishers of selling to a large corporation with significant financial resources was also readily apparent: buyers were becoming abundant and it was a fast way for larger companies that wanted a presence in Nashville to expand their depth of catalog quickly and without committing the money and time needed to cultivate a stable of staff writers. Large corporations were the only ones with sufficient resources to be able to both acquire catalogs and to continue to fund writer development, something that would become critical to the boiler rooms of Nashville's music industry when sales began to increase dramatically in 1989. The other avenue Wipperman and a few other large publishers pursued was to fund joint ventures, in this case starting a new venture with Montgomery himself shortly after Warner-Chappell acquired House of Gold Music.

Publishing has become more expensive than anything a Nashville publisher could have imagined in 1958. Aside from copublishing, which literally halves their financial return, the need to produce hits led to a major league baseball-style bidding war for some writers that has caused publishers to draw economic lines. Or at least try to, since the same competitive forces that led an earlier generation of publishers that swore never to agree to copub deals to ultimately enter into scores of them is now pushing up the advances-against-royalties numbers available to promising or accomplished writers. "The day of the two-hundred-dollar-a-week advance is gone," says Wipperman. "If someone's gonna eat you can't pay that kind of money." That, he explained, is why a Nashville publisher needs deeper pockets than their pop-oriented publishing counterparts. "Pop [publishing] deals tend to buy acts with current record company contracts. The returns are more immediate since they're going to release a record and the mechanicals from sales still mean more in pop music. In country, it takes a full three years of the [writer's contract] term to even start recouping at a time when writers are looking for more copyright participation. You wind up paying off a new writer with the money you make from the one you signed before him." It's a lot to think about, he says. Meanwhile, the fish in Wipperman's tank keep circling.

"It Gave Me An Idea"

Pat Higdon worked for Wipperman at Warner Chappell in the 1980s as a creative manager and song plugger. Higdon, a native of Nashville, started his music business career in the early 1970s working as a recording engineer at Woodland Recording, now Woodland Digital. Such a career track would more likely lead toward the producer's chair these days, but Higdon's work there as an assistant engineer brought him into daily contact with publishers and songwriters doing their demos, something that was still a major revenue source for large studios in the days before inexpensive personal recording equipment changed that market.

Higdon engineered songwriter demos in between working as an assistant to engineers such as Kyle Lehning, Brent Maher, and Garth Fundis, all of whom have become major producers in country music. But two things put him on a path toward publishing. Like almost everyone else in town, Higdon had both a personal production and a personal publishing company. Neither accomplished much for its owner until someone else decided that the name he had chosen for his publishing company would look better on theirs. "That was the first dollar I ever made in publishing," Higdon says of the transfer of the name. The second circumstance occurred when Higdon took a job at Cedarwood Music as in-house demo engineer on their four-track recording equipment, first part-time, then as a staffer. Cedarwood owner Bill Denny proved less accessible than Don Gant, who was then at Tree Music and became a mentor to Higdon through the 1970s. Higdon got more involved in the publishing side of the business at Cedarwood, convincing Denny to add writers' rooms like those at Tree. "I perceived Cedarwood as more of a place that took care of a songwriter's business rather than their art, with a go-write-them-somewhere-else sort of attitude," he observes.

Higdon left Cedarwood after two years, moving to MCA Music and working the company's small demo studio and plugging songs for seven years. He eventually acquired a vice president's title under Jerry Crutchfield, who was both running MCA's publishing division and producing several artists, including a very young Tanya Tucker. "Jerry wound up being a producer/publisher, so I ended up being the day-to-day guy," he says. "During that time I signed Don Schlitz ("On The Other Hand"), Russell Smith ("Old School"), J.D. Martin ("Two Car Garage"), and Lisa Silver ("One Promise Too Late")."

It was during this time that the performing rights societies' funding issues were coming to a head. The advance pipeline's spigot was shutting down and publishers were selling off catalogs for capital, opening the way for large corporate publishers to begin their domination of Nashville publishing. "I began to see that affect the writers I worked with," says Higdon. "Some of the older writers had been used to living off advances and not off earnings. And when BMI and ASCAP stopped the advances, their earnings never quite caught up. I saw a lot of writers fall by the wayside because of that. Meanwhile, at MCA, I saw a publishing company that was immune to this because it had corporate funding. MCA grew from almost nothing over a five-year period to being publisher of the year, and we did it with about seven writers. It gave me an idea."

The idea was to establish a small publishing company funded by a larger one, using corporate capital to replace BMI and ASCAP funding. The concept had been around in limited form—several publishers had funded publishing companies for producers and artists' managers, such as one between Warner Brothers Music and record producer Blake Mevis. But there had been no overt joint ventures with an out-and-out song plugger—someone without a direct connection to a record or a record company—up to that point. Nonetheless, Higdon put together a plan with his attorney and, after giving notice at MCA in 1985, presented it around town to mixed reviews. "They weren't going to do it with another song plugger because they thought it might cut into their own business," explains Higdon. "At the same time, those corporate publishers were building their market shares by acquiring catalogs. Each acquisition seemed bigger than the last. I saw a climate developing in which it wasn't going to take much more than service to sign some good but dissatisfied writers."

Initial indifference to the proposal forced Higdon back into the conventional publishing world as an employee at Warner Music, which was now Warner-Chappell, under Tim Wipperman. He kept the joint venture publishing idea in a mental closet through two-and-a-half years of a three-year contract at Warner-Chappell, but noted that the acquisition fever sweeping Nashville publishing hardly abated throughout that time. "Instead, it fed on itself to the point that there were no more small publishing companies."

In 1988, Higdon presented Wipperman with the idea for a second time (he had shown it to him three years earlier and been rebuffed) and this time Wipperman and Warner's went for it. Higdon was given a three-year contract with an annual budget for operations' and writers' advances. Revenues would be split evenly between Higdon and Warner-Chappell. He named it Patrick Joseph Music, after his own first and middle names. "I think what put it over this time was that, in addition to all the mergers that were happening, there were more small start-up companies being created by people with money but no publishing experience. I thought about that myself for a moment but then realized I didn't have the experience in the world of high finance. But I think that Wipperman and

Warner's saw that they were part of an environment that had a lot of paranoid writers at companies with lots of writers walking around town wondering who was going to be working them on a day-to-day basis. They saw my idea as a way of extending themselves into a boutique sort of situation where writers would get better service."

Patrick Joseph saw a half-dozen number-one country records from its writers' songs in its first three years of operation, including Patty Loveless's "I'm That Kind Of Girl," "Walk Away Joe," recorded by Trisha Yearwood, and Doug Stone's "I Thought It Was You." Their writers included Tim Mensy, Matraca Berg (whose contract was brought over from Warner's), Jim Photoglo, and Vince Melamed. Fifteen hundred songs were cataloged in three years, with 300 of them getting recorded, a better-than-average ratio even for Nashville. Contractually between Patrick Joseph and Warner-Chappell, there were no copublishing arrangements permitted in the beginning, although that later changed in some cases, with the writer, Patrick Joseph and Warner's each taking thirds. "The relationship with Warner-Chappell was restrictive in the sense that I was limited as to what kind of deals I could make," says Higdon. "But there were a lot of writers who, while they knew they could go to Warner's or Sony or EMI and make copublishing deals and get X amount of dollars, knew that they would get their songs serviced here and not be thrown in with a pack of other people and have to fend for themselves. So I was able to sign some people on terms more favorable to all of us in the long run." Like the American business model itself, Nashville publishing was turning into a service-oriented economy.

After the Warner-Chappell agreement expired in 1991, Higdon shopped the idea around elsewhere, looking for better terms based on his success. He found them at a Japanese-funded company called Windswept Pacific, a division of the Fuji Corp., a major Japanese consumer hardware electronics manufacturer, and started by, ironically, Chuck Kaye, former president of Warner Brothers at the time of the Chappell merger.

"We Were Like A Mosquito, I Guess"

"I've made a career out of being confused about what's going on here, and as a result I suppose my perspective on the publishing industry here is a bit warped."

So says Gary Velletri, sitting comfortably behind a nondescript wooden desk in a very cluttered office. A photo of Rosanne Cash surveys the controlled chaos from above the fireplace. The Bug Music office is in one of the many frame houses on Music Row's east side that looks like any number of other publishing concerns on Sixteenth Avenue South, right down to the sign that tells those without appointments that unsolicited material is not accepted. "We were like a mosquito, I guess," he says with a trace of a New York accent still identifiable after nearly a decade in Nashville. "We weren't popular with the other publishers in town when we got here. I could feel it."

The source of Velletri's discomfort in 1985 was the very core of Bug's existence. Rather than act as a traditional publisher, taking half the copyright in exchange for providing a weekly advance and pitching services to the writer, Bug's premise asked only for an administration percentage, an amount usually around 10 percent, in return for working writers and their catalogs. In the structured cannons of Nashville publishing, this was tantamount to heresy. Administration had long been one of the functions reserved for a traditional publisher, even in copublishing deals. The administrative 10 percent is a vague area of headroom in a publishing deal, putatively included to cover filing and other clerical costs and one that is rarely intensively questioned or audited. "The difference between Bug Music and administrators is that we work as publishing administrators but act like publishers," Velletri explains. "We don't own the copyright like a publisher, but we do get out on the street and plug the songs."

One annoyed publisher commented on Bug, "A writer looks at it this way: 'Bug wants to do it for ten percent; why should I give it to you for fifty percent?' An administration deal amounts to leasing a song for four or five years and working your butt off for it and in the end the writer turns around and says *sayonara*."

The company was formed in 1975 by Dan Burgoise, a former United Artists Records A&R man soured on label politics. That and his one-man odyssey to help longtime friend and singer Del Shannon recover the royalties due him from Shannon's 1960's hit "Runaway" and other compositions brought him into the publishing business, but with a decidedly nontraditional take on it. He sought out and found a truly eclectic collection of songwriters in his original home base of Los Angeles. T-Bone Burnett and Asleep At The Wheel were among the first to sign with what could be regarded as the Ben & Jerry's of music publishing. Burgoise made frequent trips to Nashville over the next ten years, and despite his unorthodox ways started lining up some of Nashville's burgeoning underground country, including Rosanne Cash.

Velletri came down to Nashville from New York almost equally disillusioned about the music industry; the job that brought him here disappeared upon arrival and he spent three months looking for another. Velletri and Bug were a perfect match. As Burgoise devised a unique publishing strategy, his new Nashville office chief Velletri was implementing tactics on an equally ad hoc basis. "I literally had to invent this office," he recalls.

Writers John Prine and John Hiatt came with the office, and Velletri began a chain of signings, including Nancy Griffith, Marshall Chapman, and Fred Koller. "People were curious," he says of that time. "They came to us. But it also seemed that every time a writer that wasn't country came to BMI or ASCAP looking for a suggestion about a publisher, they said, 'Go see Bug.'"

At a time when the industry was rallying around Randy Travis, Ricky Skaggs, and other New Traditionalists, Bug was perceived as swimming the wrong way, despite Emmy Lou Harris going top-ten country with a T-Bone Burnett and Billy Swann song, "Drivin' Wheel," and Rosanne Cash hitting number one on the country chart with John Hiatt's "The Way We Mend A Broken Heart." It wasn't until Kathy Mattea had a hit with Nancy Griffith's "Love At The Five & Dime" in 1985 that Bug began to become regarded as part of the country network. In the high-volume world of Nashville publishing, the major record labels try to be relatively selective in giving out all the information about which artist is looking for material to prevent literally truckloads of songs arriving from hundreds of independent publishers and songwriters, even before the various pitch sheets around town get a hold of it. "I knew we had become established when we began getting that kind of inside information from the larger labels," says Velletri.

Nonetheless, Bug remained an oddity until recent years, breaking the rule that most Nashville publishers had subscribed to—you don't pitch pop songs in Nashville and vice versa. "You can almost hear a publisher in Nashville calling a guy in an L.A. record office and saying, 'I got a hit for Bette Midler' and you can see the L.A. guy rolling his eyes on the other end of the line." Velletri laughs. "And you could see the same thing happening in reverse, when the L.A. guy calls and says he has a country smash and the Nashville guy thinking, 'I hate it when these L.A. guys think they know country.'"

In the course of its years here, Bug has begun to conform to the Nashville way. As Velletri talks about needing to protect Nashville from some of the excesses like cowriting gone wild with some recording artists now having as much interest in participating in copyrights as in picking the best songs, and ever-smaller percentages of the charts available to publishers, he begins to sound a bit like publishers of an earlier generation. "Hey, look, I am a Nashville publisher at this point," he agrees after a moment's pause. "I'm not trying to be a renegade or a controversial figure. People start out wanting to change things when they get here and I was like that, too. But any sense of change that I want to accomplish now is different."

"It's All Percentages"

It is early afternoon on a weekday and Chris Dodson is walking around the deck that envelops the rear of his office in a house on Music Square West. He is setting off bottle rockets. Every now and then, he looks over at the house next door, in which an architectural design firm has its offices. "They don't like it when I set these things off, but it's the only way I can keep the birds from shitting all over this deck," Dodson mutters, as he lit another fuse with a borrowed cigarette. Someone has written the simplest of rules on the side of the rocket, ones that could also apply to music publishing: LIGHT FUSE. GET AWAY. LISTEN FOR REPORT.

The shot scatters the small blackbirds that have been roosting in the hackberry tree behind the office. Within moments, though, they're back on their perches. The bottle rockets are almost as loud as the Boeing 727s passing overhead at full power as they lift out of Nashville International Airport ten miles to the east. The birds have gotten used to them, too.

Dodson is relaxed as he goes about this task. He is from Nashville and has spent his life on the Row, more or less. His father was a music business attorney who represented Jim Reeves, Loretta Lynn, and other country stars from the 1950s and 1960s. Chris Dodson got his start in the business at the age of fourteen working in the mailroom at Starday Records, an independent label whose back room was the birthplace of the first Nashville mail-order record business, Cindy Lou's Record Club. Along the way, he finished law school and tried his hand at songwriting and playing in rock & roll bands. The legal field being as crowded as the songwriting one, he finally wound up as a song plugger at Tree in 1977.

Dodson's story could have gone on to parallel those of hundreds of others who got into the publishing business with a major company. But it took a turn in the late 1970s when Michael Murphy, a songwriter and performer whose catalog had been signed to Tree years earlier, came in looking for some songs on an act he was going to produce. Dodson played him a few songs, including "Ace In The Hole," which was from Murphy's own catalog. Murphy had forgotten all about that song, buried beneath his own output and the output of hundreds of writers knocking out three and four songs a month for years. Dodson played him a few more and Murphy suggested that he might consider pitching Murphy's catalog on the side, cutting Tree in for a piece of the writer's publishing that Murphy had retained in his original Tree deal.

There's no hard number on the independent song pluggers in Nashville. Dodson, who represents songs for Mac MacAnally, Robert Byrne, Rodney Crowell, and Bill Anderson, asserts that he was the first, and there's no reason not to believe him. As the publishing business became one of conglomerates, the smaller publishing houses, spawned in the late 1960s and early 1970s as country music expanded, became the objects of desire as larger publishers, infused with out-of-town capital, bought them up to increase their catalog bases. The third wave of publishers came from a round of writers grown rich off their work and from starting their own companies, which developed into a new generation of small publishers, as well as developing new relationships between entrepreneurial publishers. But even that proliferation of publishers couldn't handle the increasing number of writers appearing in Nashville. Independent plugging deals vary from individual to individual; in Dodson's case, he gets paid a monthly retainer and bonuses for a song's chart performance. "It's all percentages," he explains. "Except in a couple of isolated instances, I've never done it for a piece of the copyright. I'm like an independent promotion man."

Independent song plugging is a way for writers to keep their material from drowning beneath a sea of songs that pile up at publishing houses as a result of catalog acquisitions and the output of staff writers. It's also a way to keep a song out there for the time it takes to get it cut. Unlike the trendiness of pop music, country songs have what Nashville calls a "long shelf life." Recycling old country songs is a staple of Nashville, à la The Kentucky Headhunters' recut of Hank Williams's "Oh Lonesome Me," but even the songs that haven't been cut yet get second, third, and fourth chances as country goes through its seasonal lyrical and tempo cycles. "A couple years ago, everybody wants an 'Achy, Breaky,'" observes Dodson. "At one time, everybody wanted a 'Gentle On My Mind' and at another time they wanted 'The Dance.' They want different kinds of country songs at different times and it always comes around again. I take a song, I'm prepared to pitch it for a real long time, 'cause that's what it takes. But country songs last a real long time."

Typically, independent song pluggers are people with a lot of ambition, some access, and a phone. Preferably a cellular phone. They provide some tactical mobility for a publishing business that's dominated by large institutions surrounded by smaller publishers dependent upon them for their capital, keeping songs and songwriters riding above the depths of songs that country generates. Despite the monthly retainers, they're basically working on a contingency basis. As with any service in which there are far more sellers than buyers, it's opened the doors to scammery, what they call "pay-to-listen" services that will evaluate songs for a fee, usually around $25.

"It's hard to draw the line at what's legitimate and what's not," says Dodson, referring to both publishing services and songwriters. "Here's a guy running your errands and cleaning out ashtrays and he calls himself a songwriter. Some guy named Kris Kristofferson. You go into a restaurant and your waitress tells you she's a singer and you kind of quietly laugh and it turns out it's Kathy Mattea. She used to wait on me at Friday's restaurant . . . It's hard to know who or what's going to happen . . . You just do whatever's happening, whatever's going to light up the phones."

The Musicians

Here the sidemen are richer than the
stars they record with. They should be—
they work a hell of a lot more.
—HOMER & JETHRO[1]

T HE ALARM GOES OFF in the red brick two-story house in the Bellevue section of Nashville at six A.M. It's late November and a trace of frost is on the now hay-colored lawns. The radio is tuned to WMOT, a PBS jazz and news station out of Murfreesboro. Glenn Worf gets up and makes breakfast for his oldest daughter, Mandy, before she leaves for high school. About an hour-and-a-half later, he's joined by his wife Susan and they get their three other children ready for school. Worf moves out of the kitchen and picks up first the Nashville *Tennessean*, then his 1960 Fender Precision bass, which he bought for $200 years ago in Kentucky, a scarred piece of wood and metal that has been rehabilitated by a local luthier.

A self-admitted creature of habit, for the next forty-five minutes Worf plays scales, until 9:15, when he tosses the Fender and a few other items into the back of a 1994 Volvo station wagon, a suburban favorite for people who have to transport kids, dogs, and the occasional six-foot acoustic double bass. Worf takes the I-40 East to town, cruising past Junk Row on the right and the edge of Music Row on the left. The session call for today had come in three weeks earlier,

---

1. *JCM*, Vol. No. 16:3

which is cutting it a little close in Nashville, where bookings for an in-demand session player tend to run closer to three months in advance, and where musicians usually get picked for a recording before the songs do. "The Los Angeles players who've moved here, like Dann Huff, tell me that, as much as they worked out there, they're still amazed at how you can get booked so far advance here," Worf says, making the left onto Seventeenth Avenue South. "It's a nice feeling to know you've got that work coming."

The studio, Nightingale Recording, is on Seventeenth Avenue, the west side of the Row. (The studio, which changed ownership in 1996, is now known as Seventeen Grand Recording.) It shares a duplex with a travel agency in a low-slung white single-story building. Studio owner Joe Bogan is the engineer for this series of sessions. Upon entering, the studio presents an efficient, anonymous face, gray carpeting and wood trim. But there is a comfortable lounge with a small kitchen off it, and a television set that seems to be always on.

The first sessions began the day before. Drummer Paul Leim arrived at 8:30 A.M. to set up his kit and get sounds with Bogan, to be ready for the rest of the musicians and the ten A.M. start. The drum sounds will be refined as the sessions move along, using both Leim's own tunings as he stretches and loosens drum heads with a chrome-plated key, and Bogan's tonal equalization on the recording console and his placement of microphones around the kit—the way drum sounds have been recorded since recording began. Leim's acoustic kit, though, is augmented by an electronic one, a black-topped pad to his left divided into segments that can electronically trigger any one of hundreds of drum sounds that reside in sound modules in his five-foot-tall electronics rack. Behind Leim's drum throne is a shelf holding scores of three-and-a-half-inch floppy disks each containing digital samples of drum sounds, augmenting his arsenal of sounds into the thousands. Some will be triggered by hitting the pads, others will trigger off sensors mounted on the acoustic drums themselves. When Leim hits the snare drum, three drums will actually be heard in the control room: his acoustic snare and two snare drum samples. The sampling of sounds via digital recording has been ethically, artistically, and legally controversial since affordable sampling technology became widely available in the early 1980s, with rap music taking the heat for pulling entire vocal and instrumental lines off old records and inserting them onto new ones. Court cases continue to drag on asserting copyright infringement based on sampling. But among musicians, the use of samples, which are often traded among them like baseball cards, is now a commonplace technique.

The drums dominate the recording room, set up in the center on a low-rise platform. Leim sits facing Worf, who has his two bass guitars leaning up against his own rack of sound effects. To his right Dan Dugmore, another Los Angeles transplant and formerly with Linda Ronstadt's band, sits at his double-necked Sho-Bud pedal steel guitar, his effects rack feeding directly into the recording console rather than going into a guitar amplifier. Sitting in glassed-walled isolation booths around them are electric guitarist Larry Byrom, pianist Matt Rollings, and acoustic guitarists Chris Leuzinger and Billy Joe Walker, who is the coproducer on the session with Asylum Records head Kyle Lehning. Lehning also produces Randy Travis, including the artist's seminal *Storms Of Life*, and began as an engineer himself, at the Glaser Brothers' studio one block and one lifetime away.

Lehning, like everyone else on the session, is dressed casually. By 10:30 he is running the day's first song down, listening to a guitar and voice demo of a Jim Lauderdale ballad that was slated for then-newly signed Asylum recording artist Bryan White, who sat calmly in the control room watching the well-choreographed process of what would become his first record. White would go on to have two platinum albums for Asylum and become the youngest contender for the CMA's Male Vocalist of the Year in 1996. But at this moment, Lehning was looking for Asylum's first major hit and White was the novice in a recording studio ritual similar to ones that had consumed three previous generations of artists, producers, and musicians in Nashville.

The players huddled around a Formica-topped desk in the center of the room following along on charts filled out with the Nashville number system. Lehning asks to hear the Lauderdale demo but it's nowhere to be found. His assistant, Jason Stelluto, hustles on the phone and calls Glen Campbell's publishing company, requesting a cassette copy. Meanwhile, the players keep discussing the song. Walker suggests a rake part, a technique used to arpeggiate a strum on an acoustic guitar to make it sound bigger. "That's him, the Rakemaster," chirps Leim. "We should package you and sell you."

"Right," adds Rollings. "Put ten picks on a strip and pull them across the strings. Call it the Rotary Rakemaster—three picks on a power drill blade for continuous raking."

After a couple of dry runs in the control room, the musicians file out into the studio. Bryan White heads into an isolation booth in the far corner, puts on headphones, and prepares to lay down a reference vocal. Just signed to Asylum Records, he is nineteen years old in 1994 and both looks and sounds more like a choirboy than a country music star. He has a perfect complexion and a heavy dose of Oklahoma in his accent. But he has what Lehning calls a "perfect sense of phrasing" for the music. His mother was a jingle singer in Oklahoma City and sang with his father, a guitarist, in a lounge band there. Bryan was playing drums at the age of five, and it was his guitar teacher who sent a tape of him singing to Billy Joe Walker.

The song is played down in pieces—the verses get run through until a consensus develops about its feel. It's then coupled with the chorus and the two pieces are run together several times. On the other side of the glass, Bogan is soloing different instruments by muting all the others on the console as he fine-tunes each instrument's sound.

Lehning is staying out of the traffic; the musicians are working out intros and turnarounds between verses among themselves. Rollings and Leuzinger decide to double each others' part on the intro. The parts assemble themselves into a complete pass, then a take as Bogan hits the Record button on the remote control to the Swiss-made Studer 24-track tape recorder sitting in a glassed-in machine room.

The players file in to the control room for the first playback. Lehning listens with them, standing behind the console, his head bowed between the speakers on the bridge along the top of it. The track is already confident—partly because these musicians are arguably the finest collection of nonclassical musicians in the world. They do this day-in and day-out, working on more records than any of their peer groups anywhere else.

But the confidence borne of experience comes from repetition. The world of country music recording studios is an assembly line where many parts are right out of a standard inventory, varied slightly according to the emotion the singer might offer, the moods and creativity levels of the ensemble cast and, for all anyone knows, the weather. And the technology of modern recording has changed it, as well: a verse, a chorus, a turnaround vamp, a verse, a solo becomes a low-pressure event from a guitarist who knows that it will be over-dubbed again later. There will always be the special moments, the scores of accidents and momentary inspirations that produce something sparkling and new at each session, but those moments can now also be time-shifted by overdubs done at everyone's leisure or cobbled together as a waveform on a computer monitor screen.

Nonetheless, there's a invigorating sensation in the familiarity of the environment, particularly the environment found in Nashville on a country record, where it is a group of musicians rather than one technologically adept auteur making the music—as is increasingly the case in pop music—and where the songs almost always offer an instantly recognizable structure. You've never heard this song before, yet it's a comfortable fit. It's an intimate support for the lyrics that drive country. And rap, for that matter. The similarities are striking: both can create almost infinite musical permutations from a limited array of elements. Musically, they're predictable; they're supposed to be. But a good track in either genre is never tiresome. It's all in the execution.

There's a precision here tempered with a genuine enthusiasm, a professional pride combined with a palpable desire to please: the producer, the artist, and themselves.

The musicians' initial boisterousness at the start of the playback gives way to a quiet analysis as the tape rolls at thirty inches per second past the playback heads on the Studer deck. Lehning looks up and nods his head. "It feels really good, but there's a couple of arrangement thoughts I had," he says. Lehning makes a few comments about the structure. "By the time we start the second chorus, we need a break from it. We need to let the track breathe in between choruses." White mentions that this pass felt a bit too fast. Drummer Paul Leim says it felt good to him.

"You sound like Porcaro or Marotta," Walker tells him, referring to a pair of other Los Angeles session drummers. The remark would be vague to an older generation of musicians that never knew anything but Nashville, but an inside joke with L.A. references is easily appreciated these days.

"Fuck you, I got my part," Leim replies with mock ferocity, a studio retort that would be understood by the pros of any generation.

Back in the studio, Leim and Worf are back at their positions first. They kick into a salsa groove, a suddenly rhythmic stab of color in a country session where the drums and bass are the anchors rather than the featured instruments. Lehning looks up from the console on the other side of the glass and says deadpan into the talkback microphone, "Let's cut that one next."

Leim's count-off for the second take slows down minutely between "one" and "four," taking the band by surprise. He hadn't forgotten White's comment. But within a half-bar of the intro they're locked into it. A playback produces agreement on the tempo but Lehning suggests switching the pedal steel solo for a guitar solo. "And Bryan's vocal should come in sooner at the end of the solo," he says. Larry Byrom's solo is rock-tinged, capped with one of the triple-stop R&B licks he's peppering the track with. He is a former member of late 1960s hard-rock band Steppenwolf, and with Leim, Walker, and

Dugmore tips the character of the band further toward a Los Angeles vibe.

The third take is the keeper, Lehning decides. "There's a couple of train wrecks in there between Larry and Matt, but nothing we can't fix."

The rest of the track is tweaked with overdubs, including fixing a drum fill by Leim, trying to match it to an acoustic guitar figure. While each musician takes his turn fixing parts, the rest gather on a pair of couches in the lounge. Leim has commandeered the remote control and is flipping channels between CNN and CMT. If a song comes on that one of them has played on—an almost sure bet if the television stays on more then twenty minutes—they might mention it. Martina McBride is singing "My Baby Loves Me," and Dugmore, the quietest member of the crew today, speaks up for the first time. "That's me on guitar," he says to no one in particular.

Back in the control room, Bryan White is listening to the fixes as they go down, apologizing for the fourth time for what he says is a closed throat. His friend Scott from Oklahoma City is sitting across from him. "Quit bitchin'," he says. "You got a record deal." Nineteen and a year of singing publishing demos around Nashville and he has a record deal. Adds Scott, a singer himself, "I'm twenty. But I'm not in any hurry."

Chris Leuzinger is walking past the two of them on his way to the lounge. The control room is the common ground for the artist and the musicians. Bryan White does not join the players in the lounge, however. There is and always has been an invisible wall between the musicians and the artists in Nashville. A good voice is not sufficient for entry into the musicians' fraternity. A few have breached it, such as Vince Gill, who is a superb picker and who won even more points among the brethren for turning down a pop career offer from Dire Straits leader Mark Knopfler to stay with Nashville.

The old saying in the music business is that you get a lifetime to write your first record and six months to write the second. In Nashville, as in New York, Philadelphia, and other recording centers of the '40s, '50s, and '60s, you generally got about three days to make any record, first, second, or last. The idea that the Beatles were taking an entire week per song to make *Revolver* in 1967 amazed some American engineers at the time. One reason for that was because the recording studio was on the cusp of evolving into the musical instrument it has become. The primary technological reason records were beginning to take longer to make was the commercial introduction of multitrack recording systems. Recordings had been made monaurally until 1958, when stereo was introduced. Taped recordings were still competing with recordings made directly to lacquer discs, as they had been for the previous forty years. But once tape technology opened up the potential for more tracks, professional tape recording decks went from two to three to four, eight, sixteen, and twenty-four tracks in the space of fifteen years. Once professional digital recording decks became common after 1980, that number soon rose to forty-eight separate tracks on a single machine, which could then be lined for parallel operation for up to ninety-six tracks to be used on a single song. Digital nonlinear systems, using computer hard drives, entered common use a few years later, adding even more tracks to the mix plus random access. More tracks meant more options and thus more time, and cost more money. But it was the makers of mainstream music—particularly rock records—that both pushed the envelope of the state-of-the-art in recording and had the sales to warrant the budgets that new technology and longer stints in the studio required. Niche music genres, such as jazz and country, lacked the financial resources—or, as their adherents sometimes put it, retained the discipline—to make records in less technologically excessive environments. Multitrack recording became common in Nashville by the mid-1970s, but until the first contemporary rock influences that touched the city took hold, Nashville's studio technology base lagged behind those of New York, Los Angeles, and London, as did country music's recording budgets. As a result, the need for a musician corps that could make records quickly remained at a premium.

The musicians of Nashville are legendary. You have to be good to get the gig, and you have to love the music to put up with the conditions of the career, which up until the late 1940s centered around touring—driving 300 miles in a twenty-four-hour period between gigs, sleeping in the back of the car with the band instruments hitched to a trailer. Pay was $10 dollars a week for Joe Talbot when he was Hank Snow's steel player on the road. Talbot had a relatively cushy gig, playing with a member of the Opry. Their touring range was limited because Snow and his band, like the other Opry stars, had to be back in Nashville for the Saturday night show. "You only got two Saturdays a year off from that," Talbot recalled. "The only excuses accepted were death or serious illness, preferably your own."

As Nashville's status as the center of the country music industry evolved in the 1950s, the recording emphasis had shifted from scattered sessions in New York, Cincinnati, Dallas, or Chicago, or from field trips to more remote locations by label engineers and A&R men, to recording in Nashville itself. From this evolved the team of session players that both shaped the country sound and allowed the truncated country recording budgets that persisted until relatively recently to be met.

"A Cadillac With Air Conditioning!"

Bob Moore, Ray Edenton, Buddy Harman, and Charlie McCoy are sitting around an office in the one-story red brick building that houses Local 257, American Federation of Musicians, at the top of the Row, the organizational home to Nashville's 3,700-plus registered musicians. It is a warm, late summer afternoon and the bustle of Music Row is deadened by the thick glass of the union's meeting room. The four have not seen one another for some time, a few years in some cases, but they greet one another warmly and with intimacy.

If this had been the same day but thirty years earlier, the greetings would have been of a similar tone and nature.

It would have been in one of the dozen studios in Nashville at the time, and they would have been carrying musical instruments instead of paunches and memories. This original nucleus of Nashville's session players, such as guitarists Grady Martin and Hank Garland, worked some of the first sessions of modern country music. They created the music and the sound as they went along. They helped make up the rules.

"And the first rule was, you don't put drums or horns on country music," says Ray, a guitarist, with a sly look at Harman, small and wiry and almost lost behind a large, cluttered desk. Harman was the first drummer allowed to play on the Opry stage. "Allowed," because Bob Will's drummer stealthily cornered that honor several years earlier in the late 1940s when he eluded detection until showtime by Opry management. "I had a snare drum and two brushes; that's all they would let you have," says Harman, who began his career out of high school as a big band drummer and a road musician with Marty Robbins and Carl Smith. It was Smith who had tried to get Harman and his drum kit on stage with him at the Opry in 1954 and was told by Ernest Tubb that his career would be ruined for his effort. The effect of percussive censorship on drummers like Harman was a lighter touch on the drums—when they did creep into the music—that lasted for another decade. One current country producer recalls that as a young assistant engineer, he was amazed when he noticed during a session years ago that Harman did not play his kick drum—the fundamental part of the drum kit along with the snare—until the songs reached the choruses.

Ray Edenton smiles, something he does a lot of. "The way they took care of rhythm on records back then was the guitar player. In those days you [loosened] the strings down on an arch-top guitar and hit it hard and got like a drum beat. There was no tone; [key changes] meant nothing. You just played to keep the beat."

Most of them had their first recording experiences outside of Nashville, at local radio stations that recorded country singers to lacquer discs for later rebroadcast. Bob Moore, possibly the most recorded bassist in all of country music, did his first session at a radio station in Knoxville in 1949, and did sessions with Red Foley in Cincinnati in the '40s.

There were around a dozen players who made virtually all of the records during the early days of modern country recording. There were plenty of musicians in Nashville after World War II, but only a handful developed or intuitively had the musical, personal, and social gifts that would be required to make records under the circumstances in place then. And even though there are far more records being made now and more musicians than ever in Nashville, that same requirement for special skills—musical and otherwise—remains to this day. A lot of great players never made the studio cut because they had what Edenton called "studio fright"—"They just froze up when the red light went on. They could go onstage in front of fifty thousand people and just blow you away, but they couldn't hack it in the studio."

The studio was and is an intense environment, despite the ambiance of loose camaraderie the Nashville musicians bring to it. The musicians union mandated that sessions could last no longer than three hours before going into overtime. That three hours was worth $41.25 in 1949 to a musician. It's hardly kept pace with inflation; today that same three hours at single scale nets a player $256.13—$543.34 for session leaders—plus $27 in health and welfare benefits and miscellaneous items such as equipment cartage. Compared to the peanuts many of them had made on the road, though, it was a small fortune. As the number of records increased, so did the amount of work for this small crew. They were doing as many as four three-hour sessions in a day, five days a week. "A young producer once asked me how we got so tight," says Moore. "I told him, you play five hundred sessions a year with the same people, you'll get tight." The intensity of these relationships increased by the fact that at many sessions as late as the early 1970s, some producers would not allow musicians into the control room; they listened to the playbacks on monitor speakers inside the recording room.

The success many of these musicians experienced quickly and radically changed their lives. "Can you imagine a poor boy from East Nashville all of a sudden driving a Cadillac?" asked Moore.

"A Cadillac with air-conditioning!" McCoy shouts in response, loud enough to be heard through the door where union secretaries turn their heads at the sound of his voice.

". . . And listening to yourself on the radio playing on a number-one song!" Moore adds.

Their attitude is still resonant of that of the cocky young musicians they were thirty-five years ago: scuttling between sessions for Patti Page, Eddy Arnold, Red Sovine, Ferlin Husky, Lefty Frizzell, Jim Reeves; stopping in the afternoon to have lunch together at Marchetti's on Lyle Street where the Midtown Cafe now is; then playing from dusk to dawn at the Carousel Club in Printer's Alley, because they loved the music as much for itself as for the power it was giving them.

"You'll never see the likes of that again," says Charlie McCoy, a harmonica player whose first session gig in Nashville was in 1959 and who went on to have a successful solo career as an instrumentalist and to be the musical director for television's *Hee Haw* for nearly twenty years. "You'll never see that happen here again where it lasts so long. Careers of artists that used to last for forty years now last for five, and so do the careers of the musicians."

For all the power they were acquiring, they still felt put in a place apart, a well-padded prison in which constant attendance was mandatory, lest someone else take their coveted spot. A few went on to produce records, joining that aspect of the power structure, including Jerry Kennedy and Billy Sherrill from that generation, a path others in later generations would follow. Others, like pianist Floyd Cramer from those days and Mark O'Connor of the current class, left the studio grind to pursue artist careers. McCoy also made solo records, but continued to be one of the boys in the crew. His first encounter with the A-Team of country music eloquently explains the motives behind his and others' desire to be and stay a part of it.

"I came here in 1959, to audition as a singer," he recalls. "That wasn't working out, but in the meantime someone took me to a session these guys were doing. I was about eighteen years old and I watched them cut a record with Brenda Lee— 'Sweet Nothings.' That day changed my life forever. I watched that session, the way these guys worked with each other, and said I gotta be a part of this. Somehow, someday, some way, I gotta be a part of this."

The way they worked together became intuitive, says Edenton. "It used to be that they were seated in the studio in such a way to be looking at each other all the time during sessions, and that no one wore earphones. Unconsciously, we would all decide to push a certain beat at exactly the same time during a song. We did it without saying a word to each other, even without thinking it to ourselves. It just came naturally."

Adds Moore, "Ray could be sitting in the session and . . . I would just watch him change one string and I'd know where he was going."

They had their relationships with the original cadre of producers in Nashville, and their estimation of the members of that group seems to hinge upon how involved they perceived each one to be. Owen Bradley still commands a tremendous amount of respect from them all. "Owen would literally be at every minute of a session," says Moore. "He knew every note he wanted played before the session even started. Chet Atkins, he would sit in the control room and read a magazine."

Edenton tempers Moore's assessment, adding, "He was hands-on in the beginning. They all were. I remember someone once asked me why Chet wasn't in the control room during a session and Chet replied, 'I've got six producers in there for me.' He trusted us. Billy Sherrill got that way later on, depending upon the great songs that he wrote and [pianist Hargus] 'Pig' Robbins to give him a sound."

In those days, producers routinely completed as many as thirty or more album projects in a year, which makes the half-dozen to a dozen they do now seem paltry by comparison;

still, contemporary country producers have an output that dwarfs that of pop producers. Coproduction, as with cowriting, became the modus operandi that allowed Nashville's record industry to be so fecund. Such prodigious output was also encouraged by the technology of the time, which was two- or three-track recording and mono mixing though the mid-1960s. You simply played the songs over and over until you got a take everyone was satisfied with. And with the caliber of musicianship that was evolving among Nashville's A-Teams, if that "keeper" take wasn't gotten by the fourth or fifth try, the song itself became suspect. But the musicians were, in effect, the originators of coproduction, though without any formal recognition of that. Along the way, the musicians nudged the song's arrangement, changing a chord here or there, or sometimes manipulating the very DNA of a song by altering a melody line or even a lyric. "Owen Bradley rewrote lots of songs that don't have his name on them," says Edenton. "The same goes for the musicians. None of the writers resented it back then." But there is still a lingering sense among some musicians that they haven't gotten their due.

The pool of players that formed the earliest A-Team would be broken up into session groups according to a combination of personal preferences of the producers and on their own availability as demand for their services steadily increased. The four musicians gathered in the union hall this day, augmented with Hargus "Pig" Robbins, was a typical configuration. But later in the afternoon Moore might show up at a session with Hank Garland on guitar and Floyd Cramer on piano. They were almost interchangeable; seeing and working with each other day-in and day-out ensured that there were few secrets—new guitar licks or bass playing techniques—that were not part of everyone's repertoire within weeks. It was as much the characteristics of each producer and the demands of the song and the artist as the differing styles of the musicians themselves that kept the music from sounding completely the same.

Despite the premium put on them by their exceptional

abilities and small numbers, they learned early on to form alliances with different producers and to handle them all with a certain amount of caution. Moore recalls a session when Ferlin Husky asked him to bow the final note of a song on his upright bass without mentioning this change to the producer, Capitol Record's A&R chief Ken Nelson. Moore complied and was rewarded with a tongue-lashing by Nelson. "As soon as the take was over, Nelson hit the button in the control room and said something to the effect of, "Where in the world did you get the damned stupid idea to put the bow in that?'" Moore simply said he thought it might sound good, keeping Husky out of the line of fire and mollifying Nelson, whom Moore said later apologized about blowing up. "But it shows you how you had to please them no matter what."

But within their own ranks, the A-Team moved through the three- and four-session days secure in the knowledge that the records wouldn't get made without them. They also knew that a feel was being developed that was becoming innate rather than simply mechanical. A&R men would come down from New York and sometimes made disparaging remarks about the lack of sight-reading ability they found among Nashville musicians, then boasting about the reading chops of New York session players. "There were a lot of them came down here who could play and read their asses off," says Moore. "But they never learned the one important thing: what *not* to play. One New York arranger came down and Ray left a part off that was written out on the chart and the guy came out and said, 'Can't you read music?' And Ray says back to him, 'Not enough to hurt my playing.'

The Nashville Number System

The Nashville number system, a methodology of reading music that developed there in the 1950s, might on the surface seem to be one more step in the process of codifying the studio crews into a secret society, opaque to outsiders.

In reality, says Charlie McCoy, its main attraction was that it allowed songs to be arranged and keys changed to fit the artist quickly and easily, thus keeping the factory-like schedule of sessions running smoothly. And the number system, which is still in everyday use in Nashville, was easily accessible to any outsider with a grounding in basic music theory. McCoy, at the time, was one of the few with any of that in Nashville, though.

"I had been in an accelerated music theory program in high school in Florida," he says. "At this session in the late 1950s, someone introduced me to the [four-member vocal backup group] Jordanaires. I really didn't know who they were at the time, even though they were some of the few people who played on records that got any credits on the sleeve of the album back then. Anyway, I glanced over at their music stand and asked Neal Matthews of the Jordanaires what the numbers they had scribbled all over the paper meant. He said it was a code they used, but then I recognized it as something I had studied in school."

The "code" is based on the tonic note of the song's key and the numerical relationships between it and other chords. For instance, if a song needs to be moved from the key of C (the tonic or I chord) to D, the IV chord of the new key changes from an F to G and the V chord changes from a G to an A, but their numerical relationship to the tonic remains the same. So all anyone has to do is call out a key and the number charts tell the musicians what chords to play.

McCoy began using it, along with other musicians in Nashville, and he'd share the system with initiates, as would the others. By 1962, it was commonplace in Nashville sessions. But the concept has remained confined to Nashville; after a 1994 recording session in Nashville, Long Island native and singer Billy Joel remarked to *Tennessean* columnist Tom Roland about the system as, "This number thing that looks like algebra to me."

The A-Team was getting recognition outside of Nashville despite the dearth of album credits and the major labels' reluctance to even mention that noncountry records were

being recorded in Nashville. Elvis Presley continued recording in Nashville as he transitioned from country to rockabilly
to pop, and Moore and Edenton played on several of his
recordings there. The most sincere adulation seemed to come
from the artists in rock. McCoy and others of this crew played
on Bob Dylan's *Nashville Skyline* recording in 1968, a record
that opened the floodgates for a stream of other artists to
come to Nashville to record, including the Byrds, Linda
Ronstadt, and Neil Young. "I think Dylan coming here was
one of the single most important things that happened to
Nashville as a recording center," McCoy asserts. "It made it
all right for all the other artists. It removed the stigma that
many of them saw in country music. And they came for a lot
of reasons, but mostly they came for the musicians."

McCoy was instrumental in getting Dylan to Nashville.
McCoy had been hired by New York songwriter Bob Johnston
to record demos for him. Those demos led to Johnston getting
a shot as a producer for Columbia Records. Johnston had a hit
right out of the box with Patti Page on the theme song to the
film *Hush, Hush, Sweet Charlotte.* Columbia gave him several new artists to work with, including Dylan and Simon &
Garfunkel. "Johnston found out real quick that the way to
work with these people was to stay out of their way and let
them do what they did," says McCoy. On a trip to New York in
1965, McCoy called Johnston and the producer suggested that
he stop by a session for Dylan at Columbia studios. Dylan had
one of McCoy's solo records and asked him to sit in on the
date, which consisted of Dylan on guitar and harmonica and
a bass player. McCoy was surprised he wasn't asked to play
harp but instead directed to another acoustic guitar by Dylan.
The track was "Desolation Row" and it was done in two takes.
Bringing these new contemporary pop artists to Nashville
introduced them to the country recording methodology.
McCoy says *Nashville Skyline*'s principal recording took all of
twelve-and-a-half hours at Columbia's Studio A.

The money was good, but it wasn't always enough to keep
you sane. Mack Gayden was one of the most sought-after
session guitarists in Nashville in the 1970s, a slide guitar

player nonpareil. Sitting in a Japanese restaurant on Second Avenue one afternoon in 1994, he remembers the moment he decided to hang it up, unsure of the year but definite about the decision. "I was doing a session for Billy Sherrill, and it was the day that the new Cadillacs came out. The salesman for the dealership came into the studio with the Caddy brochures and Sherrill stopped the session and everyone gathered around to look. That's when I realized that everyone on that session, including every one of the Jordanaires, had a brand new Cadillac and that this was becoming as important as anything else to them. I just snapped." Gayden quit sessions to form a band with other session musicians called Barefoot Jerry, which later splintered off the Nashville group. He has since continued a solo music career.

"I Was Doing About Six Hundred Record Dates A Year"

During the 1960s, growth in sales and multitrack recording induced a demand that exceeded the original A-Team's ability to supply. The next wave of musicians to Nashville studios was vanguarded by players from Muscle Shoals, Alabama, and Memphis, Tennessee, cities that had also developed and maintained their own groups of studio bands, thanks mainly to the fact that blues and R&B acts centered there continued to use session players through the 1960s and 1970s far more often than rock and pop acts, which were becoming increasingly self-contained units that generally called on the occasional session player to augment their own playing. (New York's elite crew of session players was becoming more and more oriented toward broadcast commercial jingle work during this period, and the eventual transition of commercial music to private studios and music houses using electronic instruments has left New York's once-large cast of session players significantly smaller today. In Los Angeles during those decades, that city developed its own session player base. But as it progressed as the capital of rock music, L.A.'s session players were increasingly members of their own bands. The most successful of these elite groupings was Toto, which won seven Grammy Awards in 1983 and one member—bassist David Hungate—would become a major Nashville session player later in the decade.)

Norbert Putnam was part of the Muscle Shoals crew brought to Nashville by future Elvis Presley producer Felton Jarvis in 1965 that included keyboard player David Briggs, drummer Jerry Carrigan, and saxophonist Billy Sherrill. They would become Nashville's second generation of session players. Putnam, a bassist, became a musician simply because, he says, "There was nothing else to do in that town back then. If you didn't play music there was nothing to do. It was such a small town that if you stole a car they'd know who stole it."

Muscle Shoals, a small town tucked in the hill-and-lake country in the northwest corner of Alabama and about a three-hour ride from Nashville, was a momentary blip on the peripatetic journey of R&B music on its way to Detroit and crossing over into pop, leaving behind a small but talented collection of white Southern musicians and writers on whom R&B's voodoo had a lasting effect. The first hit black artist the town produced was the late Arthur Alexander and his recording of "You Better Move On." Alexander was the bellhop at the Muscle Shoals Hotel. The manager of the local movie theater, Tom Stafford, would offer the musicians free passes to the movies in exchange for playing on his demos, recorded in the dilapidated offices above his father's corner drugstore. The musicians played to an old Roberts mono tape recorder with only enough microphones to record half the drum kit and a Heathkit recording console with no volume fader— the fadeouts were accomplished by turning the console off and letting the tubes die out. "We'd hang out with Tom, go to the movies, then go upstairs over the drugstore," says Putnam. "Occasionally he'd go down to fill a codeine cough syrup prescription and share it with us. Arthur Alexander was coming over and bringing songs to Tom. Tom got Arthur together with Rick Hall [a future music producer and publishing magnate who would go on to produce Alexander and other country, pop, and R&B artists], who was the bass player in a band called the Fairlanes. Billy Sherrill [who went on to produce Tammy Wynette and run Columbia Records in Nashville] was the sax player in that band. Rick called up Briggs, Carrigan, and I. We did two songs and got in his car and drove to Nashville and played the tapes for Chet [Atkins] and Owen [Bradley] who said they couldn't do anything with it because it wasn't country. So Rick found Noel Ball, the leading DJ in Nashville. He had a sock hop on a local television channel on Saturday. He was the Dick Clark of Nashville. He also worked for a record company." The 1962 record made the top-ten two months later on Dot Records.

"That launched Muscle Shoals as a recording center," says Putnam. "It wasn't as soulful as Memphis. We were listening to Burt Bachrach and Bobby Blue Bland. We had experience playing black music, but it didn't come out as black as Memphis.

"The profits from that record funded Rick Hall's Fame Studio," Putnam continues. "It also attracted Bill Lowery out of Atlanta with his R&B acts. He brought Joe South, Billy Joe Royal, Ray Stevens, Jerry Reed, and Tommy Roe and his bubble gum hits. It was black music but with a white rhythm section. Felton Jarvis would come down to do Tommy Roe for Bill Lowery. Once we got there, we ended up playing for Fred Foster on sessions for Presley and Roy Orbison."

Through the 1960s, the Muscle Shoals musician club grew, based mainly out of producer Rick Hall's Fame Recording Studios (actually in nearby Florence, Alabama; the name Fame was an acronym for "Florence, Alabama Music Enterprises"), and they played on over 500 hit records of all genres. The core of the musician group—drummer Roger Hawkins, bassist David Hood, guitarist Jimmy Johnson, and keyboardist Barry Beckett—remained after others moved away to Nashville and other cities, setting up their own studio, Muscle Shoals Sound, in Sheffield, Alabama, which became a mecca for many rock and pop acts through the early 1980s that included Paul Simon, Rod Stewart, Cat Stevens, and the Rolling Stones.

The musicians from Muscle Shoals who moved to Nashville started out playing demos for producers Wesley Rose and Jerry Bradley at RCA. "From those demos came all the master sessions. The producers hired us based on those demos," says Putnam. "By 1970 I was doing about six hundred record dates a year." Those sessions included Bobby Goldsboro's "Honey," Tony Joe White's "Polk Salad Annie," JJ Cale's "Crazy Mama," and several Presley hits, as well as the Monument artists Orbison and Boots Randolph.

"Go Home, Flash,"

The intuitive abilities of the original A-Team members to move the groove around without so much as a wink and a nod among themselves during sessions became an offensive weapon that delineated the first generational gap among musicians in Nashville. Drummer Jerry Carrigan sits in his comfortable Nashville apartment, sipping white wine and pulling off a cigarette, recalling his early sessions as a testing ground not only for his musical chops but his breaking point, as well. "We were cutting a song called 'The Bridge Washed Out' [a number-one record on the country chart in 1965] with an artist named Warner Mack in the old Columbia Studio A," he says. "Owen Bradley was producing, so it was for Decca Records. I was the new kid in town on the date, which included Floyd Cramer, Bobby Moore, Ray Edenton, and Grady Martin. Grady and Floyd started moving beats around on me, dropping measures and shifting grooves and driving me nuts. Owen came out of the control room after a couple of takes and I thought he was gonna let me have it. Instead, he turned to the other players and said, 'Gentlemen, I asked this guy to be on the session. He's a friend of mine. If you don't quit fooling around with him I'll ask you all to leave and he and I will finish the session together.' That was the end of that. The record came out and was a smash."

It wasn't quite the end of it, however. Carrigan would walk

into dates and find notes laying on his snare drum conveying sentiments like "Go home, Flash," a reference to the harder-edged musical sensibilities that the Muscle Shoals musicians were bringing to Nashville. "We played differently from the Nashville musicians who were here before us," he remembers. "For instance, shuffles. I play shuffles like the black guys played them; [the Nashville musicians] were playing eighth-note triplets with the middle triplet out, which kind a sounded washed out. One day one of them came over to me and grabbed my brushes, which I had taped up so that only the very tips were showing, which let me pop the drum harder. He pulled the tape off and fanned the brushes out and said, 'Try it *this* way, kid.' It lost all the punch but it made me sound the way they wanted it to. It's when I realized that, if I wanted to keep making a living here, I had better conform a bit." He pauses. "And they were still moving beats around on me when they felt like it."

Carrigan did become one of the crew eventually. His studio log reads as good as any of them, from Eddy Arnold to Faron Young. There was no epiphany, no turning point at which he realized his full acceptance, just a gradual process in which he incrementally modified his style enough to fit in with what Nashville wanted at the moment, while the extra rpm that his generation's R&B and pop background brought became another spice in the Nashville sound.

The introspective epiphanies came closer to the end of his session days, as they did with the original A-Team. After a little over fifteen years of multiple-session days, which only once allowed him to take a seven-month working hiatus, Carrigan began to see his work tail off as the next round of players and musical influences came in to Nashville and to country. Bob Moore's comments about drum sounds have a resonance of their own in Carrigan's mind. "As the sounds of the records got better over the years with new technology coming in, I was pulling down double sessions, coming in in the morning to get drum sounds and then doing the date in the afternoon," says Carrigan. "But in the early eighties, I was getting as many calls for sounds but fewer for the actual sessions. When you get called in just to tune a man's drums, you definitely get the sense that the torch is getting ready to be passed. I mean, I knew in the back of my mind that I wouldn't be playing sessions forever, but in another way I guess I thought that it would never end." Carrigan took a road gig with John Denver in 1981 and stayed out almost continuously for ten years. He's now trying to kick start a career as a producer in a Nashville he knows has changed dramatically. "I know it's the same as starting all over again. But, you know, no one ever really retires from Nashville."

"It Was A Whole 'Nuther Thing To Actually Be A Part Of It"

Carrigan, Briggs, Putnam, and other Muscle Shoals musicians were the first wave of the second generation of Nashville session musicians, and any cultural adjustments necessary to broaden the player base of the town were vented with their arrival. The Muscle Shoals crew had made an edgier pop influence more palatable to Nashville, so the transition for those who came after was smoother. The next round arrived in the early 1970s, some from the decimated recording scene in Memphis, others from the Midwest. They were younger, and rock and R&B music was an integral component of their styles and attitudes. But they had feet planted firmly in both camps—while they had musical styles that incorporated structures beyond the I-IV-V chord patterns of country music, many were Southern-born and country music was part of their youth. They also knew the reputations of and lionized members of the original A-Team.

Reggie Young spent the early part of one morning poring over the operations manual for his Bradshaw guitar rig. The rack-mounted component amplifier was set in an isolation booth at Soundstage Studio, next to a three-way guitar stand holding his 1957 Fender Stratocaster and a pair of vintage Gibson guitars: an ES 335 and a gold-top Les Paul. The Stratocaster and Les Paul are the same guitars that he used to play the smooth double-stop R&B lines on Dobie Gray's 1972 classic "Drift Away."

That was the year Young arrived in Nashville to stay. He picked up the guitar twenty-two years earlier in Oceola, Arkansas, at the age of fourteen. In high school he would rush home in the afternoons, and if meteorological conditions were just right he could pick up WSM's "Two Guitars" broadcast, featuring Chet Atkins, Jerry Byrd, and a guest guitarist. He wouldn't buy a record unless Atkins was on it. While still in high school in Memphis, he joined a local rockabilly band called Eddie & The Stompers and rode the song "Rockin' Daddy" up the charts in 1956, opening shows for the grand-masters of the rockabilly/country axis, Roy Orbison and Johnny Cash, and occasionally sneaking away with the band to Nashville to record.

In the late 1950s, Young joined up with the Bill Black Combo (Black had been Elvis Presley's bass player before Elvis was drafted in 1959), which had a string of instrumental hits including the million-sellers "Smokie (Part 2)," "Josephine," and "White Silver Sands," and which, along with Willie Mitchell and Booker T.'s band, formed the nucleus of one of the three Memphis crews of studio musicians. In Memphis, Young, bassist Tommy Cogbill, drummer Gene Crispin, keyboardist Bobby Inman, and guitarist Chips Moman (a Muscle Shoals session alumnus) were hired as the house band at Royal Recording Studios, also home of High Records. There they played on tracks including Gene Simmons's "Haunted House" and Joe Tex dates produced by Buddy Killen, one of several Nashville producers who were coming regularly to Memphis and Muscle Shoals. Jerry Wexler, president of Atlantic Records, also came down from New York, and eventually brought this rhythm section back to Atlantic's studios in New York to cut tracks at $100 a day, much more than the $50 a week Royal was paying them. Moman eventually opened his own recording studio, American Studios, which became their home in Memphis and was the source of over 500 charted singles, from Dusty Springfield to Neil Diamond.

The Memphis scene didn't last, however, and Moman suggested they move the entire act, studio and all, to Atlanta. "We figured we'd all retire in five years because we'd have the only thing going on in Atlanta," Young remembers. "Unfortunately, we *were* the only thing going on in Atlanta at the time. It was a total blowout and I bailed out."

Young passed through Nashville on his way back to Memphis and stopped in on David Briggs at Norbert Putnam's studio, Quad Recording. Briggs had come to Nashville with some of the Muscle Shoals crew seven years earlier and had become a fixture as an arranger and organist on country and pop sessions. "He asked me if I was interested in playing a session for the Adressi Brothers, a pop act. I said yes and I've been here ever since," says Young.

Young found that Nashville's recording scene had become more open to a range of styles and musical backgrounds. "Drift Away" was one of the first sessions he did, produced by Mentor Williams, followed by six months of pop sessions before he played on his first country record for Charley Pride.

In Memphis, it was common to spend an entire day on a single song, playing it, talking about it, playing it again, deconstructing it, and reconstructing it to fit the Memphis groove model. But this process of making records was completely outside the realm of the country way, and as more musicians crossed the camp lines, they saw the differences in methodology illustrated clearly and without reservation.

"I started doing country dates with guys like Bob Moore and Billy Sanford and Grady Martin and I'd be scared to death," Young recalls. "I thought a song took five hours to do and they did four songs in three hours. And no mistakes." In addition to the pace, the approach to the arrangement was different, too. In Memphis, parts were arrived at by a dialectic of repetition, section by section of the song, but Young would walk into a Nashville country session and be told where to put his fills. "It was a formula, very structured. I'd heard about it and knew that this was how Nashville worked, but it was a whole 'nuther thing to actually be a part of it. I never said a word, though. You just conformed."

But the diversity of Nashville at the time more than made up for its structured approach to record-making. Where Young might do three songs on a three-hour country date with Owen Bradley in the morning, he would likely work on a pop song at Quad all afternoon. And both sessions would sometimes have a mix of Nashville originals and recent transplants—a rhythm section could be Briggs on keys and Young on electric guitar coupled with Ray Edenton on acoustic, Bob Moore on bass, and Kenny Buttrey, who was the leading country/rock drummer in Nashville in the 1970s. "Memphis was all closed groups and cliques, including our group at American Studios," he admits. "No one got in to those groups and they didn't mix up the players. In Nashville, it was always mix-and-match musicians. All the Memphis players I worked with at American were here. I always wondered why they didn't hire us as a section together. I would have thought that would have been an advantage. But they did it their way in Nashville, and it worked."

By the late 1970s, Young was well-established as a Nashville session player, as were many of his colleagues who came to Nashville attracted by the steady work for studio musicians. Among them, Young was at the center of one of the most fundamental changes to the lives of studio musicians in Nashville—the double-scale issue. Union scale, based on the national AFM contract rate, was $137.21 for a three-hour session in 1979. At three sessions a day, five days a week, with the occasional overtime and doubling (playing more than one instrument on the session), that was over $2,000 a week, and very good money for the time in any profession. So it wasn't necessarily for the money alone that Young and drummer Larry Londin began talking about requiring twice that amount from producers per session. They weren't anywhere near ready to hang up sessions, but the amount of work was taking its toll on personal lives. "We figured, if we lost half our work, we'd still make the same money. It was the only way we could think of to slow down and not burn out but still not lose money."

The issue was sensitive enough for Young to test-market

it on two levels. He called several of his regular accounts, including producers Billy Sherrill and Jimmy Bowen. "They didn't all want to go for it at first," he recalls. "Some of them said it was okay as long as it just showed on the card that I was getting regular scale. They didn't want the other players to know. Some suggested that I take a leader spot, which automatically pays double scale. But I didn't want to knock anyone else out of that spot."

That was Young's other concern. In a tightly knit group that had some specific rules about how far an individual could stray from the pack, Young was worried about how he'd be viewed by his peers. "I called Billy Sanford and a few other guitar players. They all said to go for it." Young did. Since then, double scale has become fairly standard for the A-Team players, although it took a while for the practice to circulate. Like the practice of copublishing with older generation publishers, it continued to meet resistance among record producer and budget-watchers at record labels, but the move represented a break with a past tradition that ultimately coincided with the expansion of recording budgets in Nashville in the mid-1980s. Today, triple scale is not uncommon for some of the more in-demand players.

"It's As Much Psychology And Attitude As It Is Music"

One of the people who Young called to discuss the double-scale move was Steve Gibson. Gibson's input was important since he moved easily between the camps of the older, more traditional country musicians and the more recent musical immigrants from Memphis, Muscle Shoals, and—increasingly—Los Angeles. Gibson was one of the youngest regular A-Team members, sliding in with the crew soon after his arrival from Peoria in 1971 at the age of seventeen. His acceptance was abetted by the recording experience he gained working out of a small studio near Chicago, when Quincy Jones, The Buckinghams, Chicago, the Cryin'

Shames, and a number of other rock and pop music acts called Chicago home and briefly made it a major center of mainstream contemporary music.

Another fortunate occurrence was renting an apartment in the same building as budding young songwriter and artist, Dave Loggins. After a year or so of playing demos and jingles in Nashville, Loggins called his nineteen-year-old neighbor to play acoustic and electric guitar on "Please Come To Boston" in 1973. "It was the first hit I played on," says Gibson, who was only recently succeeded as the guitar player with more top-ten record credits than anyone else in Nashville by Mark Casstevens. "That was one thing I learned very quickly: to keep getting work, you had to play on hit records. Your name got around faster and people also figured, if that one was a hit with him on it, then maybe this one . . . The formula that had worked in Nashville for so long of just picking the right song was getting more complex—now you had to pick the right musicians, too."

Gibson moved regularly back and forth between country and pop dates. His first country date was the same year; Larry Butler was producing Carl Perkins at Johnny Cash's House Of Cash studio. He was paired on acoustic guitar with Bobby Thompson. "They all accepted me pretty much at face value, despite the fact that I was a Yankee," Gibson laughs. "You really weren't judged on who you were or where you were from as much as whether or not you could get your part right and not screw up in the process. The studio was a pressure cooker from day one and you learn that it's as much psychology and attitude as it is music."

Gibson learned the rules of the A-Team and kept his playing style fluid, fitting in on a broad range of session types. "I was the chameleon in terms of playing style," he says, citing musical influences that ranged from Chet Atkins and Grady Martin to Eric Clapton and Curtis Mayfield. "I had a style, but I knew what these guys played and I thought I knew what they wanted to hear. I learned it from records and from going three times a year to see the Grand Ole Opry with my family as a teenager. I idolized Hank Garland."

Playing on a country record one day and a pop record the next gave Gibson a perspective on Nashville that helps him context the music industry there today. "I'd play a country date with Harold Bradley and Ray Edenton one day and pop date with Briggs and Norbert Putnam the next. You could see who was staying in which camp. But you could also see the town was changing. People forget that Grand Funk Railroad came down here to do one of their records. People were moving in from Los Angeles, at least until *Urban Cowboy* caused the town to implode and the record people in L.A. didn't want to hear anything that came out of Nashville, country or pop."

Now, the same thing is going on in Nashville. The next generation of musicians is arriving, and Gibson is trying to be tolerant of them. "The A-Team was tolerant of me when I first got here and didn't know anything," he says. "I'm trying to be the same of younger musicians who I work with in the studio now. They think of double scale as normal, and I guess the way I look at it is the difference between being awarded something and earning it. But they'll have other pressures to face. You might not see twenty-five-year careers for studio musicians anymore here. These new guys are going to have something more like sports careers: the money's good but you'll never know how long it's going to last."

There was enough work for the expanded A-Teams throughout the 1960s, as more labels and producers came to Nashville, but the generational gap began to make itself felt— much of it centered around the changing technology of record-making. The music industry overall was transitioning from the two- and three-track recorders of the 1950s and 1960s to multitrack systems. Some players started their own studios, such as Putnam and David Briggs, who opened Quadraphonic in 1970 and became a platform for Putnam's production career.

There is a noticeable sense of resentment about the transition of generations. Charlie McCoy bemoaned the effect that overdubbing, a by-product of multitrack recording, had on the interplay between musicians. "It got so that I had no idea who was on the record I was playing on," he says. "I was just in a room playing with a track that had been done before I got there. That's why I kept playing as much live as I could with things like *Hee Haw*; I just want to play with other people, like we always did. Now, people spend a lot more time on the sound than on what they're going to play."

The generation gap is apparent in Bob Moore's comment that, "You've got to be ignorant to spend two or three hours getting a drum sound." Today, it's not unusual to spend a half-day getting drums sounds on pop records, and while country records still don't always avail themselves of that luxury, a couple hours on drum sounds alone isn't unusual.

The older generation firmly believes they can make competitive country today using the same techniques as in 1960—sitting around in a studio, facing one another, no headphones, just intuitive and visual cues, and three takes maximum before they get it perfectly. "You can go back and make those records over again now," says Ray Edenton. "We could do it if the producers just let us play. But you can't give them any ideas today. They just want you to sit and be a robot in the studio now. There's no real creativity."

Moore, the feistiest of the group, showed another side when he observes, "It went apart the same way it came together. Toward the end maybe I was getting too tired and maybe a little too rich. [Moore augmented his session pay by having several hit records as an artist himself in the 1970s.] It's like being a boxer; you gotta be hungry for it. Once a boxer gets rich, he gets knocked off. It got to where there was people I was working with I just didn't enjoy working with. I didn't realize it at the time. I was just getting cranky. I got to be where I wanted a song to be over with. I walked out on a George Jones session once toward the end. That's unheard of. It used to be that I couldn't wait to get to work."

But after due deference to the observations of the elders of the city's musician culture—to a much larger degree than anywhere else—the records *are* still made the same way they were when Moore and the rest had their day. Despite the changes in technology, the fundamentals of recording studio design are still predicated on one primary tenet in Nashville—that the recording room will be full of musicians all playing together and that they be able to see one another in the process. Many parts of records will be overdubbed and the musicians doing those overdubs will work in the isolation that McCoy finds so distasteful, and more country records will be made in people's homes as the technology of music becomes more affordable and accessible, but if there is one striking thing that a visiting musician to Nashville notices, it is that studios full of ensemble musicians who have clear sightlines to one another is the norm. Even in the newest studios built in Nashville, the ability to visually communicate is considered paramount, and is the first thing that a Nashville producer or musician vets in a new studio the first time they enter it. On a more technical note, the cue systems in Nashville studios—the closed-loop circuits that allow each musician to make custom mixes of the recording in their headphones while playing—are the most advanced in the world, and many are developed at the studios themselves and marketed to the professional audio industry. There are no holds barred when it comes to making musicians comfortable in a Nashville studio, and in this last bastion of live, ensemble recording, the musicians of Nashville wouldn't have it any other way.

It was around the core of the studios in Nashville that the story of its musicians is wound. The recording industry in Nashville as it stands today, with several hundred conventional studios operating full-time and several hundred home-based and other private recording facilities, is traceable back to The Castle, a one-room, three-man studio set up in the dining room of the Tulane Hotel on Eighth Avenue South and Church Street just after World War II. The Castle was put together by three WSM radio engineers—Aaron Shelton, George Reynolds, and Carl Jenkins—in 1946, and took its name from one of WSM's self-devised slogans, "Castle Of The Air." The studio closed eight years later in 1954 when WSM, seeing a number of their personnel developing potentially conflicting business interests in the music industry while they were still on the payroll—for instance,

Jim Denny started Cedarwood Music while still working for the station—declared that employees had to choose between their ambitions or a regular paycheck. Denny left WSM for the entrepreneurial pastures of music publishing; the founders of The Castle went back to broadcasting, although they were also compelled by the fact that the Tulane Hotel's building was about to be demolished.

In its brief time, though, The Castle was the leading studio in Nashville; during much of that period, it was virtually the only dedicated, professional studio in the city. According to Aaron Shelton, "We produced the majority of hits out of Nashville until the studio closed." Those included "Your Cheatin' Heart" and another session with Hank Williams that produced three Top-Twenty singles. The former dining hall was divided into three sections: a recording room, a control room, and a small area for the Scully acetate lathes for the lacquer discs—there were no tape machines, initially—to which the music was directly cut. As was common at the time, the three engineers designed and built their own recording console, the main device through which electronic signals are routed. Special audio effects such as reverb or tape delay were also hand-constructed. The Castle's console was advanced for its day, with eight inputs for microphones, twice as many as consoles of the time. Shelton would divide the inputs up according to the configuration of the artist and his band; larger combos would get several microphones placed around the room with one dedicated to the vocalist and any featured instruments. Smaller country acts would get more individual attention, with separate microphones for the guitarist and other featured players, another for the rhythm section of drums and bass (on the rare occasions when there were drums), and microphones for the lead vocalist and background singers. These microphone inputs would be mixed through the console to the acetate lathes or later to the large, squat Ampex 2000 mono tape recorder running at fifteen inches per second. If the sessions got too big, The Castle's engineers would book out the Grand Ole Opry's Ryman Auditorium three blocks away and rent time on telephone company lines to bring the signals back into the studio for mixing.

The Castle was not a union studio, as were the record label-owned studios of Decca, RCA, Columbia, and Capitol, of the day, but it tried to stay within the union guidelines. The guidelines called for no more than three or four songs in three hours, during which musicians, who were more often than not members of the artist's road band and not freelance session players (a reversal of the current model in which members of artists' touring bands rarely supplant studio musicians on country records) tried their best to give the A&R men—the fledgling producers of the time—what they wanted. The sessions were mostly at night; with country music still a nascent commercial enterprise many of the musicians and artists had to have day jobs. The A&R man for each label would have picked the songs, called the musicians, and booked the session a few days in advance. The studio charged $90 for the three-hour sessions, which included engineers, acetates, and tape.

The country music record-making process was remarkably professional from the beginning, considering that the engineers, musicians, artists, and producers were making many of the technical and artistic techniques up as they went along in the recording process. There were bumps in this process, though. Red Foley and his A&R supervisor/producer from Decca Records Paul Cohen spent the time it would normally have taken to do half an album—eight hours—on one song, "Television," a parody of the then-new medium, because Cohen was convinced it would be a hit. The song barely charted. Folk singer Burl Ives used the studio at a time when folk and country genres were reported together in *Billboard*. He would start out his recording dates with a presession dinner and drinks at the 216 Dinner Club downstairs from the studio, then pick up a bottle of Jack Daniel's for the session, consuming most of it during the session. "Sometimes he made it through the session, sometimes he didn't," recalls Shelton. "He'd get high and start dancing around the studio and knocking over music stands and microphones and we'd be picking them up behind him. If he was too far gone to sing, we'd cut the tracks with the band and then bring him in the next day as an overdub." Another session was interrupted when a hotel guest forgot to turn off his bathtub faucet in a room above the studio and The Castle's grand piano was turned into a freestanding pool.

The seat-of-the-pants approach to recording at The Castle laid some of the technical foundation for what would become the Nashville sound. Invited to watch an Eddy Arnold session in Chicago, Shelton observes that the union engineers there were timid by comparison. "They were doing mostly classical recordings there and they would severely limit the volume because they were scared of cutting into and destroying the sidewall [that made up the groove] of the record they were cutting to," he says. "As a result, those records never had the dynamic range of a country record."

Recording in Nashville for the next decade took place mostly at label-owned studios such as those of RCA and Decca. But by the early 1970s Nashville's studio base had grown substantially beyond those, mainly as a result of the proliferation of independent studios that were started and owned by publishing companies and independent producers. RCA Records was still operating two rooms, Studios A and B, as was Columbia, which still had one studio in the old Quonset hut. But along the way they had been joined by Memphis native Jack Clement's Recording Studio, Monument Records's studio, Woodland Studios, Norbert Putnam's Quad Recording, and Music City Sound, owned by Scotty Moore, Elvis Presley's guitarist. The area around Nashville was also seeing satellite studios popping up during this period, such as Cinderella Sound, started by guitar player Wayne Moss in Madison, Tennessee, and Doc's Place, a small studio in Hendersonville owned by dentist Dr. William Burkes, who played accordion on The Red Foley Hour of the Grand Ole Opry and went by the sobriquet Little Billy Burkes. "It was a pretty good studio and you didn't mind going there to record," comments Lee Hazen, one of Nashville's first freelance engineers, "But as a dentist he'd talk your head off about music and you couldn't say anything 'cause he had his fingers in your mouth."

The label-owned studios were rigid in their structure: engineers were mainly former radio engineers and had to be members of the International Brotherhood of Electrical Workers (IBEW), and most artists signed to Columbia or RCA had little choice as to where their records were made. But by the early and mid-1970s, the proliferation of independent studios was accelerated as more ready-made major production equipment, such as multitrack tape recorders and dedicated music consoles (earlier ones were based on broadcast consoles), became available, eliminating the need that many early engineers encountered to be soldering and schematic geniuses and thus broadening access to the profession. This development also helped artists get into studio ownership, like Porter Waggoner's Fireside Studio and the Glaser Brothers' studio. The equipment also became less expensive as new models were rapidly and regularly replacing older ones, creating an affordable used equipment market that lowered the studio entry threshold even further. And the studios became smaller, as technologies such as digital reverb "black boxes" appeared that eliminated the need for larger rooms to add ambiance to recorded sounds. The concept of "close-field monitoring," replacing the large, soffited monitors that required wider front walls in studio control rooms, became the preferred approach to mixing records, cutting down on the space needed to accurately listen while mixing records. These changes both allowed the new studios to occupy the one- and two-story residences along the Row, and contributed considerably to the very "dead," anechoic sound that characterized country records in the 1970s.

Less costly because of competition from their growing numbers, and more innovative than their corporately owned counterparts, this wave of new independent studios eventually pushed the larger label-owned ones aside. RCA closed Studio B in 1977, and it is now operated by the Country Music Foundation as a museum. RCA Studio A was sold and is now the site of privately owned Javelina Recording. Engineers, once mainly IBEW members and salaried staff members at studios, became and remain to this day—mostly independent contractors at the studios of Nashville. In fact, even assistant engineers, which almost all commercial recording studios have as staff employees, often freelance in Nashville, working as independent contractors for the freelance engineers.

Studio owners from the time say they never really worried about losing market share to Los Angeles studios during the *Urban Cowboy* era that saw country and country-esque records increasingly recorded on the West Coast. Aside from the fact that the musicians were centered in Nashville, "You could always tell a country record that was recorded in California," says Lee Hazen. "It just never sounded quite right."

The 1980s saw the rise of a second and third generation of engineer-owned studios, such as Glenn Meadows' Masterfonics, artist-owned studios such as Ronnie Milsap's Groundstar Labs and Roy Clark's Sound Emporium, and perhaps most significantly, the increase in the number of studios owned by producers, particularly those with label connections. While independent producers bought existing studios (Allen Reynolds, who produces Garth Brooks, bought Jack's Tracks; Brent Maher bought Creative Workshop; Garth Fundis purchased Sound Emporium, previously purchased by Roy Clark and Larry Butler), other producers, such as James Stroud built his own facility, Loud Recording, with producer Richard Landis. They started their own studios not only to ensure that time would be available when they needed it, but also as a way to maximize participation in the revenue flow of Nashville, a business concept that Owen Bradley had understood and put into practice thirty years earlier.

The independent studios of Nashville face a new array of issues, despite country's recent successes. While more new artists were being signed and bookings remained high as the country sales boom continued into 1995, the seasonal cycle of bookings became more intense as summer tours stayed out further into the fall, pushing artists into more compressed time slots to make their records. In a city already overcapacitized in terms of studios, the slack times were compounded by the fact that the rates they charge clients haven't significantly changed in nearly two decades. "It tops out at about a hundred dollars an hour, about what we got twenty years ago," groans Bob Solomon, once an assistant engineer at Woodland Studios and now the owner of Woodland Digital. "The trouble is, there's lots more equipment you have to have to be competitive and it's gotten more expensive. It costs ten times as much to outfit a studio competitively now." Two new recording facilities that opened in Nashville in 1995 and 1996—Masterfonics's The Tracking Room and Ocean Way/Nashville (an extension of two Los Angeles-based studios)— had project costs of $3.5 million and $5 million, respectively. Daylong rates, the most common rate structure for album-length projects, run anywhere from as little as $500 a day up to published rates of $2,500 for one of the four or five top-level rooms. But studio owners concede that they rarely get published rates on a consistent basis, and that the relationships with producers so necessary to business are nonetheless contingent on producers getting the price they want.

Pressure is also coming on studios from a new source. Since the early 1980s, a new level of technology, referred to in the professional audio trade as project studio recording, has eaten into the demos market, the traditional grout that filled the spaces between bookings for major studios and that remains the lifeblood of many midsize and smaller studios. The project or personal recording studios is enabled and empowered by scaled-down recording technology that offers full-scale capabilities at a fraction of the price and allows songwriters and producers to make demos and records in their own homes. Digital versions of reverbs and other signal processors cost as little as $200; digital multitrack recorders can be stacked in modules up to a 128 tracks for as low as $250 dollars per track. Sophisticated recording consoles can now be purchased for well under $10,000. The very ubiquitousness of this new generation of technology forces conventional recording studios to differentiate their capabilities in the crowded market by purchasing ever more expensive equipment. New top-of-the-line recording consoles, such as the British-made SSL 9000J, cost nearly $750,000; large-format digital multitrack tape recorders cost around $200,000. To these costs must be added the price of acquiring, developing, and maintaining the space of a conventional recording studio— the ambient recording rooms that are another critical difference between personal and conventional studios—and which in Nashville are all the more crucial to accommodate country's penchant for using live, ensemble musicians on records.

While professional recording studios all over the United States have felt the impact of project studio economics, it has the potential to hit Nashville even harder than in other cities. Annual surveys of Nashville recording facilities by the publication *Music Row* have found that revenues from demos have consistently slipped over the last several years and threaten to drop below 50 percent of total revenues, a significant occurrence in a town where hundreds of song demos a day get done.

Changes in technology and their markets have Nashville studios aroused and concerned, as do the fortunes of country music, to which, despite irregular visitations by pop artists such as Bon Jovi and Billy Joel, their futures are inextricably tied. And if these changes sometimes seem to take place too quickly or on too large a scale to address, there was at least one instance in recent times that seemed to bring them all together and at the same time throw into stark relief some of the other changes in Nashville.

In late December 1994, Reba McEntire's Starstruck Entertainment company applied to the Nashville zoning commission for permission to add a heliport to the large studio and office complex the company is building on Music Row. McEntire owns a charter jet leasing company, Starstruck Jet, so the move made sense from that perspective. However, it incensed owners and operators of studios along the Row who knew immediately that the term "soundproof" associated with studio construction would not withstand the sound pressure levels or low frequency waves generated by helicopter liftoffs and landings. On the evening of January 4, 1995, about thirty studio owners, engineers, and managers gathered in one of the rooms at Georgetown Masters, a mastering studio directly across Seventeenth Avenue South from the then-steel girdered framework of Starstruck's edifice that had been under construction for about a year. The next morning the zoning commission was scheduled to hear arguments, and the studio owners, engineers, and managers were listening to Russ Berger, the Dallas-based studio design consultant the group had retained, explain the impact of helicopter operations on acoustically oriented businesses.

"If anyone has any doubts about it, let me say now that the impact would be significant," said Berger, who had worked on over twenty Nashville studios and had, after reviewing the case, decided to do his work for the studios pro bono. "The noise will destroy session work. I don't think [Starstruck] really understands the magnitude of this."

Todd Culross, the chief engineer at Music Mill Studios, said, "Our studio is in a log cabin type of structure. It's completely ludicrous to propose such a thing. You know this business: sometimes you only get one chance to get a great take. The noise will drive smaller studios out of business."

But it was Owen Bradley, the grand old man of the business, and who with Chet Atkins owns substantial interest in properties along the Row, who realized the other significant thing about the gathering. "I've never seen anything like this happen before," he says, his eyes sparkling. "It's the first time you've had so many Nashville studio owners in one room and not yelling at each other."

The heliport was redesigned into a roof garden.

"Chicken Fights With A Dollar Bill Attached"

"I can sense a generation gap between musicians here. I sensed that from the very beginning." Glenn Worf, a member of Nashville's third musical generation, has a bona fide seat on the A-Team. There was no epiphany that identified or illuminated the moment; rather, it was a cumulative thing, a look at a session log book and a feeling of ease at recording sessions that he gradually acclimated to. The sense also of a generation gap transitioned, from being an outsider to becoming part of the limbic organism that is the corps of Nashville A-Team musicians.

Worf played bass in countless local rock and country bar bands in his native Madison, Wisconsin. An offer of more of the same from a bar band in Los Angeles almost drew him there, but he thought he'd try Nashville first. In 1977 he came to town with, as he put it, "No money, no contacts, and I could have lived without the former if I'd have had the latter." With a wife and two kids to look after, he took the first road out of town that paid anything worth making.

He came back to Nashville to stay in 1982 after five years of touring. That started almost eight years of demo and independent record sessions that form the apprenticeship foundations for a seat on the A-Team. "A lot of them were nothing but chicken fights with a dollar bill attached to them," he recalls. Nineteen-eighty-two was a year of contraction for country in the wake of *Urban Cowboy*. There were fewer sessions to go around and much of the original A-Team, such as bassist Bob Moore, were still first call for major recording sessions. Worf saw Moore at record dates at Pete Drake's studio on Music Row, where Drake, a pedal steel player and independent producer, had let Worf hang out. "Pete was the kind of guy who liked to have an audience around, but by letting me watch I learned the rules: I kept my mouth shut and listened," Worf remembers. That's when the generational divide made itself apparent to him. "I realized after a while that, no matter how good I was, I wasn't going to get their work," he states. "The older musicians had long-standing relationships with the producers. The producers and musicians were of the same generation and they had been to war together and built the town, and no way were they going to hire a kid off a milk truck. It wasn't a matter of breaking into a clique; it was a matter of human relationships."

So Worf played the demos and independent record dates, sometimes not knowing what the pay was until after the session was over, sometimes not even till a check showed up in the mail a few weeks later, and then only after a few phone reminders on his part. The generation gap offered him some hope, though, when Worf realized that all things come to an end, an end he thought he might have had a glimpse of before his predecessors had. "You could sense the burnout in the studio. The older guys thought there'd never come a day when it would end. You could see how the effort of some of them was diminishing, how well they kept up their instruments or if they even bothered to tune up. They were dropping hints with their attitude and some of them didn't realize how many guys like me there were waiting in the wings."

There was also a defensiveness among some of the older musicians that Worf sensed. Moore seemed distant, understandably so when it became clear that Worf was a bass player and an ambitious one. On the occasional sessions where Worf worked with older A-Team musicians, he said he could sense from just a look in their eyes that he was occupying a chair that had someone else's name invisibly but indelibly carved on it.

Worf's career turning point came in 1987—after a decade in Nashville—when Radney Foster and Bill Lloyd called the same players for their forthcoming record that they used on the demos, including Worf, Bruce Bouton on pedal steel, and Tommy Wells on drums. The Foster & Lloyd record proved to be Worf's own breakthrough; Foster & Lloyd's eponymously titled debut album, released in the spring of 1987, was a pivotal record in country's transformation of Nashville back again toward pop and rock influences, and it was a talisman of a generational change the music industry in Nashville was undergoing as younger producers and songwriters came into their own. It also gave Worf one of the critical credentials for A-Team membership: a credit on a number-one country record, "Crazy Over You" from that album. "I got the sense that it wasn't just my luck that had changed; the music had changed, too."

This didn't knock the walls down completely, though, Worf recalls. It wasn't until 1991 that he felt as though he had truly arrived. Records with Foster & Lloyd, several early Pam Tillis recordings, and records with country-rocker Kevin Welch—all people he had done demos with before their record deals were signed—and sessions for younger producers such as Paul Worley and Josh Leo, both of whom went on to label positions, put Worf's session career on a faster track in a way it would for much of his generation and in a manner it hadn't for generations previous. The demos were becoming more and more the templates for the records, and producers wanted to match the increasingly sophisticated sounds of the demos. And an entirely new generation of artists used to working with bands and musicians empathetic to their own musical backgrounds were having more input on who played on their records.

Worf's growing confidence allowed him to bring his fretless bass on more sessions. This gave him a sound—the aggressive growl that is implicit in the electric fretless bass—which wasn't common to Nashville records before then. "Ray Baker, who had produced Charley Pride at one point and some early Reba records, heard me play it on a demo and he thought it was a synthesizer. He called me and said 'Come do whatever you did on that demo' on this record he was doing. Before that, you couldn't give fretless bass sounds away in this town. Even some engineers didn't know how to record it. It shows you that as the music was changing, the musicians were having to rely on sounds as much as talent more than they ever did before. The original A-Team were amazing musicians, but their frame of reference was big band and swing stuff that they brought into the country sound. Our frame of reference now is drums, drums, drums."

Worf still feels a connection to those who came before him, not of a reverential museumlike quality but of a more sincere kind. In his own midforties, he understands their defensiveness and sense of immortality. He's also getting the same sort of upward pressure from these new arrivals waiting in the wings, although it's of a somewhat different nature now. "I couldn't just call Bob Moore back when I first got to town," he says. "I mean, why would he want to give it away to some kid on the telephone? I couldn't call him and ask how he tuned his bass or what strings he used or how he miked his amplifier any more than if I was a car company and called Ford up and asked how they made their new cars. Now I'm getting calls from people who want to find a place as a musician in Nashville, and I see what it's like from the other side. Some of the calls come from really great musicians from Los Angeles who want to come here. Other calls are more off the wall. They're from people who see your name on the back of an album cover and call information for your number. I got a call from a male nurse somewhere in the Midwest who said he was also a bass player and I had to tell him he had a better chance of being John Elway this time next year than of being on the A-Team. A friend of mine got a call from a brain surgeon who wanted to know what his prospects [as a musician] were. If people can't get me for a session, they can call David Hungate or Willie Weeks or Michael Rhodes. It took years to get this chair, and that's what it takes, and that's if you've got some talent to start with. Maybe studio musicians here still do look down a bit on road musicians, but I tell you, getting here is a whole kind of road itself. A long road."

"No More Red-Eyes"

Paul Leim didn't take a bus to Nashville; few people do anymore—the Greyhound station on Eighth Avenue North has considerably less traffic than it did in previous generations. Leim flew in from L.A. Or more precisely, he was flown in. Like a growing number of other musicians on Nashville's A-Team, Leim is part of the Los Angeles-Nashville connection that began in the 1980s and became a well-traversed highway during the following decade as Los Angeles pop producers such as Jimmy Bowen and Jim Ed Norman became forces in the country music industry, bringing their L.A. musicians with them.

Leim came from Tyler, Texas. After paying studio dues in Dallas doing commercials and playing sideman gigs with Johnny Carson's musical director Doc Severinson—who made his records at the now-defunct Dallasonic Studios—Leim moved to Los Angeles in 1977 and stayed there for eleven years, working on a mixture of pop records with the Commodores, film and television scores, and the tame pop-country records that L.A. was making at that point, including Kenny Rogers's and Tanya Tucker's. "Being from Texas, everyone just assumed I could play country," he laughs.

The Los Angeles connection brought Leim into contact with Jimmy Bowen and Jim Ed Norman, who called Leim to Nashville for sessions. From 1980 through 1987, Leim estimated he was coming to Nashville an average of one weekend per month for sessions. Tired of commuting and discovering a reappreciation for the South of his youth, he told his wife after an Amy Grant session in 1987 to take the rest of the weekend and look for a house.

Leim and other L.A. musicians and producers brought some sonic sensibilities to country music that weren't there before, part of what producer Josh Leo calls "Snare Wars." "Fifteen years ago, a typical Nashville snare sound was a real dull, dry, thud-sounding snare," Leim explains, making sounds using the percussive onomatopoeia of drummers. "It's all basically rock snares now. I'm triggering snare samples now that I used on the *Dirty Dancing* soundtrack."

Leim says, however, not everyone is gung-ho on the change. "Everyone wonders what radio wants. Radio is demanding multiple mixes now; sometimes they want the steel guitar on, sometimes they want it off. Radio is the ghost at every session, keeping people guessing. It actually has an impact on the way musicians play in Nashville. It's talked about mainly in the record company offices by the A&R people and the marketing guys, but its effects are felt right down to the studio level. Radio affects the very way in which records are made."

Despite his Los Angeles rock and film music background, Leim acknowledges a connection to an earlier version of the A-Team. "I felt connected to them even though I didn't know their names," he says. "It wasn't just the Nashville players, though, I still remember when I was ten years old and listening to the cross stick sound on 'By The Time I Get To Phoenix.' That was [Los Angeles session drummer] Hal Blaine and I thought it was the most beautiful sound. What you're hearing now when you listen to country is a fusion of new L.A. and old Nashville—how L.A. players play and how the old guys in Nashville taught everyone what and when *not* to play. And that's what Nashville is doing and what it's always done: bringing out on record what the feeling of the moment is. But in doing that, there's a tremendous amount of history behind every snare hit or guitar lick. When you listen to Nashville musicians play on a country record, you're listening to years and years of musical developments."

"The Triple-A League Of Music"

It's a Saturday afternoon, not a day that master record sessions are usually scheduled. In the demo mills of Nashville, however, business tends to break only for church on Sunday mornings and a drink late at night. In a city where the song is the main currency, the printing presses never stop.

County Q is Nashville's most prodigious demo factory. Housed in a gray building on a stout bluff in the Berry Hill neighborhood, a seven-foot "Q" dominates the parking lot on the sign out in front of the studio. Inside, past a small reception area and a spacious living room that serves as the lounge, the recording area is laid out like an interconnected puzzle maze: the control room is the central focus, surrounded by a number of isolation booths for drums, piano, and guitars, all windowed and facing the weathered Amek Series 70 recording console, upon which are perched precariously two sets of speakers, a DAT deck, and a rack of signal processing gear. Unlike the standard Nashville recording approach of having the musicians in the same room and with easy sightlines to one another, County Q makes them satellites and disembodied voices conferencing over the intercom system about the arrangements they put together in between takes, like hurried football huddles before the snap.

The football analogy is applicable: both the game and the sessions are restricted severely by the clock. County Q sessions run the requisite three hours, during which the musicians, led by Scot Merry and Paul Scholten—the studio owners and the bass and drum battery, respectively—shoot for up to five songs. County Q and studios like it that dot Nashville's alleys and basements are the homes for the B-Team—the Triple-A league of music.

Publishers pay an average of $300 per song for demos, inclusive of musicians, vocalists, studio time, tape, and other musical miscellany. Merry and Scholten of County Q have developed a system for this process by which they hire the musicians and vocalists (if necessary; the economics of the system encourages writers to do their own singing) and bill the writers' publishers for all the services on a single invoice. Merry seems to be the session leader today, but as he observes later, "Whoever is paying the bills on that session is the producer."

Saturday's session is for a writer named Bob Van Dyke, and by four P.M. it's not looking good for the full five songs even as the musicians pick up the pace. The last note of song number three of the day, "Heart Of Dixie," is the tonic, but bassist Merry lands instead on the relative minor and silently mouths an expletive. After the requisite ribbing from the other players over the talkback system, he punches in the correct note on an overdub even as the players gather around Van Dyke to flesh out the arrangement of the fourth song. At the same time, the engineer is doing some simple but critical math to see if the next song will fit on what remains of the reel of multitrack tape, which can hold up to sixteen minutes running at thirty inches per second. "It's gonna have to be pretty radio-friendly not to fit on this," he mutters, his way of saying that he's got three-and-a-half minutes of tape left, just about the length that country radio likes for records. At $125 for a reel of Quantegy/Ampex 456, details like tape costs make a difference in the profitability of sessions. Sometime, to save money, the studio will rent the tape to clients, erasing it after each session and then renting it again to the next. Thousands of songs pass through County Q and other studios that rely upon demos for business. And even Nashville's voracious appetite for them isn't enough to consume a single-digit percentage of what gets written and produced on the demo level. There is an acknowledgment of that in Scholten's dead-pan quip to Van Dyke in between takes: "You know, there's an implied money-back guarantee if you don't get a cut . . ."

The next track is ready. Merry kicks it off with the battle cry of the demo world, saying to the engineer as he nods toward the waiting amber LEDs of the twenty-four-track recorder, "Light 'em, press 'em, print 'em."

Other musicians wander in and out of County Q while the session is in progress. The informal atmosphere is the closest thing to an agora for musicians that Nashville has to offer; there are few true musicians' bars or hangouts in a town where many musicians have already started families, in itself an act of optimism that is rarely seen in New York or Los Angeles.

Kerry Marx has a scruffy beard and round glasses setting off an angular face. He is a guitarist out of Aiken, South Carolina, and spent from 1981 till 1992 on the road with country acts, including Johnny Cash, Ray Price, and Jerry Reed, as a touring musician. To him, a seat on the A-Team represents security. "You can't be on the road and on the A-Team," he says, reciting a long-held rule among Nashville's musician corps. "People want to know that you'll be here when they call you." He broke into the demo scene gradually, in between road trips, and he expects to do the same for master sessions over the next three or four years. But demo economics, while sometimes iffy, are not bad; while musicians usually make about $150 per three-hour session, many sessions pay the union-mandated $87.94 per hour, although some producers pay by the song—usually $50—and sometimes you find out what the rate is when you show up at the studio, or like Glenn Worf used to—when the check comes in the mail. But while many A.F. of M. locals have established optional demo scales for their territories nationally, the rate of compliance with them is nowhere near what's found in the intense Nashville studio environment.

Once the rent is paid, money becomes a secondary issue in the minor leagues. Everyone here is shooting for a loftier status, and the money automatically will come with that. The pressures are personal and mostly self-inflicted at this level. "There are a lot of frustrations, but most of them are with myself," Marx said. "You always want to walk out of a session feeling like you knocked them out, but it's rare you feel like that. It's one thing to know how *you* feel you played, but you always want to know how the producer and the writer and the other musicians felt about it. And they don't always tell you." Acoustic guitar player Michael Spriggs adds, "You're always set on 'stun' at a session."

The tapes from demo sessions become calling cards for these musicians. You don't sit down and audition for Tony Brown or James Stroud in person the way a song plugger gets to play tapes for them. But the demos function as the basic arrangement of the song, and the part you play here may draw an interested ear when the master session rolls around.

J.T. Corenflass, another guitarist, grew up playing country music in Terre Haute and has been playing demos for several years. "At the demo level, you're truly making everything up as you go along. Even if you're using a stock lick, you have to decide where and when to throw it in. We're creating the arrangements here and in many cases even fixing the song. On the master sessions, they're often following what we do here." Corenflass played on the demo for a Dave Gibson/Kathy Louvin song, "Queen Of Memphis," which became a hit for Confederate Railroad in 1993. There is a signature guitar lick that he came up with on the demo that is also part of the record. One difference is that he played it on his Telecaster and on the record Brent Rowan played it on a six-string bass. Another difference is that they each got paid somewhat disparate sums for their efforts—Corenflass $50 and the double-scaled Rowan probably ten times that. Corenflass experienced the feeling of intense ambiguity that every demo player feels when this happens. "I felt good that they liked the lick enough to keep it and make it a prominent part of the record. But at the same time, I have to say to myself, 'If they liked it that much, why wasn't I the one playing it on the record?'"

Marx has had similar experiences. On another song that eventually wound up on both Mark Chesnutt and Chad Mullins records, Marx came up with a guitar line that the publisher said he wasn't crazy about. "Then I listen to the records and I hear the exact line, just that it's played by a steel instead of a guitar," he says. "It doesn't bother me. What it does is reassures me about my song sense and session sense."

The level of awareness regarding the critical significance that the demo plays in country music was illustrated by singer Shania Twain's comment to the *Journal of Country Music*[2] in which she says, "If 'Blue Suede Shoes' had a bad demo, I bet a lot of people in Nashville wouldn't [record] it.

There is a level of urgency to demo sessions, as with all recording sessions, that becomes palpable as soon as the red lights illuminate, showing that the "record" function has engaged. But there is no detectable sense of desperation— that emotion is offset by the economic realities that are ever at hand in this strata of Nashville's music business. The writer wants the best demo possible but has to watch the clock, knowing that demo costs are charged against the writer's account and that they, along with a year or two's worth of advances against royalties, will carve up a substantial portion of revenues from a cut, especially if the song is a cowrite with one or more other composers. The musicians know they need to perform, not only for the writer but for any producers in whose hands will place this tape, and finally, for themselves.

The players seem to take some solace from a structure that, while still dependent heavily upon luck and fortuitous coincidence, moves with a glacial speed and certainty as generations change. Their time will come as a group; within that,

---

2. Vol. 18:3

it's every man for himself. You watch out for the newcomers and place silent bets on which ones will become successful producers and label heads and repeat hit songwriters. Alliances, conscious and unconscious, are formed. Personal problems are left for the evenings at home, one of the luxuries that session work allows. Sounds are worked on, as they have become as much a part of the players' arsenals as chops. The rules are learned, the same ones that were learned forty years ago. Show up on time, have your act together, listen. But there is a twist today. As Scott Merry puts it, "This is where we acquire the skill to be cool at ten A.M."

In a very real sense, musicians are the same everywhere, at every level. They speak common languages—esthetic, academic, and technical. A guitar player from Kansas City and one from Moscow will have little difficulty in communicating if there is a Fender Stratocaster between them. But the goals of musicians are much more focused in Nashville, centered around securing a chair on the first string of session players to the exclusion of all else. So long as there is not a hidden agenda—that they want to be songwriters, for instance—they do not come here to go on the road or play demos for the rest of their life. There may be some who will make more or less permanent forays into the producer's chair, but most of them remain true to the calling that brought them to Nashville—to play. And unlike other musicians' fraternities, membership comes with what is regarded as a lifetime pass. You are one of them forever. Or until someone else gets your seat.

Marketing: Radio and Video

There's a lot of country music. Big thing now where it used to be a small thing, you know.
—MERLE HAGGARD[1]

THE EIGHT-BY-TEN GLOSSIES that traditionally lay inside the pocket of the press kits that record companies hand out to introduce new artists are perhaps the most mundane of the growing and increasingly expensive slew of materials and techniques Nashville has embraced to deliver and differentiate its new artists to the public. The need to be photogenic is rapidly being supplanted by the requirement that the subject be telegenic. In fact, the printed press kit itself is appearing endangered. The EPK, or electronic press kit, has become *de rigueur* for new artists—a traditional printed information package accompanied by a six- to ten-minute videocassette combining clips from an initial music video release and interviews with the artist, audio excerpts of which are also put in CD form and sent to radio stations. Such interviews used to be done either in the local radio station or in the hotel room or tour bus, but it's a big country and it's hard to be in more than one place at a time.

Still, the combination of talent and a marketable look isn't enough in contemporary country music, where country has to both define itself from rock and pop even as it continues to incorporate more of those influences, and has to redefine itself

---

1. Interview, *Journal of Country Music*, Vol. 16:1

within its own context. In the last ten years several discernible strains of country have emerged, from the "hat acts" such as George Strait and Clay Walker that remain the core of country, to the quasi-rock bands such as Confederate Railroad and Little Texas, to the stylized retro of artists Junior Brown, the Mavericks, and BR5-49, to the Gen X females Mila Mason and Mindy McCready who appeal to a teenage audience.

There is the country music that continues to require a distinct and conservative personality of its artists. This can range from standard-issue good ol' boy patter to almost obsequious homilies to God, country, and country music, all of which remain part of the lexicon. At the same time, social issues such as AIDS and disaster relief have become part of the content between country performers and their fans as country music integrates itself further into the fabric of contemporary entertainment.

But the ear of the producer is different from the eye of the marketers, who seek to create images that may or may not match the music but will be acceptable to radio, and to manufacturers of a broad range of goods with which they can create mutually profitable linkages. "I've always felt that you improve the quality of a new artist if you can make a quality corporate association," said Steve Miller, Polydor Records vice president and general manager, in an interview in *Music Row* in January 1995. He went on to document the rationale for linking then seventeen year-old country singer Amy Comeaux with JC Penney's "Arizona" junior line of clothes: "She's been doing fashion shows, singing songs, and doing autograph sessions . . . right in the middle of malls," he explained.

It is the marketers who are as much responsible for country music's recent success as any other component of the industry. More so, some will tell you, but in strengthening the ties between music and commercial mechanisms, they have become the target of the myriad accusations regarding the homogenization that has accompanied country's success. In attempting to broaden the appeal of country music and increase the genre's sales base, they have weakened the underpinnings that have kept country music such a relatively pristine form of music over the last forty or so years. That point of view is neatly summed up in an essay by Ed Morris, *Billboard*'s former country music editor in Nashville, in the *Journal of Country Music* in 1990, at the beginning of country music's five-year ascendance in market share. "Although it is the stylists whom we remember and who end up in the Hall of Fame, real stylists are risky for labels to deal with," he wrote. "They arrive at the door with no market research in tow, and their very distinctiveness makes it impossible to transform them into something they're not. . . . The labels aren't without courage, but as marketing experts eclipse the power of A&R people . . . brave experiments are sure to decline."

"I Never Would Have Left"

Joe Galante left Nashville in 1990 to take over as the head of RCA Records's U.S. operations in a lofty New York office. For four years he ran BMG Records from this office, the German-owned parent company of RCA Records and its affiliates, Arista and BNA. It was a long time from 1982 when he was the head of RCA Records's Nashville division. Tony Brown, who runs MCA/Nashville and who worked for Galante at RCA at that time, had once asked Galante, by proxy, if he were ever coming back. Galante smiles at the question and answers quickly, "If everything that's happening in Nashville had happened eighteen months earlier, I never would have left."

In January 1995, Galante did return to the city and the music. They and Galante had embraced each other warily at first, and this second time around caused just as much circumspection. His pop music marketing ideas were regarded with some suspicion when he first began to make his influence felt in the late 1970s after working his way through an abbreviated apprenticeship in a Nashville that was worlds apart from the record business he started at in New York. It was a fortuitous time to be in Nashville—while country music was seduced and abandoned by its interlude with *Urban Cowboy*, the mainstream music world was rocked far harder by a decline in record sales in 1979, a market drop that took the record industry several years to recover from (they dropped again in 1982). One result was the reining in of rock record recording budgets, which had grown increasingly excessive as the 1970s progressed, with top acts such as the Bee Gees and Eric Clapton booking entire studio complexes for months at a time just to write songs for their next records. But while recording budgets for Los Angeles-made country records had climbed toward the six figure ones of rock, Nashville's average budget remained around $30,000.

By the time he left in 1990, Galante, a New Yorker with a degree in finance and marketing from Fordham University, had become the marketing guru of the Nashville music industry. His impact on marketing was similar to that which Jimmy Bowen had on production; both brought more cosmopolitan philosophies to country music, and both encountered initial resistance and reluctance before their approaches became part of country's modus operandi.

On a warm January day in 1995, Galante sits in a corner office facing the rising sun and a Nashville skyline that has changed considerably in the four years he's been gone. Once again he is overseeing RCA's country group of labels. The fortunes of both RCA's pop and country divisions had been buffeted by changes in both fields, and there was speculation that this was less the lateral business move and lifestyle choice Galante claims it was than essentially a demotion. (The scorecard for Galante's tenure in New York was mixed—he signed an aging, past-prime ZZ Top to a multimillion-dollar, multialbum deal with disappointing results, but also helped the label sign and successfully promote new acts like the Dave Matthews Band.)

Still, considering country's growth and RCA's failure to capitalize on it, and in light of what Galante had been able to do with the label's country division in the 1980s, the move begins to make sense for all concerned. At a time when several country labels had recently expanded and added parallel imprints to handle larger rosters, Galante's first move was to reconfigure the operations of RCA and its three-year-old sister label, BNA, compressing many of their management, publicity, marketing, and A&R functions into a core group under an the umbrella of a newly created BMG Records Group. (Arista Records, distributed by BMG and one of Nashville's most successful labels and headed very autonomously by producer/songwriter Tim DuBois, was conspicuously excluded from this arrangement.) Thom Schuyler, Galante's handpicked successor four years earlier, remained on the reorganized label group team as senior vice president in charge of A&R. The two labels had a total of nineteen artists between them, and the compression made more than a few of them nervous, particularly after Galante announced that roster cuts would be made. After reinventing Nashville's conceptualization of what it took to bring a recording artist to success a decade earlier, Galante's return seemed intended to shake the town up once again, and he was starting with his own backyard.

Galante started work in the finance department of RCA in New York in 1973, moving from there into record promotion, being assigned to some of the label's slow-selling acts at the time, including Lou Reed and David Bowie. He fully expected to move up the ladder of RCA's corporate structure, so it came as an unpleasant surprise when then-company president Mel Ilberman (who later moved on to become executive vice president of Sony Music's U.S. operations) told him in 1974 he was being assigned to RCA's Nashville operation, which was regarded as a posting to Siberia for a New York recording industry executive.

In 1973, Chet Atkins was running RCA Records in Nashville, with Jerry Bradley as head of operations. RCA had a large roster at the time, close to fifty acts, but many of them were past their prime; Galante remembers two of the label's best-sellers were catalog artists and not even on the label anymore: Jim Reeves, who had died in a 1964 plane crash, and Charlie Rich, who had already moved on to Columbia Records. The biggest current star on RCA's roster then was

Charlie Pride, whose sales were already slipping and with whom Galante felt little connection, musically or personally. (Pride left RCA in 1985, partly because, according to an article in *Billboard*, the label was spending more time and effort developing new acts and not enough time, in his estimation, on established ones such as himself.)

"There was no marketing at that time in Nashville," says Allen Butler, who used to work in sales at RCA in Nashville in the late 1970s. "Radio was your sales mechanism. And to a degree it's still that way today; a lot of labels don't have dedicated marketing staffs. Instead they call it sales and marketing. Of course, in those days you had artists with ten number-one records and they sold a hundred thousand units. Galante brought in a sense of marketing. He was very much a leader in that."

The first few months of Galante's Nashville stint were less than spectacular, he remembers. "I didn't feel like an outsider; I was told I was one," he says. "I was asked if I was a spy [for the New York office], I was asked what was I doing here. I had no history, no family, no real place there."

He also found no affinity with that generation's musical sensibilities. That began to change a year later when Galante met Waylon Jennings at his studio on Music Row near the RCA building on Seventeenth Avenue. Later that same year, 1974, on a trip back to New York, he met Dolly Parton as she whistle-stopped on the Long Island Railroad, doing promotional appearances to promote a show opening for Bobby Bare and Charlie Pride at the Felt Forum in Manhattan. The third artist that turned Galante's thinking about country was Ronnie Milsap, whom he met at a record convention. "I began to like what I was hearing," he recalls. "It was country with an edge, with an attitude."

By 1977, Galante and Bradley had forged a relatively smooth partnership, with Bradley handling more productions and Galante formulating what was to become a new marketing strategy for country. (And in the process establishing a precedent for the more common two-executive approach to label management seen today, in which a producer is paired with a business executive—a more apt model with Nashville's larger rosters and more complex economic and marketing environment. With the exception of producer Josh Leo's stint as head of A&R at RCA in the early 1990s, the label has been unique among Nashville record companies in that it has not had a country record producer at its helm since Chet Atkins left.) Up to that point, the standard sequence of events was to release a single several weeks in advance of the album, ride the first single as long as possible, then release a second, if there was one, then begin looking at the next album, the balance of which was generally regarded as "filler" material; i.e., not singles. Singles were the key ingredient in a context in which airplay, not sales, was the main source of revenue. It wasn't unusual for artists to make more than one album recording per year. In an age of limited visual exposure for country artists, only those who survived several rounds of this cycle developed lasting identities with audiences, and almost exclusively via radio.

"The A&R process was hit and miss," Galante felt. "Nashville didn't market records; they promoted them. There's a difference." He says he began to try to change that by looking to establish identities from the moment of signing. "I wanted to be able to sit down with *People* magazine and explain [the artist] in a paragraph. That's how people were beginning to look at culture. Once we had an image in mind, we could have a campaign in mind."

The first artist to be marketed in this modern sense at RCA was Ronnie Milsap. Working in concert with Milsap's producer and publisher, Tom Collins, Galante and Bradley rethought every aspect, from choosing different photographers to developing the album and other related graphics and artwork outside of RCA's own art department. "Things like positioning him at the American Music Awards, positioning him outside of what would have been his usual base of country," states Galante. The effort paid off with a first platinum album for Milsap, 1977's *It Was Almost Like A Song*. Collins, the record's producer, put it succinctly when he said, "It made [the label] commit to pop-level [promotional and marketing] money."

Nashville noticed, but was not so much taken with the marketing process as with one of its by-products— the crossover. His more aggressive marketing approach continued, however, and was slowly implemented at other labels as the process was repeated with similar success with the group Alabama and with the Judds, other new signings under Galante's regime. Marketing became more refined with each application. Galante implemented focus group market research techniques using radio station audiences in various markets, perhaps half a dozen a year, he estimates, assessing that information to determine how many singles the country music audience wanted before they would buy an album— what they were looking for in an act, what publications they read, and what television programming they watched, which in the age before widespread music video programming was difficult to correlate and appraise.

"We imaged the [artist] in terms of a logo," he says, becoming as animated about marketing concepts as a producer might about a song. "All the advertising had a special style to it. The Judds—that one was the first that we really worked the media hard for. They had a real story to tell—a mother and a daughter who had been through adversity. You swore she had been through life fifteen times. It was like putting the Ivory Snow commercial on the cover. We took the fabric of what they were and wove it into the media." Since then, other Nashville-based labels have embraced market research as a definitive tool for determining what to release and when. Rick Blackburn, head of Atlantic Records's Nashville office, said in an interview[2] that the company, whose artist roster is heavily weighted toward a younger demographic with acts like Confederate Railroad and John Michael Montgomery, now test-markets all recordings prior to release, and has remixed records based on input from such research. He adds, "When I sign artists, I tell them there are two rules: one, we make a great record; two, we have a love affair with radio."[3]

2. Music Row, July 8, 1993
3. Ibid.

The definition of what was useful media to country music was also changing in this process. "You can get an act on a hundred and twenty radio stations, but in the same amount of time you could do [*The Tonight Show*] and accomplish the same thing overnight," says Galante. "It was all a matter of reaching people. Rock was about groove and fashion; country was about people. How do you reach people? Through the media."

Galante and Bradley ran the label together until 1982, when Bradley left his position but remained a consultant for two years before signing on with Opryland Music Group, where he still works. The process that Galante started eventually gave RCA 30 percent of the country charts for a period in the mid-1980s, a share that has slipped considerably since then. RCA was listed as eighth in *Billboard*'s late-1996 country label evaluation, fifth as a marketing entity (based on the number of singles and albums a label charts in the course of a year), and it was conspicuously absent from most of the other lists in that assessment.[4]

The change in marketing country music coincided with a change in country music itself. Galante had perceived a different sort of music emerging in the songs and attitude of Waylon Jennings and others, that in turn was paving the way for another generation of musicians and artists that would transform country and bring it closer to the world of pop music sounds. The change cuts both ways, however. "As pop and rock music gets stronger, country will have a tougher time," Galante observes. "Three years ago, pop was in the doldrums. It was black and rap—middle America had nothing. Now they have some alternatives.[5] At the same time, to country's benefit is the fact that, while it was never widely regarded as a sexy format, in the last five years it's become

4. *Billboard*, October 5, 1996
5. A year after this interview was conducted, Galante's words were buttressed by the release of the Record Industry Association of America's market share analysis for 1994, which showed rock gaining nearly 5 percent to reach a 35.1 percent market share for the year. Country, on the other hand, fell 2.4 points to 16.3 percent for 1994.

one. *Urban Cowboy* didn't give country a sexy star, it gave it a movement in terms of a dance. Now we have guys who get on stage and the crowd yells for them to turn around so they can see their buns. That's never happened before."

Combined RCA, BNA, and Arista country sales accounted for nearly 30 percent of BMG's recording revenues in 1993, a number Galante estimated was down slightly from the year before because of pop's stronger showing in 1993. But by redefining marketing concepts for country music and providing country records with a more current set of rules better adapted to changes in how entertainment as a product is sold, Nashville regional record divisions were able to stand more independently from their coastal headquarters. RCA Nashville's consistency in terms of producing revenues through the lean years of the mid-1980s (much of which was, admittedly, based on sales of RCA's long and deep catalog) combined with the overall rise in country music's fortunes in the early 1990s to contribute significantly to a change in the relationship between country and the corporation. The paternalistic relationship that had been the norm for years was being broken down. "Nashville started declaring independence around 1980," Galante says. "They had really cut themselves off from New York and Los Angeles in the business sense by 1984. And Nashville has never really had to look back."

Joe Galante has a unique perspective on that relationship, as well. Now that he's back in Nashville, he looks over the city from the point of view of being the first record executive to head a country label after having already run that label's pop division. So there are a number of intersecting perspectives lacing together in his mind as he speaks. He acknowledges that RCA had been behind the curve during the initial period of country's recent growth period. "We missed the wave, no doubt about it," he says evenly. In an industry niche that fought long and hard to resist direction from the pop-oriented main offices in New York and Los Angeles, Galante concedes that for a time he became one of those distant directors, but bristles at the suggestion that RCA's fortunes in country were related to his New York-based decisions. "You can't look at me and go, 'Okay he pulled all the strings therefore he missed the curve . . .'" he says. "The marketplace had changed dramatically."

RCA had signed many successful cutting-edge and traditional acts during Galante's first tenure, including Foster & Lloyd, David Ball, Vince Gill, Restless Heart, and K.T. Oslin. But his departure left a leadership void at RCA, and the larger world of pop music distracted him and lessened his input into Nashville over the four years of his absence.

Galante has changed as much as Nashville has and the singular successes he once pointed to with pride in garnering mainstream media attention for country acts are now everyday occurrences. He's looking at more than twice the number of labels since 1990 in Nashville and is realizing that radio is in a better position than it ever was to determine which records will be hits. But he is still first and foremost a marketing person, and that is what he most wants to talk about.

"The difference [now] is that this audience has become mainstream," he says, echoing Jimmy Bowen's assessment of several years earlier. "These people are buying our records but are listening to everything . . . Kenny Rogers and Dolly Parton: that was pop; this is more organic. [Back then], we had to be on pop radio in order to get those numbers. Today you don't have to be on pop radio because people watch the videos or see them on the awards shows or read about them. We could never touch those things [consistently] before the nineties. Those things were major coups before and now they're expected. I don't think it's going to be that easy anymore. I think this is kind of like strip mining right now."

"'Country' Was A Dirty Word . . ."

Joe Mansfield, who was named CEO and copresident (with Kyle Lehning) of Asylum Records in Nashville in 1996, was not at RCA for Galante's first Nashville term. He wound up there, though, after over a dozen years in the Columbia Records organization, starting out as a regional promotion man in Texas, eventually moving up to head the label's national marketing efforts from New York before leaving in 1981 for RCA. He stayed at Columbia long enough to see the *Urban Cowboy* trend come and go. It gave him a perspective that was not commonly seen in Nashville; what remains a devastating watershed to country music's relationship with the mainstream entertainment sphere was to Mansfield in New York, ". . . just another phenomenon in a series of phenomena. That's the way it was looked upon. It was a motion picture soundtrack, so it was off to the side. Columbia always had a ton of soundtracks. You bought all the soundtracks so that nobody else could have them, and if one of them stuck . . ."

Mansfield came of age at a time when the field armies of record marketing were rack jobbers—a largely independent sales force apart from the labels whose record they worked, servicing smaller stores that didn't have the buying clout with record products that large chains did, including grocery stores, convenience stores, and anyplace where you could put a rack and a few records into it and hope for the impulse purchase. They were viewed by labels as a de facto marketing extension, but the rack jobbers themselves were interested in the same thing as the labels—selling hits. So they would "cherry-pick," as it is referred to, giving emphasis to records or artists that had already proven themselves.

His time at RCA Records gave Mansfield some A&R experience, before a power shift at the label caused him to leave in 1983. He returned to RCA in Los Angeles in 1985 and then moved to Capitol Records there in 1989 as vice president of sales and distribution. As Jimmy Bowen was assembling his team to shift from MCA to Capitol/Nashville, Mansfield joined it as vice president of marketing, making the move to Nashville in March 1990.

That was just as the initial launch of Garth Brooks was underway, a career that's taken marketing to new and different strata in Nashville. Mansfield was given a $1 million marketing budget for Capitol/Nashville's 1990 fiscal year, which began in April. Bowen's arrangement with Capitol's Los Angeles office called for any profits generated by the Nashville operation to be kept in Nashville, to be reinvested in marketing and artist development.

Mansfield acknowledged picking up the effort on Brooks initiated by Lynn Shults, who headed Capitol's A&R department in Nashville from 1979 to 1989 and who was named vice president of media relations at Atlantic Records in Nashville in late 1994, with a long stint as a columnist and editor at *Billboard* in Nashville in between. It was Shults who brought Brooks to Capitol after hearing him perform at the Bluebird Cafe in 1988. Capitol/Nashville's marketing plan was based around breaking Brooks out of Texas via the label's branch in Dallas. "We had to blow it out of Texas," says Shults. "The Dallas branch sold forty percent of [our] country artists at that time, though most people didn't realize it. That was the whole game plan: to get those people to have a stake in Garth Brooks. He was his own best salesman." Then Capitol/Nashville president Jim Fogelsong, whom Bowen would succeed, approved a $300,000 budget to cover shortfalls on the initial promotional tour for Brooks, a substantial sum at the time for such a purpose, underscoring what Shults considered a plan that was "radical for a new artist at that time." Shults was let go from Capitol in 1989 when Jimmy Bowen took over as head of the label, just as Brooks's career was beginning. Shults used the words "angry" and "bitter," directed toward Bowen, to describe his feelings about the ouster and its timing. He says he believes that he speaks for the Capitol team that was fired in the Bowen transition when he says, "I still feel we were robbed of one of the greatest moments in one's career. It's that thing they call fate."

Brooks's debut album was released later that year, spawning the single "Much Too Young," which made top-ten on the *Billboard* country chart. But it was the second single, "If Tomorrow Never Comes," that was his career launcher. "I came in in March 1990, and looked over the sales figures for the label," Mansfield recalls. "It was two pages, and the biggest-selling thing was Garth Brooks at two hundred thousand [units]. The philosophy in this town, the benchmark, was that if you did a hundred thousand units, it was great."

Brooks's success—and what distinguished him from virtually all other freshman recording artists in country music, lay in his willingness to go out and do the field work normally reserved for promotion personnel; he hit radio stations, rack jobbers, and retail stores with a personality they reacted well to. That kind of activist artist was not uncommon in earlier days in country music, when touring artists were expected to be proactive in terms of seeking out regional radio stations and spending time with D.J.s But Brooks's willingness—and his innately gregarious personality—was fortuitously timed to combine with the entry into the business of a new generation of marketing people who were willing to break the conventional rules of country music marketing in order to maximize Brooks's own efforts. "I met him in Atlanta at a branch meeting," says Mansfield. "He played three songs and went to dinner with the branch guys. He was charismatic. Most country artists . . . just get up in front of a microphone; Garth did in-store [appearances], signed autographs; he was willing to do anything that was suggested, and his management came up with a lot of ideas."

Garth Brooks went gold shortly thereafter, and his second album, *No Fences*, was being readied for release. Mansfield found resistance among retailers, who were also becoming more market-savvy, for a second record that soon. "The Dance" had become a hit via heavy rotation on CMT and was one of four successful singles off the first record—twice as many as anyone could have counted on a conventional country music record. Retailers had found a country artist that could sell pop numbers and they were reveling in it, so they didn't want an artist with that kind of potential competing with himself for sales. *No Fences* was released August 27, 1990, with "Friends In Low Places" the first of four number-one country singles from that record. *Garth Brooks* was still selling strongly. "Everybody said you're gonna kill that [first] record if you come out with a new record," says Mansfield. "That was traditional Nashville talking. That was two singles and let's get the next album out kind of thinking. This was one of those moments when Nashville changes, something that doesn't happen very often. I said, no way—I told Bowen we could sell a million records and he thought I was full of shit. But I knew that when *No Fences* came out, it would sell *four* million." By 1996, the record had attained sales of thirteen million units.

Everyone, including Jimmy Bowen, was skeptical of speculating on numbers in those ranges. "No one knew that he would do the kind of numbers he did," Bowen observed in another interview. Mike Martinovich, former vice president of marketing at Sony Records, observes, "It certainly put a lot of pressure on other record companies. I think the one thing that the Garth thing taught us all was that it can be done if everything is employed simultaneously. All the resources have to be going together. What it taught us is that marketing country records has to be done on a level that was way beyond where it had ever been before. It has to be done in a concerted, Madison Avenue sort of way, with a strategy and with tactics as part of that. The thing about Garth and the effect he had on marketing in country music is that, before he came, no one ever thought it could be done—to have a country artist sell those kinds of numbers and still be country. I mean, once Kenny Rogers had the big pop hits, you stopped thinking of him as country anymore. But that's not the case with Garth. So once you prove it can be done, then the pressure is on to do it—again and again. To find the artists that you think you can do it with. That's a lot of pressure to put something like country music under. It doesn't respond like pop music does. As good as Garth has been for country music, he opened a Pandora's box when it came to marketing."

While elements of the Brooks campaign are translatable across the board to marketing new country artists, the Garth Brooks experience also showed that the strength of personality, a willingness on the part of the artist to get involved in marketing, and the sheer limits of time and place, were the X factors that would affect how successful a campaign could be. The other factor was a general changing of the demographic that was buying country and, perhaps more importantly, the ones potentially ready to buy it. "Garth had sold out Billy Bob's in Texas and I went down to see him," Martinovich recalls. "'Friends In Low Places' was peaking and I wanted to see what the hell this was all about. What I saw was a lot of young people who were, by virtue of their age, heavy record buyers. The same people buying Guns 'N' Roses. You'd ask them if they liked country music and they'd say, 'Oh, I hate that shit.' You asked them if they liked Garth Brooks and they'd tell you, 'Oh yeah, I like him.' They like Rodney Crowell, too, and other artists like that. But 'country' was a dirty word . . ."

Martinovich, Mansfield, and others were watching a shift in age demographics and buying patterns that was working in country's favor. The percentage of record buyers in the thirty to forty-five and up age range had increased steadily over the years 1989 to 1993, and they bought 47.3 percent of the music sold in the United States in 1993, up from 35 percent five years earlier, according to Record Industry Association of America (RIAA) statistics. The over-forty-five market share increased in 1993 2.3 percent over the previous year for the third consecutive year. Meanwhile, the lower-age music buyer base—ages ten through twenty-nine—had declined from 64.5 percent in 1989 to 51.9 percent in 1993. And the critical music-buying demographic—ages fifteen through twenty-four—had shown the largest decline, from 42.6 percent in 1989 to 31.1 percent in 1993.

(Only recently has this trend varied, with a surge in younger country demographics unearthed by records from younger artists such as Mindy McCready and Lee Ann Rimes that has surprised the labels themselves and had most of them scrambling to launch their own teen-oriented artists. RCA Records own market research in 1996 states that the teenage market has grown from 2.5 percent of total country sales to ten percent of the market. But with country radio's demographics based squarely on the thirty- to fifty-year-old groups—and country radio advertisers' preference for that group's economic clout—tracking the teen market in country is proving to be a less-than-precise science, even in the era of SoundScan.)

The success of Garth Brooks intensified the process by which labels attempted to position records. "There's only going to be one number-one record a week," says Mansfield. "So you've got to stage all those records below it. The labels have to sit down and plan how these songs are going to get through the hole. A record at number one is not [initially] going to sell any more than a song that only went to number two. What number one is, it's a gift to the artist."

Martinovich concurs, adding, "What [having a number-one record] does for you is, there are certain media doors that open for you . . . If [Faith Hill] had spent four weeks at number two [instead of number one], would she have been on [Late Night With David] Letterman? That's going to help you sell more records, but at the time it was being programmed on the radio, no, it didn't mean more records. Everything is positioning and perception, because that translates into record sales."

The larger media outlets have become both more attractive to and more receptive to country music in recent years, but there remains the sense that that love affair could be as temporary as it was in the early 1980s. Country's core audience remains a touchstone that anyone who has worked Nashville for any length of time understands. Their incomes may have gone up some, but the core still lives and works in such places as Shreveport and Corpus Christi and Texarkana, not Boston and New York. So when Anderson Merchandisers, a rack jobber based in Amarillo, Texas, bought rack jobber Western Merchandising in 1993, Anderson sought to apply to the 1,400 Wal-Mart stores they service a marketing approach that had proven successful with unknown authors—essentially promoting new books with an author's tour of the stores. Mansfield and Martinovich were retained in 1994 to do on a large scale what country artist Marty Brown had done on a series of four smaller ones from 1991 through 1994—one for each of his MCA Records releases: tour scores of Wal-Mart stores to promote new records that were being left out of radio. In Marty Brown's case the idea for the first Wal-Mart tour developed out of discussions that Walt Wilson, then senior vice president of marketing at MCA Records had with students at a marketing class he was teaching at Nashville's Belmont University. "The students and I had been kicking around ideas for marketing an artist like Marty, who we had just signed and who is very, very traditional country," Wilson recalls. "And marketing a very traditional country artist in Nashville, ironically enough, was not an easy thing right then. I just brought him in as a topic for the marketing class to discuss." Via that discourse, Wilson made a connection between his own personal background and Brown's intensely rural appeal. "I come from a very small town in Pennsylvania— Meyersville—about two thousand people live there. I started remembering that when even small acts would pass through that town, they seemed big. It seemed like no one ever came to Meyersville, so when anyone did, it was a big event. And the Wal-Marts of America have kind of replaced the town meeting halls in towns like that. That was the connection."

Wilson approached one of the rack jobbers for Wal-Mart, the Handleman Co., based in Troy, Michigan, and proposed the idea of Marty Brown touring Wal-Mart stores in selected markets. The criteria were that the stores be located in cities with less than 25,000 people and that, for routing purposes, they be approximately 100 miles apart. Wilson also got TNN involved in covering the tour, which was essentially a form of promoting it. The initial responses were exactly what Wilson had hoped for; turnouts at the stores on the first tour in 1991 were good and some records were sold. Enough to continue the concept for three more Wal-Mart tours—the second cosponsored by Colgate-Palmolive and the next two with Rubbermaid as sponsor—and to keep the concept going and growing. Which it has done. In 1995 the concept was adapted to bring new artists, whose burgeoning numbers were making it difficult for them to get exposure on radio, to potential buyers. In 1996 alone, over 100,000 people saw free concerts at 260 Wal-Mart stores nationally.

But the success of the concept was not enough to keep Marty Brown on MCA, which dropped him in 1994 due to weak sales. "Marty has become a kind of icon within the Wal-Mart system," says Wilson, who was helping Brown in a fifth Wal-Mart tour since it can generate catalog sales for MCA of Brown's records. "And I have the feeling that this has laid the groundwork for Marty because a lot of people know him now. What I think is that he could go the telemarketing route, right to the people with an eight-hundred number, like Slim Whitman."

Mansfield's proposal to adapt the concept to new artists was different from the original concept that MCA had with Marty Brown only in scale: a 200-day tour involving fifty artists that commenced in Nashville on March 27, 1995, in which several, primarily new artists—the first tours included Boy Howdy, Wade Hayes, Lisa Brokop, David Lee Murphy, and Russ Taff—would each play seven Wal-Mart parking lots in seven days for free, and have their expenses underwritten by their respective record companies. For three weeks before their arrival, each Wal-Mart store on a particular artist's itinerary would have been serviced with the records of that artist and it would have been playing them regularly as part of an in-store promotion. Special CD racks, known as "end caps," holding the featured performer's records would be strategically positioned around the store.

The Wal-Mart experiment was the first major marketing tactic that proved repeatedly viable for country music in the era of proliferation of record labels and artist rosters. Far simpler than betting on new technologies such as the Internet and offering better cost-effectiveness than direct marketing on an artist-by-artist basis, it is the equivalent of rack jobbing but with the logistical apparatus of a small army—a Dick Clark Caravan from the 1950s but with luxury buses and frequent-flyer miles. Every major label in Nashville was participating to some degree, motivated by the Sisyphean scenario of large rosters pouring into the narrow funnel of radio. And it is, characteristically of such ventures in Nashville, described by Mansfield as a "win-win situation. Anderson has fourteen hundred Wal-Mart accounts and their competitor, Handleman, has nine hundred. They're trying to get more stores from each other and this is Anderson's way of saying, 'Hey, look what we're doing to increase your business.' And

Anderson has committed to buy twenty thousand units on each of the artists. You can have a marketing campaign on a new artist and never even ship that many records. Multiply twenty thousand units by the wholesale price [$8.50 to $9.00 combined CD and cassette average] and all of a sudden you've got a revenue base that you can apply to individual marketing efforts. No one loses."

It is a given, percentage-wise, that not all of those fifty new artists are going to have significant success. But that's not the point. Marketing anything, from soap to country music artists, is a game of percentages. SoundScan's[6] arrival, contemporaneous with Brooks's ascendancy up the charts, served as a catalyst to the marketing thinkers at record labels, giving them a wider latitude of action. By confirming country record sales with hard statistics, rather than subjective, in-store estimates, it changed the marketing emphasis from spending half the time lobbying stores and chains to report a certain record at number one in sales to physically positioning those records in the stores, with labels jockeying for end caps for country artists. Brooks' success and the four million units sold by Randy Travis up to that point, had shown the potential to applying pop marketing tactics to country records.

It also raised marketing budgets at labels. Those budgets are determined by labels as a percentage of sales and anticipated sales; thus, increased sales resulted in increased marketing budgets, which were looked at separately by the labels from recording and video budgets. (Both of those are charged back to the artists' accounts, and with recording budgets hovering around $120,000 per record and videos around the $60,000 mark, plus artist advances of anywhere from $20,000 to $50,000, an individual record needs to sell at

---

6. SoundScan, Inc., founded by two radio and marketing specialists in 1991, uses computerized point-of-purchase UPC bar code scanning to collect unit and dollar sales data on recordings. SoundScan's technology replaced the more subjective methods used by *Billboard* and other trade magazines to track record sales used to compose charts. The effect of this data on the perception of country music was immediate and substantial. The May 18, 1991, *Billboard* Top Albums chart had no country artists on it; *the following week's chart, dated May 25, after SoundScan had taken effect, had Garth Brooks sitting in the number three position.* Jimmy Bowen, then president of Liberty Records, told the *Los Angeles Times,* "The real statistics . . . have completely overhauled America's perception of what a pop hit is."

least 80,000 units to break even.) Though the specifics vary from label to label, the general formula for annual marketing budgets is figured by estimating the number of unit sales for a year, multiplying that by the wholesale price, deducting overhead costs and then multiplying that figure by a percentage of the overall operating budget for the year.

How this might affect country music's future is manifest in personnel shifts. The acceleration of marketing efforts has brought people with marketing backgrounds—as opposed to production ones—further along the executive road in Nashville. A prime example is the elevation of Walt Wilson, from senior vice president of marketing at MCA Records to a cochief executive position at Capitol, and the ascendancy of Mansfield to the same position at Asylum. It is also telling that in both cases, as with RCA, people with successful marketing track records—as opposed to production successes— are making the fastest inroads in the executive suites at the labels whose recent performances have been the most anemic of the major labels in Nashville. As mentioned, RCA's performance by the end of the third quarter, 1996 had it ranked tenth of the top-ten country labels in *Billboard*'s cumulative assessment (although it is listed in the number-three position in *Billboard*'s ranking of record distribution market share, thanks largely to RCA's still-considerable country catalog holdings[7]); Asylum Records is nowhere to be seen in those rankings; and when Garth Brooks's sales are removed from the equation, Capitol Nashville also disappears.

RADIO

We've entered the age of consultants.

—TONY BROWN[8]

There were eighty-one radio stations playing country music in the United States and Canada in 1961. By 1975, that

7. *Billboard*, October 19, 1996
8. *BMI* magazine, Fall 1993

figure had increased to over 1,000. By 1995, there were 2,613 stations with full-time country programming, according to the Country Music Association, which was founded in 1958 largely to foster exactly that kind of growth. It was the CMA that sent its representatives around the country in the early 1960s, looking for stations struggling in their markets and selling them on the economic virtues of country as a format. Like most other publishers, Acuff-Rose had a roving promotion man named Mel Foree who in the 1950s made long drives throughout the Southeast and central states touting records with Acuff-Rose songs. In the words of a contemporary, "Every time he saw a radio tower he'd go visit the station."

The CMA's crowning glory as far as radio is concerned came in 1973, when it convinced WHN in New York City to change to a country format. New York had been the elusive square in the checkerboard of country broadcast coverage, and despite its snubbing of country over the years remained a prize for the country music establishment because of its status as the main media center in the U.S. New York has had a country station almost continuously since then, although the most recent, WYNY, changed format away from country in February 1996, when its new ownership, Evergreen Corporation, changed the format to rock. The last country song New Yorkers heard before the station switched formats was Garth Brooks's "The Dance."

More recently, though, country radio's growth has shown signs of abatement. According to industry trade journal *Radio & Records*, country's share of the radio market had slipped steadily, from a 10.3 share for the summer 1995 ratings period, to a 9.2 share a year later. The number of stations programming country music full-time had dropped to 2,525 during the same period. The Billboard/Arbitron quarterly national format ratings, which track shares of the U.S. radio listening audience by station format among the ninety-six continuously measured markets (some markets have multiple stations in the same format) in the survey group, country had gone from a 10.8 percent share to a 10.6 share in the first six months of 1996. That same chart had country radio seeing a recent high of 13.3 percent in the third quarter of 1992; *R&R* had pegged country's high as a 16.6 share in the same period. While country music had more stations than any other radio format—nearly twice as many as fourth-ranked Adult/ Contemporary's 1,572—country radio lagged behind the leading News/Talk format with its 14.3 share, and Urban music with its 10.3 share, according to *R&R*. Larger market share even with fewer stations is based on the length of time listeners stay with the station during a given time period in a day.

The steady decline of country radio's numbers was the harbinger of a new round of anxiety on Music Row in late 1995. The apprehension was not misplaced; a year later saw the beginnings of a much-anticipated shakeout among Nashville's record labels and artist rosters. While new technologies have provided the music industry and Nashville with the highest level of real-time sales data than ever before, it was still the barometer of country radio that Music Row looked to see which way the wind was blowing.

The relationship between the country music industry and country radio is both symbiotic and adversarial. The theme at the 25th Annual Country Radio Seminar (CRS) in 1994, a radio industry symposium held in Nashville, evidenced that. Several panels had members from both sides of the fence on them, and one had Clint Black and Duane Propes, the bassist for Confederate Railroad, explaining a typical day on tour, trying to convey why it was now difficult for radio to always get the artists in the broadcast booth when they pass through town for a show, something radio had been taking for granted over the years. Other panels sought to explore why that procedure has become even more difficult in recent years as country radio experiences a new phenomenon: multiple country-formatted stations in the same market.

Historically, radio's relationships have been with the artists. The scene in *Coal Miner's Daughter* in which Sissy Spacek, as Loretta Lynn, drives up to a station with a record under her arm and spends a shift in the booth with the DJ is an accurate depiction of how the process unfolded from the 1950s into the early 1980s. Artists on tour would home in on radio towers broadcasting country as they traveled, augmenting the mailed and courier-delivered records from the labels that went out each week across the country.

It was the evolution and maturation of marketing that saw the record label become more involved in the last decade in ways other than simply servicing stations with records. Over a dozen major country labels and affiliates, their artists rosters growing rapidly with new names still unfamiliar to the public, need radio's exposure. But radio wants artists that their listeners know—on record and in person. Overwhelmed by so many new records, radio needs the opportunity to get to know the music as much as the listeners do; Lee Rogers, the program director at WQIK in Jacksonville, Florida, pointed out at one of the CRS panels that he wished record companies spent more time educating radio programmers about the artists before those artists came to different markets. "We don't like to sit and listen to their music in front of them" for the first time on visits to the station, he said, a remark that drew applause from the mostly radio industry crowd. (The labels, managers and talent agencies of country music all patrol the halls of the CRS in strength.) David Haley, the director of regional promotion for MCA Records, concurred, commenting on the same panel, "Just running an artist into a station for fifteen minutes is not going to work anymore."

Yet that's just what has happened in the last several years. Several new country artists have had hit records—in terms of airplay as well as sales—without live concert touring. Instead, artists such as Mindy McCready and Shania Twain have done "radio tours," swings through regions with the express purpose of visiting country radio stations—timed with the release of singles and their accompanying videos—and building up a listener base that would eventually transform itself into a sales base. And in the instances of Twain and McCready, the gambit has worked well, with recent album sales of nine million and one million, respectively. The difference between 1996 and 1956 is that radio tours are not based on the geography of itinerant artist tours; rather, they are part of highly detailed marketing plans that serve to both scientifically cover strategic regions to build bases and to do so more cost-effectively than hiring and outfitting a touring band and crew, renting a luxury tour coach and accruing the expenses of one-night stands.

The relationship between artist—as opposed to record label—and country radio is underscored by veteran country D.J.s such as Charlie Douglas, who began his career in country radio in 1953 at KLIC in Monroe, Louisiana. Douglas' career took a turn into spinning rock & roll several years later because the money simply wasn't sufficient in country radio. He returned to the country format in 1970 and now plays records at WSM in Nashville. "In the early days, it was very loose," he says. "It was generally left to the discretion of the individual disk jockey as to what they were going to play. There weren't that many artists." When Douglas began, the total size of country record label rosters ranged between thirty-five and fifty-five, less than a quarter of the number of artists now on Nashville-based record label rosters.

It made for an intimate relationship between radio and artist, often putting both parties on a first-name basis. "If you had a little morning show somewhere and Ernest [Tubb] or Kitty [Wells] or Ferlin [Husky] or whoever was passing through, they would come by and visit," Douglas recalls. "Simple as that. You had thirty-five or forty artists who were consistent sellers and they were members of the Grand Ole Opry. Every Saturday they'd do the Opry and the rest of the week they'd be on the road. There was and is no such thing as a label-driven piece of music. Nobody goes to the mailbox and says, 'Gee, I wonder what the new record from RCA or Columbia is this week.' You looked for a new Ernest Tubb then and you look for a new Brooks & Dunn now."

They were days in which the DJ served as commercial announcer, news reader, sports reporter, copywriter, advertising executive (many of the station personalities were sponsored directly by advertisers, rather than the station itself selling commercial air time and paying the on-air talent as employees, and sponsors would follow disk jockeys regionally from station to station) and engineer, single-handedly working old Raytheon consoles and Rec-O-Cut 16-inch, three-speed turntables as records came in on 78, 45, and 33⅓ speeds. While determining station ratings in that era was a primitive science, within the country DJ community they would establish their level of success by how many turntables a station had. Stations considered themselves affluent if they had three.

Country radio personalities emerged and became ethereal identities who were as strongly identifiable as the artists' voices themselves in the 1950s, their followings based on both the jocks' tastes in music and the level of down homeness in their patter. They were instantly recognizable by their signature lines, from the relative urbanity of Tom Reeder's "I hope you live as long as you want and never want as long as you live," to the simplicity of Bill Lowery's "I'll be home for supper, Elisabeth," (his mother's name) to the egregiously cartoonish tag line of "Texas" Tom Perryman, shouted over the strains of Spade Cooley's "Devil's Dream": "It's that time again for Tom Perryman's 'Hillbilly Hit Parade.' All of your favorite requested, recorded hillbilly tunes—old 'uns, new 'uns, good 'uns, bad 'uns, and sad 'uns; some leg-shakin', toe-tappin' tearjerkers. So let's get goin' like a turkey through the corn with the 'Hillbilly Hit Parade.' Suuuueey!"

These were not people who responded well to playlists, to being told that their personal interpretations of country music were to be superseded by market analyses and demographic studios. But that is what happened. Country radio simply underwent the same metamorphosis that other formats did in the 1970s as radio repositioned itself in an environment in which television ruled, and later in a multimedia entertainment and information culture in which radio's high degree of ubiquity and accessibility gave the medium only a limited advantage when compared with its commonplace quaintness.

The issues that first-generation country disk jockeys raised in retrospect are in many ways similar to those of the current generation; country radio is as much an apprenticeship experience as the country music industry itself in Nashville has been. Both generations speak to the concern that country radio programmers do not take enough chances and that the uniformity that results from the pursuit of market share shuts out new artists and new sounds, in turn forcing country labels to offer only what they think radio will play. Where current disk jockeys see playlists as a fixture of their universe, first-generation alumni view them as the first real estate transaction that transformed a comfortable neighborhood forever. But acceptance of playlisting is common if for no other reason than that is how the current corporate structure of the radio industry gains and keeps market share, a measurement that its on-air personalities may find distasteful but which the sponsoring advertisers view as the ultimate measure of success or failure.

Hugh Cherry, who began his career as a disk jockey at WKAY in Glasgow, Kentucky, in 1946 for $40 a week, observes, "Now a tune has to be on a certain number of lists before its aired on radio. That's unfair and unkind; the radio stations are limiting their own product. [But] they've got a scientific way of doing it [now], and they've got bigger audiences than we did. So they must be doing something right."[9] The older generation, though, seems sanguine about the future, having been through a few boom and bust cycles themselves. Says Len Ellis, who started in radio in 1950 at WFYC in Alma, Michigan, and became known to listeners as Uncle Len, ". . . like in the early eighties, the format will simmer down. Back then we kept about twenty percent of the people who came to Country during the *Urban Cowboy* phase. This time, I think a much higher percentage of people will stay around."[10]

But a post-*Urban Cowboy* Nashville did not have nearly forty record labels with large rosters. The proliferation of country formatted stations over the last decade isn't resolving the problem of more artists; rather, it's adding another complication to the equation as labels and artists now need to not only find time to make the visits but also choose from more than one station in an area and risk losing good will at the

9. *Radio & Records*, October 7, 1994
10. Ibid.

others. The sensitivity involved in that quandary was under-scored at the same CRS panel in 1994 in which a programmer from an Atlanta radio station stood up in the crowd and stated that of the four major acts that performed at the half-time show at the 1994 Super Bowl, only one—Tanya Tucker—had stopped by his station. Clint Black, who was one of the four acts on that show apologized, politely and politically, "You're right, I should have come by." (Black, acting as spokesman for the various artists who sang on Album of the Year winner *Common Thread: The Songs Of The Eagles* at the 1994 CMA Awards show four months later, was singular that night in his acknowledgment of country radio, saying, "You're doing a great job.") Panelist Gary Falcon, road manager for Travis Tritt, another of the artists on the half-time show, was a bit more protective, defending his employer by saying that Tritt had had four events scheduled for that day in addition to the Super Bowl show, and noted that a station had told him in essence, "If he can't come down, then we don't want him."

And that doesn't even begin to address the issue as to what to do with all the older country music that resides in the vaults of Nashville. There is little in the way of a format for country records that fall into the oldies category, which in country music today generally consists of anything released prior to 1985. The oldies format that has become so ubiquitous for pop music—Arbitron's 1996 ranking puts the format at seventh with a 6.4 percent share that continues to increase—has no counterpart in country radio. The stations that are doing it are relatively few, and are doing so for the most part without the imprimatur of the consultant caste that is now pervasive in country radio. As Kyle Cantrell, program director at Nashville's WSM-AM, which does play older country songs, told the *Tennessean*'s music industry columnist, ". . . we're not basing this on any kind of research or study. It's just something we've decided to plunge into." Instead, the trend is in the opposite direction, with rubrics like "Young Country" and "Hot Country," programming formats that are more current-intensive, and more established country formatted stations reversing their 70-to-30 percent old-to-current ratios. The relationship between country radio and country music has evolved into one of time and motion management and demographic analyses. As clinical as that may sound, it's the direct result of too much success for both parties.

"All We're Doing Is Playing The Records"

Moon Mullins has taken a comic strip character's name. From his Brentwood office in a Nashville suburb, Mullins and his partner Jeff Pollack in consulting firm Pollack Mullins are one of a number of analytical teams working on monthly retainer bases that lease their ability to interpret the entrails of radio's listenership back to the stations as they try to jockey for market share.

Neal Mullins, as he was born, has his own personal tastes as far as country music goes. Moon, on the other hand, his business alter ego, goes where the money is. For instance, Neal, the fan, liked the fashion-forward country of Twister Alley's "Dance." "Moon Mullins, the thirty-year radio veteran who is a consultant advising radio stations on their playlists, almost laughed at that record," he says. Neal/Moon's reaction to Restless Heart's 1992 pop hit "When She Cries," however, was unanimous, viewing the crossing over as less a bridgehead into the pop world as an incursion by pop into the sanctum of country music.

Regardless of preferences, though, singles played on the radio are still the primary means by which country music sells its records, and singles are the only format left in which positions are determined by radio airplay now that SoundScan has entered the sales reporting picture. Stations report to a number of publications, among them *Billboard Country Airplay Monitor*, a *Billboard* sister publication, which has 139 reporting stations, and *Radio & Records*, which has 216 stations, that cumulatively attempt to present a picture of where a record is in terms of radio action. Radio in general has a follow-the-pack mentality, driven by its need to keep listeners in order to sell them the products of the advertisers who keep them on the air, and country radio, with a self-admitted obsessiveness with familiarity and hit-driven programming, is the apotheosis of that kind of thinking. Country radio has turned to consultants like Mullins to keep them, if not ahead of the pack, then at least even with it. The ultimate byword has become "familiarity;" as Mullins put it in an interview published in *Music Row* magazine,[11] "Radio's aim is to increase the time that people listen to their station, not increase the number of people [that] listen. You have less of an opportunity to do that when you are playing less familiar songs. Speaking for the majority of stations in the [country music] format, it would be highly unlikely that they would change that . . ."

The labels have more control over what happens on radio than they'll acknowledge or that radio cares to admit, Mullins asserts, underscoring the sometimes antagonistic side of what has been for the last forty years a mutually beneficial and often synergistic relationship. "The labels determine . . . what publication, what chart, what criteria determine what the hits are. They'll say radio makes that determination but [it] doesn't. Years ago when *Billboard* was the primary chart which radio followed to make its decisions, the record business at one point decided it didn't like the way *Billboard*'s chart was done. [It was based partially on a rotating collection of retail and wholesale outlets, a percentage of which were surveyed each week; never the same ones, making it difficult for record labels to attempt to influence reporting.] *R&R* [*Radio & Records* magazine] came along and the labels chose that one. And radio said, that's fine with us, all we're doing is playing the records."

Putatively, the favor has swung back to *Billboard* and its recent reliance on Broadcast Data Systems (BDS), in which it is a joint venture partner and in monitoring 139 country radio stations nationally offers for airplay a slightly less absolute version of what SoundScan has done for retail sales. The system is skewed by the different sizes of markets and the vague

---

11. *Music Row*, June 23, 1995

nature of reporting terms. "One station's heavy rotation is another station's medium," explains Mullins. "It's closer to the truth, but not one hundred percent accurate." *R&R* also changed its survey methodology recently. In 1994 it shifted emphasis away from delineating activity based on rotation to asking stations to predict, within two to four plays, how many times they intend to play a record in the next week. The change in reporting and monitoring, aimed at anticipating trends rather then just reflecting them, has led to a shift in tactics by labels, which no longer lobby the publications to report heavier action on a song, or the stations to report airplay that was not given; instead, the lobbying effort goes into pushing stations to increase airplay on key songs during the period in which a label is pushing that song to the top of the charts.

If the measurement methodologies seem complicated and arcane, they are; but so is the very notion of evaluating radio, which in an age dominated by visual media has become a sort of background noise of the culture. Its very ubiquity and the lack of need to focus on its presence work against radio, and by extension, measuring its effectiveness. But for country music, for which radio remains the prime expositor of the music and which is confined to a limited number of charts, that complexity is routine.

Radio is by nature conservative; it needs to sell to a mass market and that dictates a lowest common denominator strategy. In a market fragmenting further by the year, "Young" and "Hot" country formats now represent nearly a quarter of the top 100 markets in country radio. "Radio sees country starting to fragment, and they're trying to carve out niches within it," Mullins says. What radio has been resistant to is the older artist. "Which is funny when you think about it," he adds. "Because George Jones wasn't much older than nineteen when he first came out, Faron Young was nineteen when he joined the Opry, and Hank Williams was pretty young, too. I think that nobody really cared what the artist looked like up until now . . ."

The most plaintive yet sharp riposte in the age of consultancy comes from Glen Campbell, a country star who saw both sides of the radio with hits like "By The Time I Get To Phoenix," "Gentle On My Mind," and "Rhinestone Cowboy," a country song that became a number-one pop record in 1975 that in many ways anticipated and epitomized the coming of the *Urban Cowboy* epoch. In an interview in *Country Music* magazine in early 1995, he said of contemporary country radio: "I think when they put the consultants at the radio stations and the record companies, all artistic creation probably just went out the window. . . . Check out the consultants' background—it's programming: shovin' it down their throats, the new, the bigger and the better. . . . It's outcome-based music, like outcome-based education. It isn't necessarily what's good that's gonna get played."

"It's Their Record, And The Point Is To Sell A Lot Of Them"

At the 1996 CRS Convention in Nashville, *Music Row* magazine reported a tableau that at first seemed a dazzling display of technology: producer and Giant Records label president James Stroud had set up a miniature version of a recording studio and was leading convention attendees through an abbreviated version of the record making process—tracking, overdubs, and mixing. The report ended with the comment that, ". . . as the session ended the [radio] programmers had the opportunity to feel as if they had helped create the song." It was a telling moment that went without further comment from the reporter. Radio's influence on which songs become hits is well-documented; its ability to reach behind the curtain and move the faders on the recording console is less well-known.

"Radio is a fact of life." So says Ed Seay, an engineer and producer (Martina McBride, Pam Tillis, Collin Raye) and a coowner of Nashville recording studio The Money Pit. Seay says that the perspective on radio from producers and artists is not so much that radio is a necessary evil as it is simply necessary, a fact of life. However, its influence in the music industry, and particularly in country, makes it something that frequently requires accommodation.

Seay acknowledges mixing records for radio differently from what he otherwise might have; in fact, he considers not doing so a potentially foolish move and one that can be accomplished without any significant loss of artistic integrity. In 1990, he and coproducer Paul Worley (who also shares an ownership interest in The Money Pit) were producing Pam Tillis's *Put Yourself In My Place* for Arista Records. The single "Maybe It Was Memphis" was considered by Seay, at least, to be the best song on the record. The pair arranged the song with a nine-bar Southern rock guitar solo and an extended coda, neither of which sounded particularly country but which they felt were appropriate to the song. These additions brought the track very close to four minutes in length, not terribly unusual for pop at the time but longer than the "three-minutes-and-change" that country radio usually prefers. The combination of the length and the non-traditional arrangement aspects prompted a call from Arista president Tim Dubois when "Memphis" was being considered by the label as the third single from the album.

"Tim said he loved the song but that maybe radio would have a problem with a few things about it, like the length, the solo and the ride-out," Seay recalls. "Could we shorten the song, change the southern rock guitar solo to a pedal steel guitar and loop a chorus and use that for the ending instead of the jangling guitar ride-out?"

Technically, all those changes were relatively simple to effect. The original multitrack recording was copied as a safety measure, and the copy was then edited to shorten the solo section, which then had a more characteristically country pedal steel guitar solo overdubbed into that space. Seay then took a sample—essentially a digital clone of a sound or group of sounds—of a premixed vocal chorus from another point in the song and then attached that to the end of the song, replacing the original instrumental ride-out. The track then came in at three minutes and twenty-five seconds, perfect in terms of length for radio and with the instrumental accoutrements that country radio would be more familiar with.

That kind of artistic manipulation on the part of the record company would likely have drawn animated complaints from producers and artists in other musical genres. Not that it often doesn't in country, either, considering the regularity with which it has occurred in recent years, but Seay's response typifies the reaction within the music community to accommodating recordings to the exigencies of radio. "Look, Tim was right," he says. "The [arrangement] was a little bold and we liked it and thought it was good for the song and the artist. But if a label states an intelligent case, which Tim did, well . . . it's their record, and the point is to sell a lot of them."

Which "Maybe It Was Memphis" did. And while the song's original musical coda was eliminated, the story of the remix developed one of its own. "Tim had told us that if the song went to number-one country, then Arista in New York would consider releasing it to pop radio," Seay says. In anticipation of that, Seay called guitarist Dann Huff, a Nashville session guitarist whose credits from his L.A. session days include Whitesnake and who more recently was hired by metal band Megadeth to produce their record, to play an even more blistering guitar solo than the original Southern rock guitar instrumental had been. "Maybe It Was Memphis" only managed to reach number two on the country charts, however. "We were blocked at number one that week," Seay remembers. "It was 'Achy Breaky Heart,' actually," he says.

VIDEO

Stan Hitchcock was a country singer whose twenty-year career represented the kind of experience that country had offered many of its artists through the mid-1980s: his signing to Columbia Records in 1961 was with a label that stayed with him through nearly a decade that rarely saw him move beyond the middle of the charts, after which he eased into a string of independent record deals that kept him in front of the fan base those years had built. So it is ironic that Hitchcock, who lived the model of a mid-level country singer's life, would be the one who would change the world for those who came after him.

In 1984, Hitchcock and a group of investors purchased a fledgling video production and broadcast company based in Hendersonville, a suburb northeast of Nashville. The new network came with two million subscribers and a handful of mostly self-produced music videos. Over the next seven years, Country Music Television—CMT—added subscribers to watch a mushrooming number of country music videos that the Nashville labels began to experiment with, interspersed between talk shows produced at the station's facility.

But it wasn't until 1991, when a joint venture between Group W Satellite Communications and Gaylord Entertainment—the same company that had purchased the Grand Ole Opry and relocated it to a theme park, and which also operates The Nashville Network cable channel—bought CMT that it became the powerhouse that CMT is today, with over thirty-six million households subscribing to the cable channel, and cable feeds to three continents.

Hitchcock himself summed up the main impact of CMT on country music: that it both brought a younger demographic to the music and a younger generation of artists to that audience.[12] And in doing so, it changed the country music business forever. After generations of musically praising the virtues of simple, unembellished, unpretentious plainness, it has become one of the unwritten rules of contemporary country that artists be telegenic. Visual appeal has not replaced the song, but it has become the closest secondary consideration after the sound of country records. And depending upon whom one talks to, it has become tantamount. It's impact on the sales performance of a song is visceral—

---

12. *Definitive Country, The Ultimate Encyclopedia of Country Music And Its Performers*, New York: Perigee, 1995.

76 percent of country records that become CMT Pickhit videos reach the top ten on industry trade magazine *Radio & Records*'s chart.

What video has also done is upped the ante in the cost of breaking a new artist even more in Nashville. Video budgets now average around $100,000, and can cost considerably more; Billy Ray Cyrus, for example, spent over $180,000 on "In The Heart Of A Woman," flying himself and the crew to the Grand Canyon for the shoot. In general, the cost of the video is recoupable to the extent of 50 percent against the artist's royalties. When combined with the cost of making the entire album, which can run between $75,000 and $150,000 (add another $10,000 to $25,000 for dance version remixes of songs), and other related costs such as tour support, new artists leave the gate with a debt to their record companies of a quarter of a million dollars-plus. Some artists of major stature have taken a page from pop's book and are now funding their own videos. In some cases their record labels partially reimburse them; in other instances, artists are doing the same thing that many labels are doing and releasing long-form collections of their own videos.

Video has changed the economics of country. It's produced a financial liability that in effect counterbalances the reality asset that SoundScan provided; the credibility provided by country music record sales suddenly had the potential to be undermined by the cost of keeping them competitive via video. At a time when record labels were expecting three viable singles from an album, the cost of the videos needed to promote those singles cost more than the entire album did to make.

The spending was spiraling upward through the early 1990s; in 1995, several record labels implemented internal spending caps on videos, such as Sony Records's decision that not every single from a Sony artist would automatically have a video made of it. But the rising cost of country music videos also revealed that videos had not achieved (and probably never would) the status of art forms in Nashville. Where in rock music, MTV videos are often created as esthetic entities unto themselves, in country music they are, purely and simply, promotional vehicles. The complaints about the quality of country music videos now echoes those directed toward the music itself in recent years: trend-following sameness and safeness.

The labels' apparent stinginess with video budgets is reinforced by a market research study commissioned by CMT in 1992. It delineated how various demographics integrated country videos into their lives (or "lifestyles," as the marketers would have it), using it as anything from a primary source of entertainment to a filler between shows to essentially an extension of radio, not looking at it but listening to it. The report, excerpts of which were obtained by and reprinted in *Music Row* magazine,[13] indicated that 52 percent of viewers are likely to listen while doing other things and one-third listen more than they watch. At the same time, the survey concluded that viewers most prefer story videos. The contents of the report were leaked early to labels along with a *sotto voce* verbal interpretation by a now former CMT employee that the labels needn't spend lavishly on videos since, in effect, few people were actively watching them.

That interpretation was embraced by some country labels for whom spending on promotion has traditionally been limited, and viewed with dismay by video producers. *Music Row* editor David M. Ross's analysis in the same issue of the magazine questioned the reliability of the data on behalf of video producers by asking, "If viewers aren't *watching* the channel. . . how do they know they prefer story videos? . . . How much weight should be given to research of this nature (paid for and commissioned by the subject of the study)? . . ."

The signals from CMT have been mixed, to say the least. The network's then-director of operations, Bob Baker, stated in a letter to MCA Records in 1994 regarding Reba McEntire's "Is There Life Out There," "Theatrical videos slow down our pacing . . . The bottom line? In the future we won't air (or will require major editing) for videos like the Reba project."

13. December 23, 1992, issue

"Is There Life Out There" was then placed on CMT's heavy rotation playlist.

Something else accompanied video into country music, however. The mutual attraction between youth and video has edged older performers further out of the picture. While there are few country radio formats that play older country artists, at least their records still exist and can be bought or collected into compilations. But for most artists whose prime was in the age B.V.—Before Video—it is as though they had disappeared into thin air. They are grainy black-and-white images on historical documentaries or ghostly apparitions revived by the technology of video, such as in the pairing of Hank Williams, Sr. and Hank Williams, Jr. in a clip of "There's A Tear In My Beer." In this sense, video has introduced something that the culture of the country music business never had before—a discernible generational barrier. Country songs could cross the continuum of time and space, appearing and reappearing on new records over the decades; as the publishers of Nashville like to say, a country song has "a long shelf life," and the apprenticeship paradigm that is integral to the Nashville music industry society has encouraged entire families to remain part of it for generations. But the lack of a video, or in the case of lasting artists whose careers have come of age in the postvideo era, an entire videography, creates the situation of recording artist-without-portfolio. Video has further ghettoized older country artists by ostracizing them from the cableways. And in doing so, it may contribute more critically to any potential breakup of the familial legacy of country music than the loudest snare drum ever recorded.

"A Metaphor For Life"

Marc Ball was involved in two of the more significant videos to come out of country in the last several years. Garth Brooks's "The Dance" and Billy Ray Cyrus's "Achy Breaky Heart" are both regarded as stylistically important and strategic from a marketing point of view. "The Dance" established Brooks beyond country's boundaries as a genre and spearheaded country videos on VH-1, which has become a kind of middle ground between CMT/TNN and MTV. The video for "Achy Breaky Heart" was one of the original instances which the video was incorporated into the marketing plan of the launch of a new country artist.

Ball, who in 1975 founded Scene Three, a film and video postproduction facility and Nashville's largest producer of music videos, came from an advertising video background. The Kentucky native arrived in Nashville in the early 1970s after a stint in Chicago shooting commercials and product introductions. Such a commercial, rather than a theatrical, background is common to video directors in both mainstream rock and country. His first music video was in 1981 for Gene Cotton, at a time when a $20,000 video budget was considered extravagant by Nashville labels that were initially reluctant to get involved with video at all.

"The Dance," which Ball produced, was shot in 1990 at Scene Three's studios on Eighth Avenue North in Nashville. The shoot itself was rather simple; it was the conceptualization that made it stand apart. The song was transformed into a generational metaphor by the transposition of images of fallen grass-roots cultural icons, like John F. Kennedy and country singer Keith Whitley, culled from stock footage. "It wasn't any one person's idea," recalls Ball, sitting in his softly lit, windowless office at Scene Three. "I think it was Garth's idea to use the stock footage. We were all sitting around the couch in the office, me and Kitty [Moon, Scene Three's cofounder] and John [Miller, the video's director] and Garth was on the speaker phone. Garth kept saying he wanted it to be important, that he wanted it to be a metaphor for life. But what set it apart in my mind was that it wasn't traditional country and that makes you realize about how we think about country music, how video has changed how we think about it. Is it country? Is it not country? It's just music."

If Garth Brooks came into "The Dance" on a roll, already a burgeoning phenomenon, Billy Ray Cyrus came to Ball as a cipher, an unknown artist with a song that initially set Ball on guard. "Steve Miller [vice president of marketing] at PolyGram sent the song over here and said he had an artist he thought was going to be big, and that he had an unusual marketing approach in mind. That they had a dance that went with it." Miller's thoughts were spelled out in an interview in which he said, ". . . we recognized that the country dance clubs had experienced a large growth over the past four years and that no label had previously gone out and tapped that potential. We knew that 'Achy Breaky' was a little left of what radio was doing at the time. . . . So we decided we'd go to the consumer first. . . . when we finally did take it to radio, the listener would have already embraced it. . . ."[14]

The budget that PolyGram offered Ball for "Achy Breaky Heart" came in substantially higher than most, he remembered, and that made him ecstatic. On the other hand, the song left him cold at first. "My assistant came to my door and said that here's the tape Steve had sent over. It's called 'Achy Breaky Heart.' I remember I got a knot in my throat at the title. But the truth is, after you hear that song a few times, it's fun. So we decided to have a good time with it." So did nine million others; the record stayed at number one on the *Billboard* Top Albums chart for seventeen weeks during the summer of 1992. It also signified a shift in both the music and the visual images away from simply storytelling to one of video-clip personality and physical appearance. The backlash was significant, epitomized by Travis Tritt's comment that "Achy Breaky" had turned country into "an ass-wiggling contest," an observation considered by some to be ironic, considering Tritt's own live show reliance on arena-rock gyrations. In the end, both artists continued their success, as did the more traditionally country ones. Rules were meant to be broken.

The evolution of country music videos has paralleled a trend in Nashville, and that is the increase in timidity as the genre grows more successful. Decisions by committee have become more common, as they have with virtually every other aspect of country music. "You can tell it when you premiere a

14. *Music Row*, June 8, 1993

video," says Ball, describing a scenario that could also have been any Madison Avenue advertising agency concept pitch for a corporate client. "You've got a group of people screening it for the first time. It's amazing how quiet it is until the person who needs to gives his acceptance or rejection [speaks up] and then suddenly everyone in the room thinks the same thing. 'Achy Breaky' was simple—just a couple of calls and the concept was established and it was on its way. 'The Dance' was conceived by a group of people but not by what I call by committee. [Country music videos] have become in many cases almost like television spots where there's all these people sitting around adding and subtracting from the concept and going back and forth and that's not the way to do it."

"The 'Bubba' Factor Didn't Get It. But Nashville Got It"

Music video, which went through its early evolutionary stages with various sub-genres of pop and rock on MTV, was plopped down relatively fully formed into the country music milieu in the mid-1980s. Without the benefit of some degree of evolution in tandem with country music's own conventions, it's been perceived by some as an alien form of life, and the relationships between video and country—directors and artists and labels—have been formed quickly and tenuously, without the advantage of the leisurely pace that the other relationship structures on Nashville have had.

Marc Ball had mused on a perfect world when he wistfully talked about how labels should "pick a song, pick an artist, pick a director, and leave them alone," not unlike the traditional "pick the right song, call the right players and shut up" approach to country record production. But video, like marketing, has intruded upon that stable relationship over the last several years. Both have changed the fabric of the music.

Though the relationship between record producers and recording artists that has evolved over the last forty years remains an overwhelmingly patriarchal one, country recording artists are increasingly seen as the coproducers on their own recordings, such as Suzy Bogguss and Reba McEntire, and as producers of other artists, such as Tim McGraw's coproduction on Jo Dee Messina. While the trend toward increased cowriting of songs on their records by artists reflects a desire to participate in the revenues from publishing, the motivation toward production is probably less pecuniary than artistic, since in most cases the points and producers' fees structure remains the same as it would for single producer.

While no country artist has yet had a codirectorial credit on a country music video, their input is increasing, according to some of the directors. Steven Goldmann, who was CMT's Director of the Year in 1993 and has directed videos for Pam Tillis, Michelle Wright, Martina McBride, and Kathy Mattea, has earned a reputation as a woman's director in Nashville. "Some, like Martina, want to be involved on every level of the production, from concept to cutting," he says. "And it was Pam Tillis's idea to pattern the look of 'Shake The Sugar Tree' after Maxfield Parrish." The artsy effect of that video reflected Tillis's own perception of her audience, he observed: "The 'bubba' factor didn't get it. But Nashville got it. I think regardless of the director, the artist intuitively sorts it out. They know their audience, some of them. They've become so video-savvy that some of them think they can step into the director's chair."

The costs associated with videos have increased from the $20,000 or so of the early 1980s to an average of approximately $100,000. Some have cost twice that, and artists of major stature often cross the $150,000 threshold. Considering that artists release an average of three videos per album-length recording, generally one for each single, the video budget has come to rival the cost of the entire recording process. The budgets are delineated out on a standard American Association of Commercial Producers budget bid form, which is patterned after the budget format used in feature films, with talent and scripting costs falling in the so-called "above the line" area and technical costs "below the line." Directors will generally get 10 percent of the gross cost of the video, producers 5 percent. Cinematographers charge $1,800 to $2,000 per day; camera rentals cost around $1,500 per day and post production costs—the editing and sweetening of the video after the shooting is completed—runs between $3,000 to $5,000 per day. The production company builds in between 15 and 20 percent as its profits.

These costs are one reason that video was reluctantly embraced by Nashville initially. The other, according to Goldmann, is a function of control. "Producers run the labels here," he says. "They've worried that videos can narrow-cast a song or an artist, limit the appeal. They're still not so sure it sells a song or an artist. Certainly they were concerned before CMT came along that there was no outlet for country music videos. And they really don't know anything about video, so they've tended to stay far away from it. It's the marketing departments that have been first to go for video. For them it's the ultimate tool."

The disparity of respect between video directors and record producers is one that Goldmann and other directors are noting mentally. In another published interview, Goldmann pined for a time when video directors would receive the same sort of regard that Nashville's producers get. "I'd like to be able to create an atmosphere where the artists, management, and record companies look to us with the same degree of respect that is given to the record producer," he says wistfully.[15]

"There Is An Unspoken Conspiracy..."

With innovative videos under his belt for K.T. Oslin, Alabama, Reba McEntire, and Kathy Mattea, Jack Cole is one of the few country music video directors to ask for and receive points on an artist's record. He participated to the extent of two percentage points on Linda Davis's 1992 debut recording,

15. *Music Row*, May 8, 1994

Linda Davis. The record didn't sell well, so Cole described his royalty as "negligible." But to Cole, the scenario describes the state of country music video as one that has been economically impoverished and is becoming more so creatively. Cole had done rock videos and commercials in Los Angeles prior to coming to Nashville in 1991, including videos for Joe Cocker, Joe Perry, and Journey. His first country video was for a CBS recording artist named Mark Grey, for whom he directed "The Left Side Of The Bed"—an eleven-minute opus that also introduced dialogue, plot, and character development to a music media which would dispute all three in coming years—which introduced the 1983 Columbia Records national convention.

Cole claims he's never been caught in the budget crunch situation that he said characterizes country videos, thanks to the level of artists he's worked with. The Linda Davis experience, in which the artist and her management agreed to compensate him partially through participation in album sales when Liberty Records balked at his fee, exemplifies the lengths to which artists will go to get videos beyond the norm—or to get them at all. Cole estimates the value of the country video segment of the industry at around $12 million. "That doesn't allow for any kind of growth," he says. "There is an unspoken conspiracy among labels to keep a cap on the music video industry. They acknowledge the importance of music videos in breaking an artist verbally, but not in dollars. It's actually gone backward, because the amounts spent per video go down as the industry adds more artists."

Cole, like several other directors, is also doing fewer music videos in Nashville because they have priced themselves out of the game in context of country music budgets, according to the people at labels who coordinate videos. Retta Harvey, manager of music video production at Mercury Nashville, said her budgets range from $55,000 to $75,000. Mercury has spent as much as $180,000 on one shoot, Billy Ray Cyrus's "In The Heart Of A Woman." Nonetheless, she agreed that there is a downward pressure on video costs in Nashville as a result of the number of new acts being signed and released.

The opposing pressures are labels that want to see video costs kept down and video outlets—specifically CMT and TNN—that want to minimize controversy, à la CMT's refusal to air Garth Brooks's "The Thunder Rolls" video due to its violent theme. Some established artists don't release a video for every single, and acts like Travis Tritt, Doug Stone, Garth Brooks, Restless Heart, and Brooks & Dunn have all have produced hit records without the benefit of videos for the songs. On the other hand, as more artists are signed, the labels and the artists need to differentiate them from one another, and videos have become a critical tool with which to accomplish that.

The result has been pressure for artists and their associates to fund or partially fund videos. RCA Records initially declined to pay for a second video off the Mike Henderson *Country Music Made Me Do It* record, released in 1994. Henderson's publisher, EMI Music, stepped in and agreed to help finance a video on the second single "The Want To" after the fizzle of the first release, "Hillbilly Jitters," which charted only briefly. "RCA felt they wanted to spend money in other marketing directions on Mike, and we disagreed, so we were ready to pay for the second video," states Mark Bright, creative director at EMI Music and who also produces country band Blackhawk. RCA later changed its mind and did finance the video, but the scenario is becoming increasingly common. Henderson was signed both to EMI Music and to EMI Nashville Productions, a division started under the record label in 1992 and later shifted to the publishing company. EMI did the same thing earlier on the first Billy Dean release on Liberty Records. (Though in Henderson's case RCA's hesitancy might also have reflected their commitment to the artist; Henderson was subsequently dropped from the label shortly thereafter.) The decision, though, proved useful in propelling Billy Dean's career. "It's no different than hiring an independent promotion man for the record, something that's been done for years by publishers," says Bright. "If a label signs four or five new acts, the one with the cold, hard cash to help with things like this is going to have a significant advantage." EMI also offset its costs by piggybacking the productions onto other video shoots already scheduled in Nashville, using the same crew and director, not an uncommon practice but one that video producers are reluctant to let labels get too comfortable with, lest they tighten budgets even further.

CMT plays it safe in its choice of videos, and in doing so induces yet another reverse-centrifugal force on country music, compressing the edges closer to the center. Like radio, CMT relies upon charts to determine what goes into heavy rotation (five plays per day), Hot Shot (four plays), medium rotation (three plays), and light (two airings a day). However, CMT has an even more intimate relationship with the major record labels than does country radio: it plays virtually every video they produce at least once. As a result, there are fewer repeat slots on CMT; its playlist runs around seventy videos a week versus the thirty-five or so records on an average country radio station playlist. Independent labels will have their artists' videos reviewed, but the ratio of independent to major label acts appearing on CMT is decidedly in favor of the larger labels.

Garth Brooks's domestic violence set-piece "The Thunder Rolls," ran for a week in 1992, during which the programming department fretted over whether to pull it or leave it. They pulled it. "They were just playing it safe," observes Retta Harvey, who handles videos at Mercury Records. "People don't want to be reminded of violence."

Epic Records's Gibson Miller Band never made it to the cable network with the original video version of their 1993 single, "Texas Tattoo." It was rejected after a screening at CMT as too sexually suggestive. "We are a family channel," says Tracey Rogers, manager of programming for CMT and CMT Europe, who programmed Los Angeles country station KSAN before coming to CMT in 1992. "There were several shots in that video that were over the edge. We asked the label to fix it and they did." James Carlson, director of video production at Sony Music, of which Epic Records is a part, says that the edited scenes were "semiprovacative," but he downplays the significance of CMT's request for an edit, saying the contested scenes were few and brief. But the incidents underscore the fact that CMT and TNN, by virtue of their monopoly as outlets, function as a sort of censor for country music, with all the power that connotes. And CMT will likely continue its dominance of the format; while more country video outlets spring up, via regional and syndicated television such as the California Music Channel's country spin-off channel, others fizzle, like Disney's *Countdown At The Neon Armadillo*, which was viewed as out of place for the family values of country. The same applied to the reviews of ABC television's *Best Of Country '92*. December 1992, broadcast, whose "Bad Girl Dancers" drew criticism from country traditionalists.

Backlashes against video have proliferated in Nashville. One of the more apparent ones was when Allen Butler, executive vice president and general manager at Sony Records' Nashville operations, mentioned to an industry symposium in late 1994 that Sony would henceforth not automatically authorize videos for every singles release for its recording artists. Butler later said that the announcement caught even his own employees off guard, and that several came back to him and reported a significant level of dissatisfaction from artist managers, particularly those representing new acts.

"Let me tell you what happened, how our thinking changed," says Butler, who before Sony worked at Arista Records and RCA Records in Nashville. "It used to take lots of albums to create an identity for country artists. The video came along and we could create an identity in one album or one or two songs. We saw what MTV had done: breaking new talent strictly on [video] power, on artists not getting airplay on pop radio. That was very enticing to us, so everyone jumped on the bandwagon. TNN had limited time to play videos then [Gaylord's flagship station continues to have a considerable amount of non-music programming, such as sports shows] but after CMT came out there was more opportunity for exposure."

Video was perceived as being a possible viable alternative to country radio which, despite its growth, was still a bottleneck in that it mainly adhered to a hits-based format, minimizing exposure for new acts. But video brought with it its own set of problems, financial and artistic. Butler and other operations managers had to swallow hard to accept the costs of videos and the fact that they had to commit to them as far in advance as the singles that were normally released to radio ahead of the albums, usually a month to six weeks. Releasing an advance single to radio costs virtually nothing other than mailings and promotional materials; the videos, on the other hand, can cost half of what the entire album recording cost.

These costs mounted cumulatively over the late 1980s and early 1990s. And during this time, the country labels were finding that even with video, they couldn't do without country radio. Butler first took some solace in a correlation he found between video and records sales: "Since we started using videos, look at the numbers of platinum and gold records we racked up," he says. "Before video we maybe had five platinums in the entire format." According to data compiled by the CMA, country music garnered thirty-six platinum and thirty-one multiplatinum records in 1994, as well as seventy-six gold record sales awards.

But what country does not have—yet, anyway—is the proliferation of charts to reflect the fragmentation of the contemporary music market. Pop is scattered over numerous charts in *Billboard:* the Billboard 200 (on which country, like all other genres, is tracked), The Hot 100, Adult Alternative/New Age, Adult Alternative/World Music, Adult Contemporary, Dance/Club Play, Dance/Maxi Singles, Rock/Album Tracks, Rock/Modern Rock Tracks, and Top 40 and Hot 100 airplay charts. Country, which is segregated only twice—the Country albums chart and the Country singles chart—is still regarded, by the reporting trades and the genre's participants, as a single entity. Over time Butler himself began to find that the link between video and records sales was somewhat more tenuous then originally thought. "What we realized is that CMTs penetration is scattered and fractured. It's not everywhere. Country radio is. The advance singles were getting airplay in markets where people don't have CMT. It's not as great as it once was, but radio remains the keystone [for country music]."

Butler found himself questioning more and more the connection over time, realizing that the expenditures for videos for every newly released single had become automatic, like the advance release of the singles themselves. "I started doing a reality check on what we were doing," he recalls. "I had to sell myself on the whole concept all over again and then started wondering if it made more sense to maybe wait until the second single to do the video. Why do we *have* to have a video for every single?"

And then there was the realization, appropriate for the backside of the bell curve that country sales were about to embark upon, that the financial resources are finite. "I was also asking myself, do we do more 'low-dough' videos so we can get twice as many, or spend the top dollars to do fewer but better ones? I had been challenging my people to go out and find the Young Turk directors who could do the videos for lower budgets even while the managers were saying they wanted this name or that name director to direct."

(Butler acknowledged a quintessential Nashville irony in that line of thinking: that the pursuit of less expensive videos was providing opportunities for video directors in country music; at the same time, the record producers' club remained as elite, closed, and in demand as ever.)

As mentioned earlier, the reaction to Butler's examination of conscience and its somewhat abrupt announcement caused a stir within and without Sony Records in Nashville. A&R personnel and artists' representatives will now have to sell Butler and Sony on a case-by-case basis on the need for a video for each single. Sony implemented Butler's decision as policy in January of 1995. He says that once the initial shock had worn off that Sony would go about educating its staff, artists and their representatives about its implications. But in a more Nashvillian manner, Butler says of the decision,

"We're gonna do it this way from now on. We just haven't picked who the first victim is yet."

While radio is still perceived as king in the processes that come after the records themselves are produced, the three-way combination of the medium, along with marketing and video, has created a machine that is increasingly an organism unto itself. Incidents such as Sony Records's reconsideration of how to use—and be used by—video reflect the impact that it has had on everything from artist signings to song choices. But it also indicates how the music business consciously rejects being dominated by it, at least perceptually to itself. Like the weather, everyone complains about radio, and by extension video and marketing, but no one does anything about it. In an era when country music has had to compete with other major musical genres for consumer dollars, it must accommodate the exigencies of a broader entertainment business, as well. From that standpoint, country radio's focus seems even narrower as it continues to concentrate itself obsessively on the same limited number of hit records from an ever-wider pool of artists and releases.

It's safe to postulate that radio will remain country music's primary expository format, despite the fact that everything else the record labels do seems intent on circumventing it. Videos made to break acts that don't seem perfectly tailored to country radio haven't achieved those ends on any kind of scale, with few crossing over the line to other video formats. And country music video as an industry segment, while its relatively late maturity allowed it to benefit technically and in a business sense from the experience of pop music video, has come of age at a time when the novelty of music videos has significantly worn off and also during a period of increasingly specialized television narrow-casting, in which a proliferating number of channels compete more intensely than ever for viewers and advertising dollars. MTV, which many country music executives already concede has been far more activist in helping break new music artists than CMT or TNN have, had few such issues to deal with when it began its existence.

Marketing efforts like extensive Wal-Mart tours have a radio component built into them, as well, with label marketing departments aware that radio remains the preeminent conduit for getting people into the stores and for after-the-fact follow-up, just as it does the same task for live performances. And pure marketing first-record successes like the Tractors, whose platinum-selling debut record in 1994 had radio scrambling to catch up, are few and far between. But all three— radio, video, and marketing—have synergistically combined into an entity that is more powerful and pervasive in its effect than radio was alone.

But because the power of personality—and thus the personal power—in country music resides primarily in the producers and the songs, the ultimate effect of this phenomenon is not likely to change country music's structure as it did that of pop and rock music, where the bulk of the power of personality now belongs to the recording artists themselves. In short, while the newly combined force of radio, video and marketing have become its own separate entity to a large degree, it will remain, in the universe of country, a moon orbiting the larger mass of the main structure—producers, publishers, writers, and to some extent musicians, none of whom have yet let an MBA, or a lack of one, get in their way.

"Where's the Next Nashville?"

O N A SPRING AFTERNOON in 1995 Arista Records held its fifth anniversary party beneath a large canvas tent near the company's offices on Music Circle, just off the head end of Music Row. Alan Jackson was playing truncated versions of his hits—one verse and one chorus of "Here In The Real World" and others—the way country artists do it at the Opry sometimes or when you've had so many hits that you have to compress your entire oeuvre into a six-minute medley.

In between a sip of beer and a bite of barbecue, someone wonders aloud where the "next Nashville" will be.

It is a question with many implications. On one hand, one could infer that Nashville is, like most of the urban centers of the contemporary entertainment industry, just a stop along the way in a changing, peripatetic and restless entertainment culture. Insecurity is a given in that business, and there's no reason to think that its geography is any more certain than employment in it. The question gave voice to the quiet apprehension in Nashville that all this success was some sort of chimera that could evaporate at any minute. Not just its newfound status of music megacenter, but even the central position that Nashville has long held in country music. The very success that country music experienced during its five-year run in the 1990s raised the psychological stakes that took this question from the back of the mind out, tentatively but purposefully, into the harsh light of the moment.

On the other hand, why ask such a question at all? A valid response is that there will never be another Nashville—there doesn't need to be one. Never before has a major contemporary genre of American music had so long and so deeply entrenched a relationship with a single city. The only other such relationship that comes to mind is Hollywood and the film industry that has been centered there since the 1920s, a seventy-year intimate association that has held twice as long as that of country music and Nashville. No other location has been the center of any music's production, business, personal homes and ancillary industries in recent history as Nashville has been for country music and its participants. Hollywood, too, has had pretenders to its dominion, from Vancouver, British Columbia, to Orlando, Florida, but none have succeeded in displacing it as the central core of the film business.

Hollywood itself has been affected (some might say "infected") by the culture of the film business and in doing so has become even more intimate with the film community, allowing it to exist as a society apart from the myriad other enterprises that call Los Angeles home. So it is with Nashville, where the city has provided a home to those who choose the country music industry as their life, allowing them to not only go about their business but to live their own version of life, with all its excesses, both within and apart from it. The divorce rate in the entertainment industry is well above the norm for the rest of the population. Yet in Nashville, with its higher per-capita ratio of churches than any other U.S. city, divorce and other transgressions of the religious culture of the South are overlooked, if not always forgiven. To those who live in Nashville but who are not part of the music business there, country music is sometimes the eccentric, wealthy relation that lives in their midst, enjoyed for its ability to provide a diversion to the quotidian things that make up life, and whose idiosyncrasies are tolerated because it is family. Chet Atkins walking through the Bellevue Mall at Christmastime draws second looks from shoppers, but none of them would ever think to stop him for an autograph or even a hello. In Nashville, what few paparazzi venture down there have learned to check with someone's publicist first for an appointment.

A synergy of technologies already here and yet to come—the Internet as a distribution mechanism supplanting retail record stores, for instance—as well as the changed perspectives and philosophies of business that come with them are in the process of decentralizing the larger music industry. Already present and having considerable effect are the music production technologies that permit affordable and powerful recordings to be done outside of traditional recording facilities, and thus outside the historical structure of the record industry as it's been known for the last fifty years. Entire records in the Pop, Blues, Jazz, R&B, and Urban genres are routinely done in artists' and producers' relatively modest personal recording studios—Bruce Hornsby's 1995 *Hot House* recording, for instance, was done almost completely in his home in Williamsburg, Virginia. And virtually entire subgenres of music, such as Hip-Hop and techno club remixes, have evolved into home-based industries. Such personal or so-called "project studios" are increasingly moving the bulk of record production and mixing out of traditional studios and in doing so, moving them out of the traditional power centers of music. Often, as part of advance monies paid to their recording artists, major record labels are agreeing to partially or completely fund the purchase of such recording equipment and spaces for their artists, paying not for the actual recording process, as has been the normal sequence of events, but rather for the tools of the process. The personal recording phenomenon has fueled a renaissance in the independent record sector in the last several years to the point where independent labels now collectively represent the second largest prerecorded music entity in the United States with 19.4 percent of overall U.S. sales in the first half of 1996—second only to WEA, the music division of Time Warner, which had a 21.9 percent share for that period.

WEA also had the largest share of the country music market—22.4 percent—a market in which, interestingly, independent records as a collective group have lagged behind all six major distribution companies with an 8.1 percent market share. That contrasts sharply and meaningfully with the experience of independent labels in other genres that have already felt the larger effects of technologically empowered recording artists: independent labels were collectively the fifth largest purveyor of recordings in the R&B field, with an 11.6 percent share in the first half of 1996. Country music's rigid business structure and its relative penury as a market until 1990 in a very real sense isolated Nashville's music business from the effects of this technological revolution. Country records continue to be produced through the traditional record label/recording studio model, one that has kept independent labels at bay in Nashville. What the effects of more widespread technological empowerment will be in the near future are not certain, but as more labels such as Rising Tide and Dead Reckoning—the latter a cooperative effort of recording artists, such as Kevin Welch, who have been left out or have chosen to leave the tightly packed wagons that form the record industry along Music Row—come on the scene, it's reasonable to conjecture that they could give the giants along Music Row a run for their money.

All that is a part of a future that's already in progress. Another, further-reaching, component of that future is the coming revolution in the distribution of music. Just as the fact that Pay-Per-View movies and broadcast events can be dialed up directly by consumers in the home now is undermining the future basis of the video industry; direct, digital delivery of music is likely to eventually do the same to the record store. People have recorded music for years from the radio, but that process has been blunted in its effect on sales by the fact that the choice of music was not completely at the discretion of the consumer, and by the inherent imperfections of the analog tape—the cassette tape—that had been the primary mass consumer rerecordable format. Since the advent of the Compact Disc in 1982, consumers have proven that they want the cleaner sound that digital audio has to offer and, more importantly in the age of the short attention span, the random accessibility to tracks, that the CD format provides. The only disadvantage of the CD vis-à-vis the analog cassette tape is that the standard consumer CD is a nonrerecordable format. There was a moment in the late 1980s when the Digital Audio Tape format—DAT—showed promise of becoming the rerecordable consumer digital link in the process, but concerns on the part of record companies regarding lost revenues to home taping—including Columbia Records and PolyGram Records, owned respectively by Sony and Philips, which jointly developed the CD and whose same consumer hardware manufacturing divisions both manufactured consumer DAT decks—prevented accord on the implementation anticopying technology within the decks until 1990, a delay that cost DAT an opportunity to generate any interest in the mass market.

But 1996 saw extremely rapid growth in a CD variant known as CD-R, which allows users to record once over a blank CD, and the technology to enable rerecordable CDs—multiple recordings and rerecordings on a single disc—both for audio and for video, is generally acknowledged to be imminently feasible as part of both a new variant of the Compact Disc format and of the newer DVD format and its large storage capabilities, which saw its major consumer roll-out in early 1997. A combination of a mass-acceptable, reusable disc format coupled with the imminent technologies of telephonic and fiber optical cable distribution that would allow consumers to select programming on demand and capture it digitally could eventually render the traditional record store distribution process obsolete. (Consumer retailers such as Blockbuster and Sam Goody are already responding to this vision of the future by combining audio and video products, as well as computer software, under one roof.)

The evolution of such a new business model would also further endanger the role that radio plays in breaking records. And in light of the degree of country music's tightly intertwined relationship with its radio network, the success of new models would have an impact in proportion to the intensity of that relationship, just as the personal recording model will have an equally larger impact on the traditional model of Music Row as that phenomenon progresses.

If there were no need to be in any one particular place to make music, and little or no need to have a massive, complex infrastructure to distribute it, supervise its marketing or administrate it, then what need would there be for another Nashville? What need for anything other than executive offices and accounting departments networked to a web of outsourced services, many of which, like promotion and publicity, the music industry already uses non-employee resources for? That is precisely what has happened in mainstream music: the executive management of major record labels remains centered in New York and Los Angeles while the music itself wends its way through the nation, from Minneapolis to Atlanta to Seattle and elsewhere, alighting momentarily until it is pushed by any number of social, cultural and economic forces.

Nashville has survived as the core of country music as long as it has for very good reasons, but ones that are susceptible to siege. As long as the methodology of production can withstand the onslaught of the personal recording phenomenon—as long as it's deemed necessary to make country records communally, with entire rhythm sections playing at once instead of in the piecemeal fashion that other mainstream genres are using—and as long as the system of multiple responsibilities devolving upon one person, in the form of record producers who are also writing songs and running labels, then there will always be a Nashville as it's known now, and it's most likely location will be at the juncture of Interstates 40, 65, and 24, in Middle Tennessee. In a place that is as real as the emotions its songs have historically been based upon, and as mythical as the Camelot it's become.

But the siege engines are those of technology, and technology will not be denied. The question could thus be posed instead, will geography, culture and infrastructure be able to withstand the changes that technology will effect on Nashville's country music industry? Country's incorporation of pop music production techniques has been relatively seamless but has also opened the genre up to criticism regarding its dilution in the face of new influences: is country shifting from a lyrical core to a sonic one? And will that open the door to a musical Diaspora for country music like the ones that other genres have undergone? It's a particularly trenchant query at a time when Nashville (the city, not the country music icon) is reaching higher into the municipal cosmos with its own aspirations, seeing a U.S. demographic shift southward and positioning itself—with a slew of theme restaurants and professional sports franchises—to be far more than just the mythical home of country music.

As country music continues to incorporate pop production values and marketing techniques, it runs the risk also of integrating pop's more rapid cycling of trends and all the impermanence that comes with that, bringing with it the possibility that country music will lose its identity not from without but from within. The Nashville music industry's own penchant for imitating its own success—a propensity that has been exacerbated significantly during the recent years of higher sales—will also have its effect. Every label does indeed want a Clint and Garth and a five-piece band on its rosters; it's been proven that consumers want them as well. Or at least, the image of them; categorization or "pigeonholing," as a means of finding handles for artists and rounding off rosters has always been a staple of the popular music industry, but it has been raised to a finely tuned and of-the-moment science in country music. Country has not been innocent of the practice historically, but a long tradition of developing artists based on personality and talent has seen considerable erosion in the past decade as the criteria upon which the industry chooses which artists to develop moves closer to being predicated on marketing-based stereotypes.

What is ultimately under siege—from technological, cultural, and social forces—is the rigid, familial, and benignly feudal structure of the Nashville country music industry, one that allows its initiates in the fields of production, musicianship, publishing, and songwriting to work simultaneously and/or sequentially under as many of those rubrics as they can comfortably juggle—the opposite of the trend toward specialization that is affecting the rest of the entertainment industry—so long as they have achieved those offices via a sufficiently long apprenticeship, during which one proves not only one's talents but also their personal commitment to the music, the business and the city, as well. Most of the emigrants to Nashville who aspire to be part of the club have found that doors opened considerably wider for them once they either bought houses in the area or evidenced that they were in it for the long haul. Carpetbagging is endemically and historically feared and loathed in the South, and Nashville and country music are no exceptions, particularly at a time when the streets of Nashville are perceived by many as being paved with gold and platinum. And this sense of intrusion is being heightened for some as they watch the development of Franklin, Tennessee, change from wealthy suburban retreat to a hotbed of often wealthier pop music refugees from Los Angeles and New York. Franklin is where Amy Grant made the records that crossed her over from the top of the Christian music charts to the top of the pop charts, and where former Miss America Vanessa Williams has made her pop/R&B records. Nashville's own live music environment—the mix of clubs and other venues necessary to foster musical cultures have been long quiet in Nashville due in part to the dominance of Gaylord Entertainment in its control of the few venues in the city until recently—has experienced a rebirth in recent years, part of the real estate and economic renaissance of the city's downtown area. A combination of more accessibility to more kinds of music and the continued influx of people to Nashville who are not coming to participate in country music are forming the basis for parallel universes to develop there. It's not axiomatic that those new musical cosmos will threaten the traditional structure of the country music business there, but alternatives to it will likely have their effect on it. Technology, demographic shifts, and a fracturing musical culture in America will all have their impact on the way Nashville runs its music business, and by extension, on the music itself, if only because the success of country music in recent years has tied its fortunes more closely to those of the larger entertainment industry's. And as those forces cast a new kind of illumination on Music Row, then it will become a function of personal point of view as to how that stretch of real estate will be viewed: as a fortress manned by defenders of the True Faith, or as a quaint but dated collection of storefronts whose glass-and-chrome atria will mean little as the business of music moves in the form of data streams from the homes of musicians, producers and publishers over a fiber optic network.

There is a syndrome that Nashville evokes. From the emblematic guitars and musical notes that dot the city's exteriors to the imperiousness of the facades of Music Row's new buildings to the traffic-dodging pedestrian mall that are the streets of Sixteenth and Seventeenth Avenues South as songwriters, publishers, producers, engineers, and musicians run from appointment to appointment, there is a bustle and an unrelenting sense of history and grandness to the whole thing, even in the tackiest of fronts along Junk Row. From a distance some could be forgiven for sometimes feeling that, "It's only three chords. If Hank could do it . . ."

But the reality of Nashville becomes more apparent the longer one is there. Country music has developed its own caste of exegesists, scribes who record and interpret, and who can be remarkably insightful if not completely detached about the music. As Bob Allen, a freelance journalist, wrote in the *Journal of Country Music* about the *Urban Cowboy* syndrome, in an observation that is just as apt for the current climate in Nashville, "It's hard to tell whether country music is going through a commercial renaissance or suffering through the most far-reaching case of mass trivialization in its history, as more and more 'Young Country' artists . . . who with all their flash, glitz, and Calvin Klein Cowboy duds, almost seem like throwbacks to the early eighties *Urban Cowboy* era . . . come to the fore. . . . I have this sinking feeling that mediocrity is in its full glory and the day belongs to the trend followers. I keep having these weird premonitions that the drab days of John Travolta, Johnny Lee, Olivia Newton-John, and Kenny Rogers are upon us again."[1]

Or local newspaperman Clark Parsons debating the differences between the current expansion of the genre and fifteen years earlier: "The primary difference between the *Urban Cowboy* Era and today's Suburban Cowboy ethos is that back then Nashville tried to change its sound to reach more listeners on other radio formats. If there is one great success story in the new boom, it's the way Nashville went back to its roots and made country radio so popular."[2]

Regardless of whether one agrees or not with either assessment, they reinforce the point that Nashville has and continues to have a linear perspective on itself. Where other musical genres have their genealogy mongrelized esthetically, culturally, politically or geographically, placing vantage points from as many different angles as various influences lay claim to them, country tends to look at itself as an uninterrupted timeline and generally from an of-the-moment point of view— the analogy of tape passing over a recording head is apt in many ways—as the integral and detached organism it has been all of its adult life.

Its sequestration from the mainstream has been often interrupted, either from without, as with *Urban Cowboy* or via the periodic visits by pop musicians, artists, and producers over the years, or from within its own walls, as when the commercial success of writers such as Kris Kristofferson have forced the norms of their times to be reassessed. Pop influences are nothing new to Nashville, from Fred Foster to the Muscle Shoals and Memphis players to producers like Larry Butler's forays into pop records with country artists, on through the steady stream of Los Angeles music business refugees that increasingly make up the sessions that back the singers. At least the singers are still mostly from Oklahoma

---

1. Vol. 16:2, 1994
2. Ibid.

and Texas, although one Nashville label, Giant Records, signed a British country singer, Graham McHugh, to its roster in 1994 (He was quietly dropped from the label in 1997), and at least one major label, Polydor, has signed a black female country singer.[3]

There is no hint of political correctness in these actions, nor of any latent multiculturalism; neither of those ideologies has much of a base in Nashville. They are purely designed to sell records and to move country into new markets, to cover as many bases as possible in a musical environment that relentlessly follows trends on literally a weekly basis. And in the case of McHugh, to sell plane tickets, too: his inaugural U.S. performance was at the Nashville airport concourse after he arrived on the first direct (and now-defunct) London-Nashville flight on May 27, 1994. As Edward Morris, former country music editor of *Billboard* wrote, ". . . the business of record companies is to make money. And they do this by securing acts that are willing to do what it takes to sell records. Anyone repelled by these admittedly vulgar realities would do well to imitate Emily Dickinson and thrust his or her artistic output into the far corners of dresser drawer."[4]

But regardless of the commercial aspects that country shares with other forms of entertainment, its essence has always revolved, and still does, primarily around the song. And while the drums are louder and the guitars are more distorted, it is still a music made up of songs that can be sung with a single voice and single acoustic guitar upon a stage, or on a back porch. The back porch is, after all, where they still come from, metaphorically and literally, despite the creation of what are virtually compositional production lines at the many publishing houses in Nashville. That focus, combined with the implicit linear self-perspective, will continue to provide country music with a core that no other significant

3. Pamela Foster's story in the *Nashville Business Journal* (September 12, 1994) listed over three dozen black female singers who had signed or were considered for signing over the years by Nashville labels. ". . . but none has made it to the top ranks of sales or radio airplay."
4. *Journal of Country Music*, Vol. 13, No. 3

musical strain in America has. Josh Leo's comment that "this is my idea of country" shows at once the presence and the flexibility of the rules. Even as James Stroud and Tony Brown skid away from the precepts of Jimmy Bowen, they can look with raised eyebrows at a Mike Lawler, just as the power brokers of a generation earlier looked at Foster and Norbert Putnam. And while the publishers have gotten smarter and have gone online, they still ply Music Row like door-to-door salesmen when they need to, which is most of the time.

Country's history is literally laid out like a DNA spiral, with the gene pool of predecessors found within each of its succeeding generations. Proximity plays a large part in this—it is still quintessentially a southern branch of music—but so does a quiet, unspoken compact that each of its more astute and intuitive participants seem to at least acknowledge upon their arrival in Nashville, and which everyone eventually learns. Everyone's personal version of country is uniquely their own, but it's still country according to a common definition that again owes its consistency to proximity. There are few new songs that actively conjure up the great R&B or rock of the past without sounding like calculated endeavors. As good as Billy Joel's "Uptown Girl" was at evoking the Four Seasons's sound, it had a kind of mathematical precision about it. But hearing George Strait sing anything written within the last three years still evokes the Merle Haggard of twenty years ago without even trying, just as Merle was able to conjure up the essence of Lefty Frizzell before him.

What will imperil country more is the spread of advertising. Modern country was born of advertising, as was its tabernacle, the Grand Ole Opry, and the music and its adherents have long reconciled and rationalized the connection. And the idea of making money from the process of recording and distributing music is common to all commercial genres. But the numerous pages that can be filled up itemizing the many linkages between commerce and individual artists dulls the distinction between them as much as critics claim that radio has made new artists sound indistinct from each other.

The potential is there for trivializing the music, a symptom that many maintain is already in an advanced state in the content of the music. "This is my idea of country" is a credo that cuts both ways. In the hands of the relatively small coterie of individuals—all of whom have shared an experience and an apprenticeship—whose decisions determine most of what comes out of Nashville, country can widen the cast of its net while still remaining recognizably country. On the other hand, listeners have more opportunity than ever before to make that assessment for themselves, deciding whether country for them is straight and narrow George Strait, the pop-tinged eclecticism of Wynonna Judd, the ass-wiggling of Travis Tritt doing the Eagles, or the Eagles themselves. All they have to do is twirl a dial on a radio. And as they do, the consultants track their tastes and refine their findings into a formula that gets ever more precise and confining.

Because of its origins, country music's contemporary creators cannot be blamed for simply following their instincts, and based on the admonitions of pitch sheets circulating Music Row asking for songs "à la Garth" or "à la Tanya" songs, country music tends to react far more than it acts. But it should also be remembered that this cycle of country music's expansion comes at a time of unprecedented commercialism in all aspects of American society. And it could be reasonably asked if everyone else is simply catching up to what country has known for a long time.

The absorption of new idiomatic influences has always raised flags about country's musical integrity over the years, and recent years have been no different. Rock, Folk, Jazz, Blues, and other musical idioms have all undergone schisms that have set avant-garde elements against self-appointed purists. But while country is not immune to such debates, it doesn't seem particularly vulnerable to them either. The more esoteric discourses on the state and fate of other music genres rage in publications far removed from the sensibilities of Nashville. This is not to say that the main protagonists of country music are not thoughtful individuals; they are, but they are more speculative pragmatists than pensive philosophers. Publisher/producer Tom Collins can disparage the concepts of cowriting and copublishing and at the same time accede to them when expediency demands it without any conscious conflict of interest getting in the way. The unexamined life is indeed worth living, and worth living well.

Now, what has this to do with the trains, drinking, infidelity, bad jobs, lousy bosses, love, death and other verities that have been the main themes of country songs since before it was called country? A little and a lot. The themes of country music will change as the concerns of its core constituency do: country songs have come to reflect the rise in awareness of modern problems like AIDS, spousal abuse, aging, drugs, and other late twentieth-century issues. But their resolutions within the songs are strikingly similar to the resolutions that older songs gave to older issues: that the perseverance of the individual, in concert with some spiritual reference, will ultimately triumph. You don't change that with distorted guitars and louder snare drums. Such production techniques are simply a reflex action on the part of country music's creators to both include their own generation's sensibilities in what they produce, and to follow the esthetic demands of a changing and wider audience in pursuit of a profit.

But do these changes to the outer shell augur for the end of country music? The question was posed by Tony Scherman in an article in *American Heritage* magazine in November 1994. After an accelerated overview of country's rural roots and its evolution into modern country—in which he maintains that the music has homogenized itself in the process—Scherman writes: "So it looks as if it's goodby [sic] to country music . . . as we knew it from 1920 to 1980, goodbye to Jimmie Rodgers, Hank Williams, and George Jones. . . . [H]ow far from its social origins can an art form grow before it simply loses meaning (or turns into something different)?"

So when does country stop being country? Not when the thematic issues are replaced or the sounds of the records further modernized and drawn into the mainstream, but rather when the bulk of country records stop being made in Nashville by the same handful of producers, writers, publishers, and musicians. This all leads back to one of the central and enduring facts about country music, certainly from the period of Hank Williams and forward: when so many of the critical players involved in its creation and refinement are so closely packed together, the genre takes on the sensibilities of an organism. It was that way for Soul in Detroit and before that for R&B in Muscle Shoals; it was that way for jazz in New Orleans; it was that way for the beginnings of modern rock in San Francisco in the late 1960s.

Those central cores have all passed. In the case of country, however, unlike any other significant musical genre currently, the notion that Geography is Destiny continues to be enforced. Nashville has been for nearly fifty years a magnet that attracts those who would be part of country music like no other physical/musical pairing in western music.

That country could leave Nashville and be regularly manufactured in multiple locations, as is the case with other genres of popular music, is unlikely to happen, although one cannot dismiss the possibility. In as mobile a society as this one has become, the bonds that once held families and communities together have come undone, and have been unraveling faster with each successive year and each new technological advance that propels us further into a virtual reality that no longer requires face-to-face interaction. But the fact that Nashville/Country has survived both the social trend and the establishment of temporary beachheads in the past in places like Bakersfield and Austin can be taken as a hopeful sign of its ability to continue to do so in the future.

It may be the ultimate conceit to impose a restriction on country music that it bears a Nashville imprimatur. It is arguably reactionary and unreasonable. But precisely because social changes due to the explosion in technology, communications and media have created an accelerated centrifugal effect on the cultural underpinnings of societies, country music's ability to maintain its sense of self—for its makers and its listeners—requires some kind of physical sanctuary, a tangible reference point by which it positions itself, and as a benchmark against which anything espousing to be country can be measured against. Australian vintners have recently been aggressively promoting and marketing domestic port wine, and no one says that you cannot make port wine anywhere but in Portugal. But Portuguese port remains the standard by which any other port is assessed for quality.

At a time when some in America perceive their own sometimes amorphous culture to be under attack from the influences of global multiculturalism, such an argument might seem even more expedient, especially since country music has rarely been viewed as a bastion of pluralism. But it has proved its ability to accept and absorb new influences and in doing so proves that a certain level of democracy is inherent in the otherwise merit-based oligarchic structure of the industry. "My version of what country is" is a perfectly acceptable assertion in Nashville, within certain parameters. Those parameters are imposed both by fiat and by circumstance. When James Stroud, Tony Brown, Scott Hendricks, or any of the other select group of producers in Nashville makes a country record, it is a country record by virtue of the fact that they made it and they made it in Nashville. When Bob DiPiero or Red Lane writes a country song, it is a country song because they wrote it. This is not to say that their productions and compositions cannot be viable in other genres not as country songs but simply as good songs (viz. Dolly Parton's crossover hit "I Will Always Love You," which Linda Ronstadt recorded in 1975 and which won a Grammy for Whitney Houston in 1994), or that they could not make other kinds of records or write other kinds of songs. But the fact that they have arrived at a certain level in the Nashville music structure confers upon them the ability to declare what constitutes country.

The symbiotic and often adversarial relationship between the makers of the music and country radio provides another critical circumstance. No matter what any member of the Nashville music industry elite says or does, it still requires the agreement of country radio in order to attain full acceptance. The synergy between the two, alternating between antagonistic and accommodating, provides an ongoing conflict that also helps keep a balance and a robustness in country music. What the rise in influence of the marketing component in country music will do to (or for) this balance remains to be seen.

Finally, there is country music's ability to downplay age as a criterion for success or even for acceptance. Despite the fact that the age of country artists keeps getting younger and younger—as does the genre's demographic—the fact remains that the most productive and successful producers, writers, and musicians are mostly in their thirties, forties, and fifties, some into their sixties, often twice the age of many of their pop, rock, rap, and R&B counterparts, and that many of rock's own former innovators—Peter Frampton, Felix Cavaliere, a constantly growing list of former pop icons—look to Nashville as a place to retreat to in their own middle age. While rock & roll has recently become more accommodating of senectitude—seen in the continued chart and touring appeal of the Rolling Stones, Aerosmith, et al—the ongoing merging of what was as recently as two years ago referred to as alternative music in mainstream pop (it would be difficult to call Pearl Jam's multiplatinum sales "alternative" at this stage) has returned the momentum back towards younger artists and producers in rock and other genres. Country music, on the other hand, has always been relatively unbiased regarding age. Pairings of younger artists with older ones, as with 1994's *The Bradley Barn Sessions* and veteran George Jones with Travis Tritt, Joe Diffie, Clint Black, and others on 1992's "I Don't Need Your Rockin' Chair" prove that.

Nashville has had an "averaging effect" on those who have come to it—the best chance of success is compliance with the rules of country's feudal architecture. But that effect functions as a gravitational core around which people can stray as far as their personal courage will allow. Country is far more tolerant of innovation than it is often given credit for. Heretics are rarely burned that the stake—more often than not their phone calls are simply not returned. Yet country music demands of itself and its adherents a certain degree of faith and commitment. This is often trivialized as "lifestyle" by the marketing perspective, but it goes far deeper than that. And the infusion of new ideas into country has provided it with a contrast whose light and dark shades have added additional dimensions to the genre, while at the same time confusing true believers who ponder its future.

It was all summed up nicely by pianist Matt Rollings. Leaning on the console, listening to a playback in the studio on a Doug Stone recording session, he tilted his head toward the large monitor speakers as they blared rock guitars and fat drums over acoustic guitars and a New Orleans boogie beat. Cocking an eyebrow and gesturing with a nod over his shoulder, he smiles and says simply, "Country music."

"Plus Ca Change, Plus C'est La Même Chose: A Post Script)

There have been substantial changes on the surface of Nashville's music industry, many of which have affected the people and institutions portrayed in this book. Perhaps the most exceptional of these is the arrival of DreamWorks Records in Nashville, the record label division of the multi-media Hollywood-based company started by record industry veteran David Geffen, former Disney vice president Jeffrey Katzenberg, and film director Steven Spielberg. The first announced signing for the label was Randy Travis, who was a notable part of the New Traditionalists revival of country music a decade ago. On the surface, things appear to be coming full circle.

On Friday, March 14, 1997, James Stroud announced his resignation as president of Giant Records. At the time, Stroud, who epitomizes the historical role of the Nashville producer who would work on multiple records simultaneously while running a record label and owning a recording studio and maintaining publishing interests, said that he was making the move to "simplify" his life and spend more time on record productions. After DreamWorks announced its decision to open an office in early 1997—around the same time that the Disney Corp. announced that it, too, would open a division of its recording label in Nashville—Stroud's newly "simplified" life became considerably more complex when he accepted the role of DreamWorks' new Nashville label chief. But as this book shows, contradictions are a norm in Nashville.

Many of the other people included in this book have moved on as well. Jimmy Bowen retired from Liberty/Capitol Records in 1996, succeeded by Scott Hendricks. In his book, *Rough Mix*, Bowen cited a bout of cancer of the thyroid—now in remission—as one of the primary reasons for his departure. Hew did acknowledge, though, that a bout with Garth Brooks's ego played a part. Brooks's image has developed cracks, the kind any entertainer can expect when he reaches the level of success that he has. Having transcended country music, he becomes fair game for the sharper blades that wait outside the gates of Nashville. But perhaps Bowen's characterization of Brooks as an "eight-hundred-pound hillbilly gorilla" whose ambitions will not be denied reveals that the sharpest arrows still come from *within* the walls.

Disney's arrival Nashville might have been a quiet affair—its previous record label venture, Hollywood Records, has not been exceptionally successful—had it not been for a coincidental meeting of the Southern Baptists Convention in June 1997, in Dallas, where the sect's leadership voted to boycott Disney products and services, condemning as immoral and "gay-friendly" such things as the company's same-sex employee benefits, movies such as *Kids* and *Pulp Fiction* released by Disney subsidiaries, and the television sitcom "Ellen," which runs of the Disney-owned ABC network. Disney did, though, follow the Rules by hiring its new label chief, former RCA Records senior vice president and general manager Randy Goodman, from within the walls.

The proliferation of labels and recording artists between 1990 and 1995 has slowly but inexorably created the need for new producers, if only because the existsing ones were stretched so thinly with existing artists and label responsibilities. Second-tier producers have always thrived in Nashville, though their projects are usuallly taken over by "name" producers and they receive instead what is technically knows as an override—compensation in the form of of points and/or cash. Their real compensation, is the accumulation of intangible "point" within the feudal farm system of country music; when a young producer had brought enough viable talent to labels over the years, his star eventually would land him into the upper constellations of the business. Such was the case with David Malloy who, after over 15 years of artist development and production both in Nashville and Lost Angeles, was brought together with singer Mindy McCready by veteran producer Norro Wilson. McCready's first album cleared the platinum hurdle within the first six months of its release; Malloy was hired soon after as head of production for Starstruck's artist production division. Within a successful and sophisticated organization such as Starstruck, head of production is virtually tantamount to running a record label.

New producers drawn from among the disciplines within country now included composer Gary Nicholson, who coproduced *River Road* with another veteran writer, Don Cook; Mark Spiro, who came from left field with Asylum artist Lila McCann's debut record in 1997; writer Will Rambeaux developed and coproduced Australian country singer Sherrie Austin's first record with veteran engineer/producer Ed Seay. The apprentice system remains alive and well in Nashville via coproduction, versus the high degree of autonomy that independent producers in pop and rock genres operate under. The latter's rewards may be greater if they succeed, but the ordered structure that remains in place in country music generally ensures a more tempered and longer-lived career.

Gaylord Entertainment has undergone changes, as well. After divesting itself of most of the CMT network in 1997 to its long-time partner Westinghouse's Group W for approximately $1.6 billion (Gaylord retained CMT's international operations), it renewed its interest in the record industry, this time the Christian record industry. Within a little more than a year's time, Gaylord acquired Christion label Word

Record for $120 million; Z Music, a Christian music video cable television operation; and the artist management agency that represents successful Christian artists such as Any Grant and Michael W. Smith.

As the city of Nashville, with its newly found major league sports franchises and densely theme-parked downtown, realigns itself for a new century, the geography of country is also changing—slightly but perhaps significantly. With the finalizationof the Country Music Hall of Fame's planned move to downtown Nashville, the less strategic, almost charming tackiness of nearby Junk Row has become endangered. That strip along Demonbreun Street has been targeted for development by entities both within and without the country music industry. Randy Travis may have a new record label, but his gift shop on Junk Row is gone. The Legends Hall of Fame closed in 1996, its collection of privately owned artifacts auctioned off. The site of what was Gilley's nightclub has been bought by Starstruck Entertainment. It is unlikely that visitors drunk with equal doses of ambition and Lone Star beer will ever again serenade passers-by from Gilley's karaoke gazebo.

It is equally unlikely, though, that the country music industry as it has evolved in Nashville will ever, as its core, change too radically either. The apprentice system that has been in place so long has proved both its value and its resiliency. The unwritten rules get learned by new arrivals today just as they were learned forty years ago, perhaps grudgingly at first, but then with a new level of respect for their inherent value as novitiates make their progression through an almost Masonic level of degrees. As the saying—now attributed to so many sources that it has taken on a mythic level of reverence—in the country music goes, "You don't change Nashville, it changes you."

— ·· — ·· — ·· — ·· — ·· — ·· — ·· —

SOURCES & RECOMMENDED READING

Bart, Teddy; *Inside Music City USA*, Nashville: Aurora, 1970.

Country Music Foundation; *Country: The Music And The Musicians*, New York: Abbeville Press, 1988.

Hemphill, Paul; *The Nashville Sound—Bright Lights And Country Music*, New York: Simon & Schuster, 1970.

McCloud, Barry, et alia; *Definitive Country—The Ultimate Encyclopedia of Country Music And Its Performers*, New York: Perigee, 1995.

Pareles, John and Romanowski, Patricia, Editors; *The Rolling Stone Encyclopedia Of Rock & Roll*, New York: Simon & Schuster, 1983.

Tosches, Nick; *Country—Living Legends And Dying Metaphors*, New York: Scribner's & Sons, 1985.

Riese, Randall; *Nashville Babylon*, New York: Congdon & Weed, 1988.

Bowen, Jimmy and Jerome, Jean; *Rough Mix*, New York: Simon & Schuster, 1997.

INDEX

"Achy Breaky Heart," 309-310; 311; 312

Acuff, Roy, 19; 30-32; 190-191

Administration deals, 216-217

Advances, recording artists, 325

Advances, songwriting, 136; 183

Advertising, impact of, 334

Age of artist as factor, 287; 302; 309; 339

Alexander, Arthur, 240

Allen, Bob, 331-332

American Society of Composers, Authors, and Publishers (ASCAP), 136; 147; 148-149; 188; 208-209

Anderson, John, 207

Anderson, Pete, 127-131

Apprenticeship system, 25-26; 67; 132; 153; 195; 330; 335; 338; 342; 343; *see also* Cowriting

A&R, *see* Artist and Repertoire department, role of

Artist and Repertoire department, role of, 54

Artist, marketing role, 286

Artists, advances, 325

Artists, age as factor, 302; 309; 339

Artists, image of, 273-274

Artist/songwriter separation, 154; 162; 170

Artist as songwriter, advantages of, 194

Artists, relationship with radio, 294-296; 298-299

A Team, defined, 82

Atkins, Chet, 24; 34; 35; 45; 51-58; 234

Autry, Gene, 29-30

Ball, Marc, 309-312

Barn dance radio shows, 28-29

Barnes, Max D., 143-144

Barnes, Max T., 143-144

Barnhill, Greg, 160

Beatles tribute album, 164

Beckham, Bob, 155; 192-195; 197; 198

Biddy, Shelia Shipley, 62

Black, Clint, 81

Bluebird Cafe, 170-172

"Boot Scootin' Boogie," 100-101; 104-105; 106

Bowen, Jimmy, 61; 68-77; 96-97; 341

Bradley, Harold, 46

Bradley, Jerry, 276-278; 280

Bradley, Owen, 23; 24; 34; 35; 45; 46-50; 58; 234; 235; 260
Briggs, David, 240
Briggs, John, 148-149
Bright, Mark, 44
Broadcast Music Inc. (BMI), 136; 147-149; 187-188; 208
Brooks & Dunn, 100; 103-104
Brooks, Garth, 14; 149; 183; 283-287; 309-310; 316; 317; 341
Brown, Mark, 177-180
Brown, Marty, 288-290
Brown, Tony, 45; 54; 75-76; 92-100
Buffalo Broadcasting Company suit, 208-209
Burgoise, Dan, 217
Butler, Allen, 318-321
Butler, Larry, 63-68
Byrom, Larry, 224

Campbell, Glen, 71; 303
Carrigan, Jerry, 240; 242-244
Castle, The, 33-34; 252-255
Catalog computerization, 175
CD-R, consumer use, 327
CD-R, demo use, 181
Censorship, self, 141-142; 316; 317-318
Charts, role of, 29; 161-162; 301-302; 317; 319-320
Cherry, Hugh, 298
Christian music industry, 176; 330; 342-343
Cline, Patsy, 49
Close field monitoring, 256
Cohen, Paul, 34; 47
Cole, Jack, 314-315
Collins, Tom, 199-203
Commercials, performance royalties, 188
Commitment, importance of, 330; 339-340
"Common Thread: The Songs of the Eagles," 82-83

Concert revenues, 13
Conrad, David, 203-207
Continuity, 20; 131; 332; 333; 334
Controlled composition clause, 185-186
Cook, Don, 44; 45; 106-110; 342
Cooley, Al, 195-199
Coproduction, 44-45; 235; see also Multiple producers
Copublishing, 187; 193-194; 201-202; 205-207
Copyright Act of 1909, 185
Copyright Act of 1976, 185
Copyright Royalty Tribunal, 185
Corenflass, J. T., 269-270
Country Music Association (CMA), 36-37; 70; 293
Country Music Disk Jockey Association (CMDJA), 36
Country Music Hall of Fame, 19; 24; 343
Country Music Television (CMT), 14; 306; 308; 316; 317; 342
Countrypolitan, 49; 59; see also Pop music, relationship to
Cowriting, 138-139; 140; 152-162; 167; 168; 169; 170; 183-184; 186; 193; 205; 235
Cramer, Floyd, 233; 235
"Crazy," 49
Cyclical nature of music business, effect of, 14; 84; 137; 205-206; 335
Cyrus, Billy Ray, 310-311

"Dance," 115-116; 119; 309-310
Dance clubs, 100-101; 105; 311
Dance remixes, 100-101; 104-105
Davis, Linda, 113-114
Dawson, Bart, see Rose, Fred
DeLaughter, Hollis Rudolph, see Lane, Red
Demo costs, 267; 268; 270

Demographics of audience, 286-288; 308; 330-331

Demographic studies, 279; 308

Demo production sessions, 266-271

Demo revenues, 259

Denny, Jim, 191

Digital Audio Tape format (DAT), impact of, 327

Digital delivery of music, 326-327

DiPiero, Bob, 155-158; 198

Distribution of music, 42; 326-327

D.J., role of, 296-298

Dodson, Chris, 219-221

Double scale, 247-248

Douglas, Charlie, 296

Drums, 71; 76; 87; 231; 265

DuBois, Tim, 102; 304

Dugmore, Dan, 224

Dylan, Bob, 238

Earle, Steve, 97-98

Economic success, role of, 37-38

Edenton, Ray, 230-236; 251

Electronic press kit (EPK), 272

Ellis, Len, 298

Engineers, role of, 103; 104-105; 106

Equipment accessibility, *see* Project studio recording

Equipment costs, 258-259; 325

Ewing, Skip, 176

Field recordings, 27; 32-33

Financial aspects, record production, 136; 184-188; 197; 205; 232; 247-248; 258-259; 267; 268; 270; 291-292; 325

Financial aspects, video production, 307; 313-314; 315; 316-317; 319

Foster, Fred, 121-126; 191

Fundis, Garth, 44; 160; 162

Galante, Joe, 274-282

"Gambler, The," 63-64; 65

Gayden, Mack, 238-239

Geffen, David, 340

Generational gap, artists, 309

Generational gap, session players, 242-244; 250-251; 260-262

Gibson, Dave, 165-166

Gibson, Don, 54-55

Gibson-Miller Band video, 317

Gibson, Steve, 248-250

Gilley's, 22; 343

Goldmann, Steven, 313; 314

Goodman, Randy, 341

Grand Ole Opry, 28-29

Grey, Mark, 315

Guess, John, 110-115

Hay, George D., 28; 29

Hall, Rick, 241

Harman, Buddy, 230-236

Harvey, Retta, 317

Hee Haw, 28; 251

Hendricks, Scott, 45; 101-106; 341

Higdon, Pat, 212-215

"Hill-billie" music, 27

Hill, Byron, 153

Hinton, Bruce, 54

History of music business in Nashville, 26-27; 27-30; 32-33; 34-35

Hitchcock, Stan, 305-306

Hold system, 150-151

Hollywood movie industry compared to, 324

Home recording studios, *see* Project studio recording

"I Fall to Pieces," 49

Image of artist, 273-274

Independent labels, 34-35; 42; 44; 61-62; 129-130; 132; 170; 317; 325-326

Internet, role of, 42; 174-175; 325

Jenkins, Floyd, *see* Rose, Fred
Jennings, Greg, 102
Judds, the, 279

Katzenberg, Jeffrey, 340
Kennedy, Jerry, 58-63
Koller, Fred, 162-165
Kristofferson, Kris, 125
Kurland, Amy, 171

Lane, Red, 137-139
Lawler, Mike, 115-121
Legends Hall of Fame, 343
Lehning, Kyle, 224-226
Leim, Paul, 223; 227-228; 264-266
Leo, Josh, 85-92
Leuzinger, Chris, 224; 228
Live music environment in
    Nashville, 330
Loggins, Dave, 249

Major labels, 15-16; 32; 34-35; 42;
    43-44; 61-62; 129-130; 301;
    317
Malloy, David, 342
Mansfield, Joe, 282-292
Marketing, changes in, 278-280;
    292
Marketing, financial aspects of,
    291-292
Marx, Kerry, 268-269; 270
"Maybe It Was Memphis," 304-305
McCoy, Charlie, 230-236; 237-238;
    250-251
McDill, Bob, 139-143
Mechanical royalties, 184; 185;
    197; 205
Media (local) relationship with,
    19
Melamed, Vince, 160
Memphis, Tennessee, 239; 244;
    245; 246-247
Mergers of publishing companies,
    209-211

Mergers of record labels, 15-16; 61-
    62
Merry, Scot, 267
Miller, Bruce, 170; 172-173
Miller, Steve, 311
Milsap, Ronnie, marketing of, 278
Montgomery, Bob, 210-211
Moore, Bob, 230-236; 251
Movies, impact of, 29-30
Mullins, Neal "Moon," 88; 300-302
Multiculturalism, 333
Multiple producers, 110; *see also*
    Coproduction
Multiples, 210
Multitrack recording, 56; 57; 76;
    229; 250-251
Muscle Shoals, Alabama, 239-242;
    244
Music business degree programs,
    25; 195
Musicologists, role of, 27; 32-33
Music Row, 21-26; 164; 259-260
Mythology of Nashville, 11-12; 17-
    20; 328

Nashville (city), relationship with
    country music business, 11-12;
    16-22; 26-27; 132-133; 201;
    323-325; 328; 329-331; 336-
    338
Nashville Entertainment
    Association, 69; 70
Nashville Music Association, *see*
    Nashville Entertainment
    Association
Nashville Music Consultants, 66;
    68
Nashville number system, 236-237
Nashville Online, 174-175
Nashville Songwriters Association
    International (NSAI), 136; 149
Nashville Sound, 55; 58
Neese, Chuck, 153
Nicholson, Gary, 158-160; 342

"Oldies" music, radio play of, 299; 309
Olney, David, 169-170
Orbison, Roy, 123-124

Parsons, Clark, 332
Peer, Ralph, 27; 32-33
Peer-Southern Organization, 33
Percentage points (royalties) for video directors, 314-315
Performance royalties, 184; 187-188; 197; 205
Performing rights organizations, 136; 147-149; 187-188; 208-209; 213
Peters, Gretchen, 144-147
Pitch sessions, 174; 177-181; *see also* Song pitching
Pitch sheet, analysis of, 181-183
Playlists, impact of, 297-298
Pollack, Jeff, 300
Pop music, relationship to, 18; 36; 49; 53; 59; 65-67; 76-77; 84; 88-91; 95-96; 124; 142-143; 229; 272; 329; 332
Power structure, 17; 329-330
Presley, Elvis, 197; 238
Press kits, 272
Pride, Charley, 199-200
Producer, role of, 35-36; 40-45; 45; 131-133; *see also* Coproduction
Project studio recording, 34; 41; 118; 120-121; 258-259; 325-326
Publishers, role of, 189-190; 198
Publisher's share, 187
Publishing companies, mergers of, 209-211
Publishing companies, role of, 32; 188-190
Publishing, financial aspects of, 184; 187; *see also* Copublishing
Putnam, Norbert, 240; 241

Rack jobbers, 283; 288-289
Radio, artists' relationship with, 294-296; 298-299
Radio market share, 293-294
Radio, role of, 27-29; 36-37; 161; 265; 280; 292-305; 320; 321-322; 327-328; 338-339
Radio stations, growth of, 14; 37; 292-294; 298
Radio tours, 295
Rake part, 225
Rambeaux, Will, 342
Record companies (independent labels), 34-35; 42; 44; 61-62; 129-130; 132; 170; 317; 325-326
Record companies (major labels), 15-16; 32; 34-35; 42; 43-44; 61-62; 129-130; 301; 317
Recording equipment, accessibility of, *see* Project studio recording
Recording industry, relationship to larger, 13
Restless Heart, 88-89
Revenues, 13; 15; 259; 281
Reversion clauses, 136-137
Reynolds, Allen, 44
Robbins, Hargus "Pig," 234; 235
Robertson, Eck, 32
Rogers, Kenny, 65
Rollings, Matt, 224; 340
Rose, Fred, 31; 190
Rose, Wesley, 190-191
Royalties, songwriting, 136; 183-188; 197; 205
Royalties, video directors, 314-315
Rural roots of country music, 29

Sales data, 13; 15; 319
Sampling, 105; 224
Satherly, Art, 33
Scholten, Paul, 267
Scruggs, Randy, 44
Seay, Ed, 303-305

Second hold, 150

Sequencers, use of, 116-117; 120-121

Session players, role of, 82; 229-230; 232; 236; 239; 242-244; 250-251; 260-262

Sessions, 78-79; 222-228

Sessions, financial aspects of, 232; 247-248; 258; 268

Shaped note music, 27

Shedd, Harold, 61-62

Sherrill, Billy, 61; 234; 240

Sherrill, John Scott, 157

Sholes, Steve, 34; 52-54

Signing bonuses, songwriting, 136

Singer/songwriter separation, 154; 162; 170

Singer as songwriter, advantages of, 194

Singleton, Shelby, 59

Snare Wars, 87; 265

Society of European Stage Authors and Composers (SESAC), 136; 147; 149; 188; 209

Song pitching, 80; 166; 196; 220-221; see also Pitch session

Songwriting, apprentice system, see Cowriting

Songwriting, financial aspects, 136; 184-188; 197; 205

SoundScan, role of, 186; 291

Spielberg, Steven, 340

Spiro, Mark, 342

Staff writers, 136; 183-184

Stapp, Jack, 191

Stereotypes, 29; 273; 329

Stevens, Ray, 24

Stroud, James, 45; 75-76; 77-84; 340-341

Studio design, 251-252; 259-260

Studio musicians, see Session players

Studios (independent), 255-259; see also Project studio recordings

Studios (label-owned), 255; 256

Studios, number of, 34

Studio time, cost of, 258

Swaim, John, 151-152

"Synch" licenses, 188

Talbot, Joe, 230

Tankersley, Brian, 104-105

Television, marketing tool, 280

Television, performance royalties, 188

"Tennessee Waltz," 31

Themes of country songs, 336

"Thunder Rolls, The," 316; 317

Tillis, Mel, 74; 139

Tippin, Aaron, 177

Tomlinson, Troy, 175-181

Tourism in Nashville, 21-22

Tours, early, 230

Tours, financial impact of, 13; 15

Tours, radio, 295

Tours, Wal-Mart store, 288-290; 322

Tractors, the, 322

Twister Alley, 115-116; 118-119

Van Dyke, Bob, 267

Velletri, Gary, 216-218

Video producers, role of, 312-313; 314

Videos, financial aspects of, 307; 313-314; 315; 316-317; 319

Videos, impact of, 164; 305-321

Videos, self-censorship of, 316-318

Vienneau, Jim, 177

"Walk Away Joe," 160-161

Walker, Billy Joe, 224; 225

Walker, Clay, 134-135

Wal-Mart store tours, 288-290; 322

"When She Cries," 88-91

White, Bryan, 224-225; 228

Williams, Hank Sr., 18; 22; 122

Williams, Jody, 147-148
Williams, Kim, 135
Wilson, Walt, 289; 292
Wipperman, Tim, 201-202; 207-
    212; 214
Wood, Jeff, 167-169
Worf, Glenn, 222-223; 227; 260-264
Writers Group, The, 79-80

Writer's share, 187
WSM Barn Dance, 28
WSM radio station, 27-28

Yearwood, Trisha, 162
Yetnikoff, Walter, 42
Yoakam, Dwight, 126-128
Young, Reggie, 244-248